D0301801

Frank Lloyd Wright's Sacred Architecture

Faith, Form, and Building Technology

Frank Lloyd Wright's Sacred Architecture

Faith, Form, and Building Technology

Anat Geva

Routledge
Taylor & Francis Group

LONDON AND NEW YORK

First published 2012
by Routledge
2 Park Square, Milton Park, Abingdon, Oxon OX14 4RN

Simultaneously published in the USA and Canada
by Routledge
711 Third Avenue, New York, NY 10017

Routledge is an imprint of the Taylor & Francis Group, an informa business

© 2012 Anat Geva

The right of Anat Geva to be identified as author of this work has been asserted by her in accordance with sections 77 and 78 of the Copyright, Designs and Patents Act 1988.

All rights reserved. No part of this book may be reprinted or reproduced or utilised in any form or by any electronic, mechanical, or other means, now known or hereafter invented, including photocopying and recording, or in any information storage or retrieval system, without permission in writing from the publishers.

The authors and publishers gratefully acknowledge those acknowledged in the figure captions for permission to reproduce material in the book. Every effort has been made to contact and acknowledge copyright owners. The publishers would be grateful to hear from any copyright holder who is not acknowledged here and will undertake to rectify any errors or omissions in future printings or editions of the book.

British Library Cataloguing in Publication Data
A catalogue record for this book is available from the British Library

Library of Congress Cataloging in Publication Data
Geva, Anat.
  Frank Lloyd Wright's sacred architecture : faith, form and
  building technology / Anat Geva.
    p. cm.
  1. Wright, Frank Lloyd, 1867–1959—Criticism and interpretation.
  2. Church architecture. I. Title.
  NA737.W7G48 2011
  726.092--dc22   2011003028

ISBN13: 978-0-415-77508-3 (hbk)

Typeset in Myriad Pro
by Keystroke, Station Road, Codsall, Wolverhampton

Printed and bound in Great Britain by
TJ International Ltd, Padstow, Cornwall

Contents

To Nehemia

the love of my life

Acknowledgments

I enjoyed writing this book – it was exciting to research an extraordinary architecture, collect data, visit the buildings, analyze their special designs and explore their uplifting spirituality. Most of all, though, I enjoyed the involvement and support of my family, friends, and colleagues. Each contributed time, thought, and skills with love and support. I would like to take this opportunity to acknowledge and thank all of those who helped me during this mighty endeavor.

I wish to thank my family with tremendous gratitude. A very special thank you goes to my husband Nehemia Geva to whom I have dedicated this book. Without his help I would have never completed my work. Our invaluable discussions, his endless encouragement and critiques, and his editorial work made it all possible. I must note that we traveled together to most of the building sites where he helped document, measure, and photograph the buildings and pertinent documents. In fact, some of his great photographs are part of the book.

Eternal thanks go to my parents Charlotte (1920–2002) and Hans George (1918–2002) Mintz who taught me to love and admire beauty, art, music, and literature. This book is an answer to my father's admiration of my collection of books and articles on Frank Lloyd Wright. I thank my mother-in-law Pnina Gutenberg (1916–2000) for her interest and constant encouragement and support of my work.

I thank my grown children Uri and Roni, and their spouses Gali and Rick, who encouraged my "workaholism" and supported my professional endeavors. Special thanks to my daughter Roni who accompanied me on my travels to Illinois and Wisconsin, and who was my first copyeditor. Her insightful editorial revisions and corrections strengthened my writing. Her encouragement meant a lot to me. Thanks to her husband Rick who helped behind the scenes with the editing of especially difficult passages. Thanks to my son Uri who photographed the First Christian Church in Phoenix – the images are included in this book. Thanks to my daughter-in-law Gali who was the first graphic designer of both the cover and the sample layout of the book. Her help with the design contributed to the book's beauty. Finally, a special thanks to my granddaughters Maya and

Ella, and my grandson Ilan, who always bring me happiness and light, especially in moments of stress.

Special thanks to my dear friend Belinda Bragg who was the first to review my book. Her constructive comments enriched the book and its meaning. Her encouragement meant a lot to me.

I would like to acknowledge Dr. Jorge Vanegas, Dean of the School of Architecture at Texas A&M University, and Dr. Glen Mills, previous head of the Department of Architecture at Texas A&M University, for their encouragement and support. Many thanks to Melinda Randle; Hala Gibbson; Ginger White; Mallroy Schramm; Jose Vega, the friendly and helpful staff members of the Department of Architecture office at Texas A&M University.

I thank my five graduate students who, over the years, took an interest in helping with the project's research and drawings (Akshay Kini, Anuradha Mukherji, Lu Zhipeng, Jong Hoon Kim, and Jacob Morris). Special thanks to Lu Zhipeng for his help with the CAD redrawing of some of Wright's drawings, to Anuradha Mukherji for her help with conducting computerized lighting simulations of Unity Temple, and to Jacob Morris for his help in scanning all of the pertinent original drawings/documents obtained from the archive of The Frank Lloyd Wright Foundation.

I would like to take this opportunity to thank the organizations that supported my project(s) exploring Frank Lloyd Wright's sacred architecture: *The James Marston Fitch Charitable Trust; The Program to Enhance Scholarly and Creative Activities, The Office of the Vice President for Research, Texas A&M University; The College of Architecture Research and Interdisciplinary Council Grant Program (CRIC), Texas A&M University;* and *The Religious Studies Faculty Fellowship in the Glasscock Center for Humanities Research, Texas A&M University.*

Thanks to all of the professionals and staff working in the different religious buildings designed by Frank Lloyd Wright who opened the buildings' doors for my visits, and provided information, pamphlets, and pictures with heartfelt passion. Thanks to the Frank Lloyd Wright's Foundation Archive staff in Taliesin West for their help with my archival study. Thanks to Janet Hicks from ARS for her help in acquiring the copyright for the images taken from the Archive. Special thanks to Routledge's Caroline Mallinder who signed my book's contract; to Katherine Morton, who used to work at Routledge, for her patience and understanding; and to Fran Ford, Georgina Johnson-Cook, Kyle Duggan, Ann King and the entire Routledge team for their professional work.

Introduction

And the captain of the LORD's host said unto Joshua, Loose thy shoe from off thy foot; for the place where on thou standest is holy. And Joshua did so.

(Joshua 5:15)

This book examines Frank Lloyd Wright's sacred architecture in the context of the broader subject of religious architecture. Although Wright claimed that all his architecture is sacred, the focus of the book is on his built and unbuilt religious projects. Wright designed more than thirty such projects, but only ten were built (see list of projects in Appendix). In its essence, the book examines buildings devoted to religious rituals – buildings where people worship God.

A religious building is the culmination of humanity's attempt to reflect Divine presence and create the intersection of heavenly and earthly realms. Since the house of worship is a visual representation of the dwelling of God within humanity, and since it may be considered as one of the cultural values expressing the collective cognition of a congregation, this type of structure becomes distinct from all other buildings (Conover 1948; Rapoport 1969; Yi-Fu 1974; Altman & Chemers 1980; Upton 1986; Robinson 1989; Mann 1993; Geva 1995; Dubbelde 2006).

A house of God is built to symbolize the meaning and accommodate the rituals of a particular belief system of its time. It is interesting to note that although the variety of interpretations of religious motifs is astonishing, the similarity of fundamental themes is equally remarkable (Barrie 1996). For example, in his book *Church Building: A Study of the Principles of Architecture in Their Relation to the Church* (1924) Ralph Adams Cram describes four common themes as the fundamental qualities of church architecture: the church as a house of God, "a place of His earthly habitation . . . a visible type of heaven itself" (p. 6); the church as a place set apart from the mundane; the church as a space that evokes spiritual experiences; and finally, the church's function as a gathering place for the congregation to convene and "listen to the instructions of its spiritual leaders" (p. 10). These common themes are expressed in sacred buildings through architectural features and dimensions, such as the sacred path (procession), plan, verticality, geometry, and proportion. In addition, some aspects of building technology such as materials, light, acoustics, and thermal comfort accentuate the spiritual experiences in all religious buildings and enrich their sacredness.

William Turner (1979) claims that the fundamental common themes of the sacred place across faith are based on the central place of religion in the life of the individual and the community. The religious building serves as a symbol of a people's traditions, culture, and heritage. For example, my research on nineteenth century churches built by different ethnic groups of immigrants arriving from Europe to south central Texas and to south Australia shows the significance of their houses of worship. The immigrants retained the meaning and original forms of their churches in the new frontiers: "The remarkable visual memory of the settlers, able to replicate on the frontier the great masonry churches they had left behind" (Fitch 1982). I show that the tendency to preserve one's life and community's collective memory is so dominant that building these churches as an icon of the community's culture, history, and heritage was more important than accommodating local environmental conditions and extreme constraints such as the Texas summer heat (Geva 1994, 1995, 1998, 2002b, 2005, 2009a).

Given the importance of the religious building in the spiritual life of the individual and the community, I was intrigued to learn how a prominent American architect such as Frank Lloyd Wright shaped his sacred architecture.

In the study of Frank Lloyd Wright's architecture, I repeatedly encountered three principal architectural concepts reflected in his theory and design: Nature, Democracy and Freedom, and Wright's Holistic approach to design. Kevin Nute (1996: 99) interprets the concept of Nature as an environmental adaptation of architecture; the concept of Democracy and Freedom as a metaphysical and social interpretation of architecture; and the concept of a Holistic approach to design as architectural aesthetic wholeness. Joseph Siry (1996: 234) claims that Wright had already developed those "canonical ideas" in 1894 and used the 1906 design of Unity Temple as an embodiment of these concepts. My study of Wright's architecture suggests that Wright continued to return to these design concepts throughout his career. I found it interesting to study how these design principles interplay with religious principles and manifest themselves in the built form. This book investigates how Wright applied these three concepts to his design of holy buildings.

Nature served as the context and inspiration for Wright's innovative theory of organic architecture as well as an integral part of his design: "organic architecture – is a natural architecture – the architecture of nature, for nature" (Wright 1953a: 226). In Wright's point of view, Nature represented God's creation. Therefore, nature is featured predominantly in Wright's sacred architecture. Moreover, Wright looked to nature as an expression of the American landscape and local environmental conditions. For these reasons, I have investigated Wright's sacred architecture as a representation of the American natural environment and as his environmentally conscious design. In my analyses of the interrelation of nature and his sacred architecture I address his print on the landscape, the relationship of the inner sacred space and the exterior environment, and his use of materials and systems to cater to natural lighting, acoustics, and thermal comfort.

The concept of *Democracy and Freedom* was the basis for Wright's search for a new style of architecture that would reflect the fundamental American soul. Throughout his career, Frank Lloyd Wright searched for a style that would convey America's culture as one of freedom, democracy and individualism: "America, more than any other nation, presents a new architectural proposition" (Wright 1910/1992: 106). As such, I was interested to study Wright's sacred architecture as an expression of a style that permits an experience of American democracy and freedom – a symbol of a new national consciousness. This expression highlights Wright's sacred architecture as a unique style that departed from the traditional church design of his time. Furthermore, Wright's non-traditional style in his religious projects demonstrated his different interpretations of the history and heritage of each faith, as well as the common themes across religions, such as his special treatment of the sacred path/plan, the vertical axis, light/shadow, and sound/silence.

Wright's *Holistic* approach to design is apparent in each of his religious projects where the interwoven relations of faith, form, and building technology create a whole project: "all buildings would be integral parts . . . according to place and purpose" (Wright 1958a/1995: 251). As a practicing architect, I think highly of this holistic approach in architecture. I believe that a design concept where the whole is the equilibrium of its parts enhances the three-dimensional architectural experience. As such, in sacred architecture it enriches the spiritual experience in the religious building. The design of these buildings, their systems, details, and ornaments as integral parts of the whole sacred space, increases the significance of the sacred place.

I visited and surveyed each of Wright's ten built sacred buildings and collected data, including photos, drawings, pamphlets, and documents. I have studied at the Frank Lloyd Wright Foundation Archives, Taliesin West, where I collected documents and drawings pertinent to both his built and unbuilt religious projects. The visits, the archival study, and the literature review of his writings as well as publications by others on his architecture and the few on his sacred buildings made me more appreciative of Wright's sacred architecture. I was impressed by these projects, each for a specific reason. Most of all, I was captivated by their "True Beauty" as Wright would say. This beauty characterizes all of these projects and expresses the fundamental shared universal symbols that define a sacred place and enhance its spiritual experience (see Part 1, Conceptual Model).

In addition to the functional and tectonic aspects of his design, Wright included a poetic side to each of these projects to express his belief in "True Beauty". Dimitri Tselos (1969: 72) claims that "[Wright's] achievement [reflects] most of the time an extra measure of capacity for poetic interpretation of shape, materials, and space". Indeed, Wright's poetic aspects in his sacred architecture may be attributed to the following factors: (1) Wright's abstraction of geometry as driven from nature – God's creation; (2) his interpretation of the shapes and symbolism of ancient religious monuments; (3) his understanding of the essence of materials and the power of natural light as beautifiers of the religious buildings; and (4) his expression of an American architectural style that would depart from the conventional European church design of his time and link his poetic design to the American landscape.

Some would argue that there are close parallels between Wright's design conceptions of secular projects and places of worship (see, e.g., Lipman 2005: 264–285). I can see the reasons for this observation. First, and as mentioned before, Wright considered all of his architecture as sacred. Second, he applied his theory of organic architecture, which thrived to reveal "Beauty and Truth" to *all* his projects. In his 1908 article 'In the Cause of Architecture' he wrote: "Buildings like people must first be sincere, must be true, and then withal as gracious and lovable as may be" (Wright 1908/1992: 88). Moreover, he believed that "architecture is not just building. It is the living spirit that builds" (Wright 1958a). With his designs, he tried to manifest "the ancient understanding of building as a sacred act, and buildings as sacred places" (McCarter 2005a: 12). The third reason for finding similarities between Wright's sacred and secular projects is that his holistic approach to design, his environmental consideration, and his search for a unique American style underlay *all* his projects. For instance, when Wright introduced a typology of his roof designs, he included sacred and secular buildings in that list (Wright 1908/1992: 93). Other examples are his introduction of the cruciform floor plan both in his sacred and secular projects (Storrer 1993: 91); and his use of the triangular unit system in the Unitarian Meeting House in Wisconsin and then in his Usonian houses (Hamilton 1991: 23). This mutual use is expressed by Wright's belief that "The power of the types will have translated the beauty of the cathedral to the homes of the people: a broadening of the base on which the growing beauty of the world rests" (Wright 1896/1992: 29). Although I acknowledge this aspect in Wright's architecture (see some examples in

Part 5, Conclusion), this book focuses on Wright's religious projects as the essence of his sacred architecture. The book illustrates how "Wright went to great lengths to obscure the physical reality of structure, surface, and edge" and to create the "transcendental level of existence" (Lipman 2005: 271).

Numerous books and articles attempt to illustrate the various sources of inspiration and the causal influences on the design/built form of Frank Lloyd Wright's architecture. These attempts include diverse ideas such as the influence of educational psychology (e.g., Wright's exposure to Froebel kindergarten training); his relations with his family, apprentices and clients; Wright's travels (e.g., Wright traveled extensively to Japan and Europe); the impact of archeological and historic precedence on his work; and Wright's participation in nineteenth century American transcendentalism. Some of this work provides substantial support for their hypotheses, some are speculative and base their reasoning on anecdotes, and others propose these influences as open questions. Most of the approaches to write on Frank Lloyd Wright's personality and/or work tend to reflect strong opinions on the subject described.

It is not the intention of this book to add to the effort of finding the causal reasons for Wright's creative work of design; neither is it to discuss Wright's personality or his relationships with the people around him. In addition, it should be noted that this book does not attempt to pass any judgment on the man and his architecture. Rather, I step back and analyze Wright's religious projects through his architectural concepts and designs. I use his huge volume of written material, archival drawings and documentations, and visits to his built houses of worship as my sources for this analysis.

I put my analysis in the context of the vast number of publications on Wright's architecture as well as the few works on his religious buildings.[1] I use this material to reveal his religious projects, and to illustrate the interaction of faith, form, and building technology in his sacred architecture.[2] This broader approach builds on studies that focus on a single house of worship, such as books on Unity Temple, Oak Park, Illinois by Joseph Siry (1996) and Robert McCarter (1997); on publications that briefly mention his houses of worship as part of Wright's architecture (Pfeiffer 1990; Storrer 1993; Hertz 1995; Levine 1996; De Long 1998; MacDonald et al. 2007); and on the few articles/ essays focusing on one specific house of worship, such as Unity Temple, Illinois, Annie Pfeiffer Chapel, Florida, and the Steel Cathedral, New York (e.g., Siry 2004; Graf 2005; McCarter 2005a).[3] Therefore, the unique contribution of this book is my attempt to provide a comprehensive study of Wright's sacred architecture.

The layout of the book includes this introduction, five parts and their chapters, bibliography, and index. The first part, "Faith, Form, and Building Technology: A Conceptual Model of Sacred Architecture", introduces the theoretical framework of the book. The conceptual model introduced in Part 1 focuses on the interwoven relation of faith, form, and building technology while examining how Wright's sacred architecture reflects each of these themes. The model incorporates the context of time and the environment as influential factors on building technology, form, and form's sacred ambience. Furthermore, the model specifies five elements of sacred architecture: sacred path/plan, sacred verticality, light, acoustics, and thermal comfort. Sacred path/plan and sacred verticality are an integral part of the sacred three-dimensional form. Light, acoustics, and thermal comfort create the sacred ambience and are achieved by the systems of building technology.

Each of the next three parts of the book (parts 2, 3, and 4) separately addresses the main topics of the conceptual model: "Faith", "Form", and "Building Technology". Every part includes an introduction to the specific topic, and three chapters that analyze Wright's sacred architecture along his main design concepts *Nature, Democracy and Freedom,* and *the Whole as the Equilibrium of Its Parts.* While Part 2, "Faith", includes only the above-mentioned chapters, Part 3, "Form", includes two additional chapters, which focus on the *Sacred Path/Plan* and the *Sacred Verticality* in Wright's sacred architecture. Part 4, "Building Technology", consists of three additional chapters: *Light, Acoustics,* and *Thermal Comfort.* These parts of the book and their chapters illuminate how Wright's sacred architecture complied with his major design ideas.

The final part of the book, Part 5, "Conclusion", is organized along three central themes. First, I provide a summary of Wright's sacred architecture as a manifestation of his main architectural design concepts. I show that Wright created unique religious projects through his holistic design, which integrated faith programmatic tasks, American landscape and freedom, building production, and spiritual experiences. Second, I discuss the significance of Wright's sacred architecture as expressed in the continuing use of his built houses of God for worship services rather than their adaptation to other religious or secular use. In addition, most of these religious buildings are now listed on the American National Register of Historic Places and are designated by the American Institute of Architects as contributors to American culture. The third theme of the Conclusion illustrates some examples of the similarities of Wright's sacred architecture and his secular projects. All of these concluding points demonstrate the significance of his sacred architecture. This significance may serve as the justification for the preservation of Wright's built religious buildings and the conservation of his drawings of the unbuilt sacred projects.

This book was written with love and respect for Frank Lloyd Wright's sacred architecture. Observing and absorbing his poetic design in his religious projects lifted my spirit and bolstered my admiration for this type of architecture. However, since I am not a poet, although I appreciate poetry, my approach to this book represents a scholarly point of view where I attempt to offer an extensive conceptual framework of research and analyses of Wright's sacred architecture.

Notes

1 Due to the large amount of written material by Frank Lloyd Wright and by others on his architecture, I apologize if I have omitted some references.
2 Although Wright designed more than thirty houses of worship, very few scholars have written about them.
3 A recent DVD entitled *Sacred Spaces: The Houses of Worship Designed by Frank Lloyd Wright* provides a chronological survey of images of the ten built religious structures and how the congregations still use them.

Part 1

FAITH, FORM, AND BUILDING TECHNOLOGY

A Conceptual Model of Sacred Architecture

1
FAITH, FORM, AND BUILDING TECHNOLOGY

A Conceptual Model of Sacred Architecture

Frank Lloyd Wright, 1867–1957. Love of an idea is the love of God.
(Wright's gravesite marker, Spring Green WI)

The pursuit of the sacred is one of the universal characteristics of human beings: "Whether therefore ye eat, or drink, or whatsoever ye do, do all to the glory of God" (1 Corinthians 10:31). Sacredness is associated with the spiritual spheres of humanity, where man/woman seeks meaning to the complexity of life that can transcend daily reality. The concept of sacred may be vague and elusive for operational definitions. Yet, it seems commonly accepted that while the expressions of what is sacred and/or divine change with time, geography, and religion, people accept the sacred as part of their humanity (Eliade 1959/1987; McNally 1985; Wilber 2006; Barrie 1996, 2010). Moreover, at times, the *sacred* captures critical influences of the cultural and social markings of a given society.

Commonly, people tend to generate a concretization (physical manifestation) of their abstract values to gain a more tangible experience of the spiritual (Wilber 2006: 101). There are numerous rationalizations for the need to employ tangibles to "capture" spiritual entities. Whether we use sacred geometry and mysticism as a means for the simplification of complex values by "[revealing] the divine source in its manifestation" (Barrie 1996: 54); or whether it is done to facilitate the communication of inner undefined needs through prayers, holy text reading, hymn singing/chanting; we always find comfort in the concrete three-dimensional space of the house of God. The religious building is the juxtaposition of the physical (tangible) and spiritual realms, and represents the multi-faceted sacred experience of the worshiper. As Fr. Richard S. Vosko explains: "The worship space is a story-book of old tales and many still unwritten" (Crosbie 2000: 9).

Indeed, some claim that the sacred is awakened through the phenom-enological experiences of specific architectural archetypes, which work as symbols and enhance the spiritual meanings of a place (Eliade 1959/1987; McNally 1985; Barrie 1996, 2010). Thus, the sacred is intensified through the association with an established house of worship or an object in it.

This type of architecture expresses the Divine's presence, serves as the intersection of heavenly and earthly realms, and is a place of cosmological myth built as the earthly representation of the celestial system (Eliade 1959/1987; Yi-Fu 1978; Turner 1979; Mann 1993; Barrie 1996; Kieckhefer 2004; Wilber 2006; Benedikt 2008). In other words, the sacred place enables the worshiper to communicate with the other world, "the world of divine beings or ancestors" (Eliade 1992: 107; Wilber 2006: 101).

Although the phenomenological experiences of sacred architecture result in a variety of interpretations of religious motifs, we can still trace a remarkable fundamental similarity between the relation of faith and form in sacred architecture. As the thirteenth century Persian poet and theolo-gian Jalāl ad-Din Muhammad Rumi summarizes in his poem "One Song":[1] "All Religions, All This Singing, One Song," and claimed that the same sunlight shines on all. He believed that "The Differences Are Just Illusion And Vanity" (Green 2005).

The commonalities of sacred architecture reflect both the physical and spiritual realms, and stem out of the basic definitions of a sacred place; the shared fundamental universal symbols across faith; and the relation of the house of worship and people's spiritual experiences (Durkheim 1912; Eliade 1959/1987; Yi-Fu 1974; Turner 1979; Mann 1993; Barrie 1996; Kieckhefer 2004; Wilber 2006). Some scholars believe that the similarities in the sacred architectural form across faith are based on geometrical patterns, which serve as the grammar of the sacred space (Wright 1912; Von Franz 1972; Critchlow 1980; Lawlor 1982; Campbell 1988; Mann 1993; Barrie 1996). Some refer to this grammar as "sacred" geometry, while others examine the basic fundamental core of geometrical patterns (Critchlow 1980; Lawlor 1982; Barrie 1996; Tabb 1996).

And still, the imprint of sacred architecture on the physical landscape echoes specific faith rituals and symbolism (Cohn 1981). Scholars are cognizant that houses of worship do manifest the particulars of specific religions and their cultural underpinning (Cram 1924; Conover 1948; Schwarz 1958; Roberts 2004). As such, the specific requirements of each faith illustrate cultural and historical differences, and the diversity of specific rituals, all of which lead to different forms of houses of worship.

These aspects address the relation of faith and form in sacred architecture and serve as the blueprint of the conceptual model introduced in this book. The model consists of an additional major set of relationships that depicts the interaction between form and building technology. The mutual relation of these major aspects of sacred architecture illustrates the achievement of the desired sacred built form. The model also addresses additional factors such as ambience of the sacred space and its context that influence the interrelation of faith, form, and building technology.

The Conceptual Model

The book's conceptual model on sacred architecture highlights the main relations between the three elements of faith, form, and building technology (Fig. 1.1). It also shows how additional factors such as the sacred ambience and the building's context influence these relationships. Specifically, the conceptual model shows how faith's functional and spiritual requirements are expressed in the built form and its ambience; and how building technology is used to accommodate the sacred form or how it determines the form of each of the religious houses and enhances the sacredness of the ambience in these buildings. Thus, the model depicts the physical and spiritual realms as integrated in architectural religious projects (Fig. 1.1). These sets of relations serve as the framework for my attempt to decipher the design principles underlying Frank Lloyd Wright's sacred architecture.

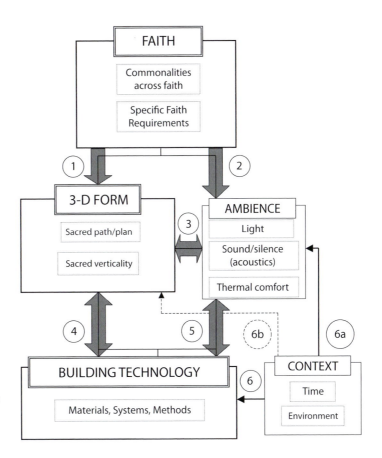

1.1
Faith, Form, and Building Technology: a Conceptual Model on Sacred Architecture.

The first major part of the model illustrates the relationship between faith and form. The term faith is derived from the Latin word *fidem* or *fidis*, which means trust. It expresses a set of beliefs, rituals, and trust in God. As such, faith introduces functional and spiritual requirements that are translated into the built form. These aspects of faith will be explicated later in my analyses of the influence of both the universal commonalities across faith and the specific requirements of each faith on the sacred form. This relation is illustrated in the conceptual model by a one-sided solid arrow, numbered 1, pointing from Faith towards Form (Fig. 1.1).

Form is defined as the shape and structure of an object, or as a three-dimensional composition that produces a coherent image (Ching 1996). As such, it includes the horizontal and vertical axes of the space, which in the model are depicted as the sacred path/plan and sacred verticality. These axes create the three-dimensional dynamic form of the sacred place and influence the spiritual ambience of the space, which answers some of the physical and spiritual faith requirements. Arrow 2 illustrates the relation of faith and ambience. On the other hand, certain ambience demands such as light, sound/silence, and thermal comfort as associated with faith can impact the three-dimensional shape of the sacred form. This mutual relationship between form and ambience helps to shape the sacred space and its spiritual experiences. It is illustrated in the conceptual model by a two-sided arrow numbered 3 (Fig. 1.1).

The second major part of the model shows the mutual relation between form and building technology. Form directs the selection of building technology. However, often building technology serves as the major factor in determining the built form. "The forms were sculptured from materials according to the nature of construction and the life of the time" (Wright 1949/1994: 336). This mutual interaction between form and building technology is illustrated in the model by a solid bi-directional arrow numbered 4 (Fig. 1.1).

The definition of building technology consists of materials, systems, and methods. Thus, the ambience aspects of light, sound/silence, and thermal comfort are part of building technology systems. As such, the mutual relation of building technology and the ambience of the sacred place is depicted in the model as a bi-directional arrow numbered 5 (Fig. 1.1).

This mutual relation of building technology and ambience helps to achieve a form that expresses a faith's spiritual and programmatic requirements. While requirements of faith lead the creation of light and sound or silence and cater to or ignore thermal comfort, building technology accommodates these systems and provides the pragmatic and practical solutions.

These systems, as other developments in building technology, are directly influenced by the context of time and the environment of the building. As time progresses, so do developments in building technology. Different environments have their conditions impact upon the development of building technology or the selection of the specific technology to be used in the construction of the religious building. The conceptual model shows this relation with a direct arrow pointed out from context to building technology and is numbered 6 (Fig. 1.1). Time and environmental conditions also influence the ambience factors (e.g., light and sound quality, and thermal comfort) of the sacred place. Therefore, this influence of context on ambience of the sacred place is illustrated in the model as a direct arrow numbered 6a (Fig. 1.1.).

The model acknowledges the influence of context on form by a dashed arrow pointed out from context to form and numbered 6b (Fig. 1.1). Changes in timely fashion styles of sacred architecture, political and religious powers, and environmental constraints influence the design of the sacred built form. As mentioned before, these relationships are embedded as part of the text associated with the major three elements of the model. For example, I elaborate on the notion of style in my analyses and descriptions of Frank Lloyd Wright's religious projects' departure from the European traditional church design of the time. Political factors in relation to sacred architecture are discussed in my analysis of Wright's design concept of democracy and freedom. Examples of Wright's environmentally conscientious design are addressed in Chapter 14 on thermal comfort (Part 4, Building Technology).

Faith and Form

The first major part of the conceptual model focuses on faith and its relation to sacred form. This part of the model captures a large volume of scholarly work written on sacred places and their expression of religion. Numerous scholars have examined the relation of faith and form along two levels of inquiry (Eliade 1959/1987; Yi-Fu 1978; Turner 1979; Mann 1993; Barrie 1996, 2010; Kieckhefer 2004; Wilber 2006; Benedikt 2008). The first level of this scholarly work addresses the commonalities and shared features of sacred places across faith. These commonalities express the relation between spiritual experiences in general and the sacred space. The second level of this scholarly inquiry addresses the idea that "A sacred building comes into a relationship with human worshipers through ritual action" (Humphrey and Vitebsky 2005: 60). The existence of diverse specific rituals and symbols represents distinct programmatic/functional needs. Consequently, many forms are developed to express the interrelationship of a faith and its sacred built form.

Faith Commonalities and Shared Features of Sacred Places

Already at the end of the eighteenth century, the German theologian and philosopher Friedrich Schleiermacher, known as the "Father of Modern Protestant Theology," defined religion as a spiritual experience rather than a doctrine (Lamm 1996). Multiple studies show that the spiritual experiences across faith reach beyond the sacred place's physical realm and bring humans closer to the Divine. Therefore, and as mentioned before, many believe that the sacred place expresses the Divine's presence. It serves as the intersection between heavenly and earthly realms, and as a place of cosmological myth (Turner 1979). Thus, one can expect certain commonalities across faith, such as the perception of the cosmos/universe and how it is manifested in the house of worship; the shared fundamental universal elements that create the universe; and the idea that a sacred space is set apart from the mundane (Eliade 1959/1987; Yi-Fu 1978; Turner 1979; Mann 1993; Barrie 1996; Kieckhefer 2004; Wilber 2006; Benedikt 2008).

Cosmos/Universe and Sacred Architecture

The word cosmos is defined as "an orderly harmonious systematic universe," where universe is considered as "the whole body of things and phenomena observed or postulated" (Merriam-Webster Dictionary). In other words, the universe and all that exists within it are one interrelated and interdependent whole. The dictionary also points out that the definition of the cosmos as synonym to universe includes "a systematic whole held to arise by and persist through the direct intervention of divine power." As such, the concepts of the cosmos and the universe are used in all religions in a reference to God, God's creation, and its spiritual forces.

The perception of the cosmos as a spiritual symbol created myths, which in turn expressed faith ritual practices (Smith 1894; Frazer 1935; Barrie 1996: 5, 52). Throughout history, human thought on the cosmos has evolved from magic rituals and myth, to religion, and even as part of science. The relation between myth and rituals was the main focus of nineteenth century anthropologists such as Sir James Frazer. Since the twentieth century scholars have begun relating myth, its symbols, and rituals to *architecture,* showing how these concepts are embodied in the dynamic three-dimensional sacred spaces (Lévi-Strauss 1963; Lane 1988; Barrie 1996, 2010; Kieckhefer 2004; Tabb 2007). In his studies of universal approaches to myth, Claude Lévi-Strauss (1963) observed that the meaning of mythology as well as the meaning of sacred architecture reside only when all the universal elements are integrated into one composition. This notion brings us back to the definition of the cosmos/universe as a systematic whole, which perfects the direct intervention of God's power. A strong example of the relation between the perception of the universe and sacred architecture is the belief of Native Americans that the universe is perfect only when the Temple is perfect. This perfection in their point of view can be achieved by creating a spatial hierarchy and sequence that brings the worshiper through a clearly defined threshold into the inner sanctum separated from the profane.

Scholars such as Yi-Fu (1974) and Altman and Chemers (1980) studied the perceptual arrangement of the universe. They claim that the universe is perceived as a central core. Euclid, the Greek mathematician from the third century BC philosophized that the central point is the beginning of a circle, which may be considered as a center that has the freedom to extend in any direction. Thomas Barrie (1996: 53) addresses the establishment of the center as the main part of creating a sacred place. He claims: "The creation of a sacred place has principally provided the existential means for people to establish a center and thus define their place in the world."

The central core of the universe includes horizontal and vertical axes. The horizontal axis expresses the lines of earth that "belongs to anyone who stops for a moment, gazes, and goes on his way" (Colette, twentieth-century French novelist). The core of the universe and its horizontal axis may be perceived in sacred architecture as the sacred plan and its path. The plan represents the center of the world, while the sacred path (the horizontal axis) leads to the core and thus creates the boundaries of the journey from the secular to the sacred (Turner 1979; Humphrey and Vitebsky 2005). The vertical axis of the universe links the underground, earth, and heaven and brings humans closer to the Divine (Wright 1958b; Barrie 1996; Ching 1996; Humphrey and Vitebsky 2005; Andrews 2007). "The sky above was just a hole, the clouds drizzling us with the lightest of rain, as the earth and grass released their imprisoned scents" (Eng 2008: 140). As such, this verticality represents the archetypal cosmic center and creates the world axis – the *axis mundi*. This axis expresses "a series of hierarchically descending radiations from the Godhead through interme-diate stages to matter" (Merriam-Webster Dictionary). In Genesis, the story of Jacob at Bethel depicts the notion of the vertical axis representing a place for communication with God. In his dream, Jacob saw a ladder ascending to heaven and heard the voice of the Lord. Here, the vertical axis is perceived as the upward movement reaching to heaven and the downward movement toward the ground. The expression of this move-ment in the sacred place triggers the spiritual experiences in that space (Tabb 2007).

The translation of the universe's structure into sacred architecture shows that geometry, order, symbolism of shapes, and horizontal and vertical axes are the major elements of the sacred form. The combination of these aspects generates three-dimensional dynamic solutions to sacred architecture and creates the sacred space in the image of the world – the *imago mundi*. For example, the central plan of the Ziggurats of ancient

Mesopotamia presented the core of their universe and the stairs of these monuments were believed to lead to heaven; the Pyramids of Egypt rose from the desert plateau on a square representing earth, and used circular shapes as part of their Gods' images and celestial systems; the longitudinal plan of the Gothic cathedrals became a three-dimensional space soaring to heaven; the sacred timber pole of the Shinto shrine is considered a sanctified column. An additional example of the translation of the universe's structure into sacred architecture is the Buddhist Temple of Borobudu in Java. The Temple's stacked square plans support its *axis mundi*. Each of the various vertical levels of this Temple is decorated with sculpted stones that symbolize the path and transformation from the mundane to the sacred, starting at the base of the Temple with the symbols of day-to-day life, and reaching through a vertical procession to the sacred summit where the three Buddhas sit with "Eyes closed in contemplation. Legs crossed. Hands symbolically placed" showing where the spirit lies (Osmen 1990: 188; Grabsky 1999: 15).

The language Wright used in his sacred architecture expressed the horizontal axis of the cosmos as growing parallel to earth, and the vertical axis as bringing God's creation into the sacred building (Rogers 2001: 8) (see Part 3, Form, this volume). This language was based on pure geometry with its associated symbols, its balanced interdependent volumes, and its meaningful dimensions, such as "continuity" for length, "breadth" for width, and "depth" for thickness. Wright acknowledged the earthiness of the square, which he also considered as a double triangle. This triangular doubling process can go on infinitely and create the universe (Suzuki 1999). The triangle in these projects represents the beginning of all forms. The circle in Wright's sacred architecture symbolizes infinity and the universe. Wright believed that these geometries were driven from nature and as such could help in understanding the celestial order, as well as synthesizing architectural features and their harmony with the environment. This understanding represented the cosmos/universe to Wright (Wright 1932a; Casey 1988; Green 1988; Alofsin 1993; Hertz 1995; Barrie 1996; McCarter 1997, 2005a).[2]

For Wright, the universal ordering principles that can be found in nature created "the *cosmic order* as clean integrity in the terms of living" (Wright 1958b/1992: 228). This notion was amplified in Wright's sacred architecture since in his view the sacred place expressed nature, which "is all the body of God we are ever going to see" (from Mike Wallace's TV interview with Frank Lloyd Wright, September 1957). Moreover, Wright claimed that "Nature is God" and "[t]hrough nature we can sense anew the universal pulse, the inner rhythm of all being" (Wright 1958b/1992: 231).

It may be concluded that Wright studied nature, its order, geometry, and rhythm as the representation of the universe and its cosmic order. He followed the historic notion that sacred architecture replicates the cosmos (Yi-Fu 1978: 84; Barrie 1996: 4; Humphrey and Vitebsky 2005: 10), and translated the structure of the universe into his sacred architecture. This translation, in addition to his inspiration from ancient religious monuments, which he believed were tuned to cosmic concepts and Nature, reveals his major design concepts and the geometric grammar of his sacred places. However, the perception of the cosmos/universe is not complete without the introduction of the four fundamental universal elements that create the universe, and hence impact on the structure of the sacred built form.

Shared Fundamental Universal Elements that Create the Universe

Another common aspect across faith is the perception that four fundamental elements create the universe: "[the] totality of the world is divided into 4 elements . . . with four to eight qualities, which unite" (Von Fanz 1972: 333–334). The literature on sacred places indicates that the four main universal symbols of earth, water, air, and fire reflect the structure of the cosmos and represent the sacred values associated with heaven, earth, and hell (Vitruvius [1960]; Eliade 1959/1987; Yi-Fu 1978; Turner 1979; Altman and Chemers 1980; Mann 1993).

Earth represents the element of life that surrounds us. Gary Snyder portrays this in his poem 'Earth Verse':[3]

> *Wide enough to keep you looking*
> *Open enough to keep you moving*
> *Dry enough to keep you honest*
> *Prickly enough to make you tough*
> *Green enough to go on living*
> *Old enough to give you dreams.*

Earth is often worshiped in its own right with its own unique spiritual traditions. Earth also represents stability, permanence, and materiality. Therefore, economic and political powers are associated with the element of earth.

Water represents the liquid state of the energy of life as well as purity. Water is perceived to carry away wastes and sins (Humphrey and Vitebsky 2005: 111). Thus, many religious rituals use water for physical and spiritual purification such as to reflect the light of enlightenment. One spiritual metaphor for water is the Ocean of God where each individual is a drop of water. Moreover, water is also seen as an additional dwelling of God beside mountains (Mirsky 1976: 9).

Air is a mobile and dynamic element without form, which is a key to human existence. Since it represents heat and cold it is situated between fire and water. Air is often associated with the sky and thus with heaven. Air is also associated with the Latin root of the word spirit – *spirare*, meaning "to breath."

Fire has the power to transform the state of any substance. It can burn and destroy, but it can also heal and create, and therefore it is associated with hell on the one hand and with godly power on the other. Throughout history the transformation of fire was celebrated across religions with rituals and symbols.

The four elements (earth, water, air, and fire) already appear in antiquity as a set of archetypes that explain patterns in nature (McNally 1985).[4] The idea was that everything was formed out of these four elements. The Greek philosopher Plato added a fifth element called *quintessence*. He explained that the cosmos and all celestial bodies are made of this element (Plato, *c.* 360 BC as translated in 2000). Aristotle, a student of Plato, called this fifth element *aether* and placed it in the middle of the four elements. He claimed that this fifth element is constant, while the others have their dynamic changes (Lloyd 1968). Recent scholars such as Joseph Campbell (1988: 63) wrote about the sequence of the elements in creating the world: "air, then fire, then water and earth." Claude Lévi-Strauss (1963: 206-231) strengthened the significance of these universal characteristics by finding similar myths about them in different parts of the world. Indeed, the same four elements are found in Hinduism, Buddhism, and Japanese religions. Like the ancient Western philosophers, these Eastern (oriental) thinkers added a fifth element in the center of the four, which they called "space" or "void."

Scholars such as Keith Critchlow (1980) and Robert Lawlor (1982) discuss the relation between the four elements and sacred architecture. They refer to the four elements as the factors defining sacred architecture and relate sacred geometry to these elements. I associate the aspects of sacred ambience (light, sounds, climate comfort) and their pertinent building technology to the four sacred universal elements (fire, water, earth, and air). Specifically, I see *fire* as the representation of the sun and therefore as a generator of sunlight. This powerful association contributes to the sacred ambience of light in the house of God. In addition, fire is linked with the physical and spiritual meanings of the eternal burning light. As mentioned before, *air* is associated with the sky and as such represents heaven. In addition, air is a major element in generating fire. Therefore, we can see air as the illuminating force of the sacred place; or even more dramatically as a major factor in the light of enlightenment.

In my analysis, I associate *air* and *water* as acoustical techniques that enhance the sacred ambience of sound/silence. Air and water can create sounds; carry rays of sound from other sources, or block surrounding secular sounds. In other words, air and water contribute to the establishment of boundaries and/or thresholds between the sacred and the mundane.

In addition, I associate *water, air,* and *fire* with thermal comfort. All three elements are part of external climate conditions, and influence the techniques of creating micro climate and thermal comfort in the building. Since water determines the level of humidity in the air, it should be considered a contributor to thermal comfort. Water is also used to cool or heat a building; fire is utilized to generate heat; and air represents temperature, relative humidity, and serves as the major force in distributing heating or cooling effects.

Finally, I refer to the combination of *earth, water,* and *fire* as part of the construction materials, such as brick, and the way they are produced: "Make the walls of bricks that fire touched to tawny gold or ruddy tan, choicest of all earth's hues" (Wright in Pfeiffer and Nordland 1988: 53).

Richard Joncas (1998a: 101, 103) describes Frank Lloyd Wright's depiction of the universal elements as "a display of . . . color, light, water and sound." In Wright's mind these features enable the conversion of a house of worship to a "spiritually uplifting theater of worship." Although Wright did not address specifically the classical four elements of earth, water, air, and fire, he did interpret them.[5] The analysis of some of his religious projects reveals their direct relationship with the four elements (earth, water, air, and fire). For example, his design proposal for the Memorial to the Soil Chapel in Wisconsin shows the building growing out of the earth – parts of it even designed as parallel lines to earth. Its square shape represents a solid and powerful image similar to the symbols associated with earth (Fig. 1.2).

Wright utilized the element of water in some of his religious projects to create boundaries and/or thresholds between the secular and the sacred. A more in-depth analysis of his use appears later in this section. Air as associated with sky, and fire as associated with light can be traced in Wright's design of the translucent pyramidal roof of Beth Sholom Synagogue in Pennsylvania (Fig. 1.3), in the skylights of Unity Temple in Illinois (Fig. 1.4), and Annie Pfeiffer Chapel in Florida (Fig. 1.5). In these examples Wright combined the spiritual symbolism of the sky (heaven) with light.

Wright's use of bright colors in some of his glass design and the way it captures light can be associated with fire, which encompasses a spectrum of colors. See, for example, the skylight colored glass of the First Christian Church in Arizona,[6] which combines red, blue, and white in Fig. 2.3.6 in Part 2 (this volume); and the red and gold colors of the glass behind the prow in the Minor Chapel in Florida in Fig. 2.1.1 in Part 2.

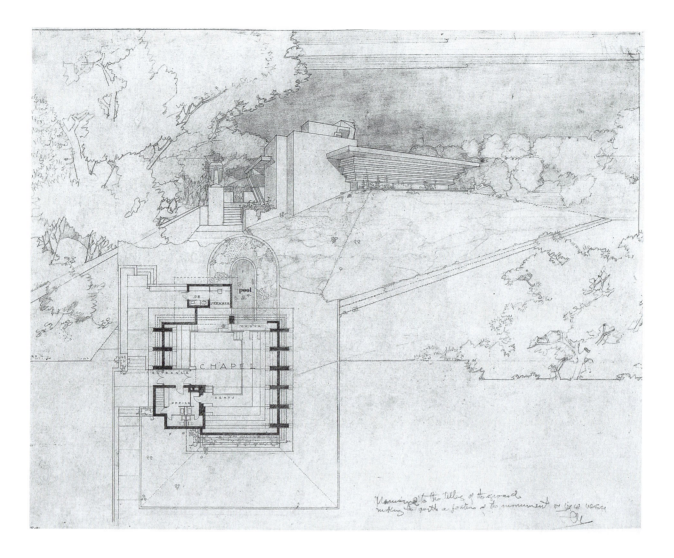

Wright believed in the unity of all elements both in religion and in architecture. His design proposal for the Steel Cathedral in New York is an example of his unification of all faiths under the same roof. This design highlights Wright's belief that all faiths share the same universal elements and therefore Wright named it the "church of the elements." If built, once the worshipers entered the Cathedral they would be embraced by light from the pyramidal translucent roof, water from fountains in the ground level, sounds of water, air, and rituals, and processional ramps, which create the thresholds between the common sacred space and the specific chapels of each faith. Setting apart the sacred common space from the profane and the specific chapels from the common areas also strengthened his design of faith unification.

1.2

Elevation and Plan of Frank Lloyd Wright's Proposal for the Memorial to the Soil Chapel, Wisconsin (1936) (© 2009 Frank Lloyd Wright Foundation, Scottsdale, AZ/Artists Rights Society (ARS), New York).

1.3
Beth Sholom Synagogue,
Pennsylvania (1954).

1.4
The Interior of Unity Temple, Illinois
(1906).

The Sacred Place as Set Apart From the Mundane

The separation of the sacred place from the profane is an additional common aspect of sacred architecture across faith. Yi-Fu (1978: 84–85) based this conjecture on the meaning of the Latin source for sacred – *sacer,* which means an area set apart and pertaining to God. In addition, the root of the Latin word *templum* is *tem*, which means "to cut out"; while the literal meaning of profane is the ground before and outside the temple (Yi-Fu 1978: 85). It is interesting to note that the Hebrew word kodesh (*k-d-sh)* means "holy" and is interpreted in the Bible as separation: "I am set apart and you must be set apart like me" (Leviticus xi, 46). These linguistic definitions reinforce the interpretation that sacred architecture is distinct from other building types.

In his seminal book *The Elementary Forms of the Religious Life* (1912/1915), Emile Durkheim proposes that sacredness expresses things that are set apart and are forbidden. In his book *The Idea of the Holy* (originally in German, *Das Heilige* (1917)), Rudolf Otto describes the spiritual experience as a frightening and irrational power, which is manifested by divine rage and is separated from the profane. Otto (1917/1970) continued to describe these experiences as *numinous* (in Latin numen: God) or "wholly other," expressing *mysterium tremendum* (the great mystery), *majestas* (majesty), and *mysterium fascinans* (fascinating mystery). Ralph Adams Cram's theory of theological aesthetics (1924), which is described in his book on church design, focuses on the house of God as a place set apart. The building creates "spiritual emotions . . . [that] lift men's minds from secular things to spiritual, that their souls may be brought into harmony with God" (Cram 1924: 6–10). In his book *The Earth, the Temple, and the Gods: Greek Sacred Architecture* (1962), Vincent Scully examines the sacred space as a threshold of communication with God – a place in which to find one's inner soul. The house of God "reach[s] down inside the worshiper and bec[o]me[s] a place where the currents are flowing from the places towards the soul, where the whole atmosphere is charged" (Osho as cited by Osmen 1990: 3).

Mircea Eliade (1959/1987) followed Otto's notion of setting apart the sacred place from the profane. In his book *The Sacred and the Profane – The Nature of Religion,* Eliade explains, "The sacred is pre-eminently the Real, a wholly other Reality which does not belong to this world even though it is manifest in and through it." He sees the sacred as a place where gods reveal themselves and thus the space is differentiated from the profane or "remains 'the opposite of the profane'" (Eliade 1958/1987: 459). Tuan Yi-Fu (1978: 84–99) elaborates on the definitions of the sacred place as set apart from the profane, and reinforces Otto and Eliade's expressions of the "other Reality."

Sacred architecture can be considered in all faith as the rite passage from the profane to the sacred and as a place for spiritual transformation. The sacred space invites the worshiper to take a pilgrimage or a journey, leaving the secular and entering the sacred realm where he or she can reunite with God. Thomas Barrie (1996: 29) claims that the act of separation is perhaps one of the most significant components of the pilgrim's journey. This processional journey from the mundane to the sacred is characterized by physical boundaries and symbols, which create a threshold space. "A sacred place of pilgrimage is a unique experiment . . . In such a place, if you do nothing else but throw open your sails, your journey will begin" (Osho cited by Osmen 1990: 3). The sacred colonnade procession in Hindu temples, which is part of the pilgrim's journey, acts as the threshold space. The sacred sculptures decorating this path set the mind of the worshiper to prepare for the sacred sanctuary, leaving behind the wordy world.

Gardens and water can serve as natural elements that create these thresholds; and man-made bridges can serve as a clear link between separated places. Often, such a bridge may be found in Zen Buddhist temples and is called *gen-kan* (Barrie 1996: 57). Such is Wright's proposed design of an elevated walkway with a fountain beneath it of the Wedding Chapel in California. This design is an example of Wright's vision of the separation of the sacred (the proposed Wedding Chapel) from the secular (the Claremont Hotel in Berkeley, California) (Figs 1.6 and 1.7). Thus, Frank Lloyd Wright used both natural elements (e.g., water, gardens), and man-made paths to create the thresholds that separate the sacred from the profane.

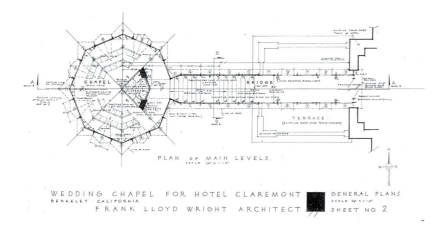

1.6

Frank Lloyd Wright's 1957 Proposed Plan of a Wedding Chapel and its Bridge, California (© 2009 Frank Lloyd Wright Foundation, Scottsdale, AZ/Artists Rights Society (ARS), New York).

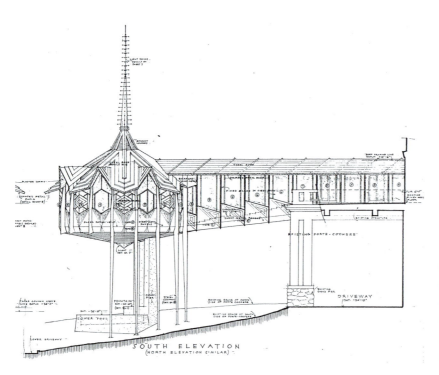

1.7

Frank Lloyd Wright's 1957 Proposed Bridge and Elevation of a Wedding Chapel, California (© 2009 Frank Lloyd Wright Foundation, Scottsdale, AZ/Artists Rights Society (ARS), New York).

Some of Wright's other unrealized projects that include a design of natural and man-made thresholds between secular and sacred places include the Johnson Desert Compound and Shrine at the upper edge of the Mojave Desert in Death Valley, California (1921? 1923? 1924–1925?),[7] the Memorial to the Soil Chapel in Wisconsin (1936), and Taliesin Unity Chapel in Wisconsin (1958). In the Johnson Compound proposal, Wright designed a triangular pool in front of the main entrance to the complex. Pumped water from this pool would cascade down to form a base for the terrace of the main house and chapel. The octagonal shrine with its herringbone-decorated spire directs the viewer's eye to a circular fountain, which terminates the diagonal axis of the project (Levine 1996: 178). In the Memorial to the Soil Chapel in Wisconsin, Wright designed a pool that is set as an exterior protruding terrace in the earth berms surrounding the chapel. The location of the pool and its reflection of light were intended to provide a background to the choir in the chapel (Pfeiffer 1988: 350), thus separating the interior space from the outside ordinary world (Fig. 1.2). In his design of Taliesin Unity Chapel in Wisconsin, Wright proposed two reflecting pools. The first is a narrow longitudinal pool along the walk toward the entrance to the chapel. This configuration would prolong the sacred path toward the entrance of the Chapel and set the mood of the worshiper (see Part 3 on Form, this volume). The second reflecting pool is situated in the back along a walk that separates the building from the rest of the secular world (Fig. 1.8).

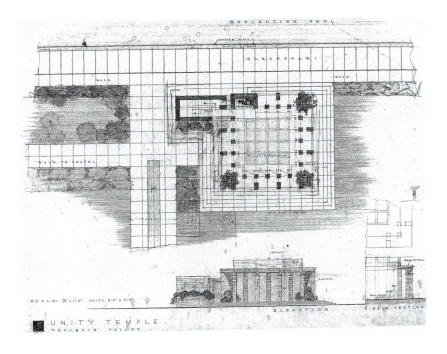

1.8

Plan and Elevation of Frank Lloyd Wright's Proposal for Taliesin Unity Chapel, Wisconsin (1958) (© 2009 Frank Lloyd Wright Foundation, Scottsdale, AZ/Artists Rights Society (ARS), New York).

In all of these examples, Frank Lloyd Wright utilized water elements as a boundary for the sacred path, and as a threshold space between the sacred and the mundane.

The location of the sacred site can also contribute to the separation of the sacred place from the profane (Lane 1988: 19). This notion already appeared in the Old Testament (Exodus 3: 5): "Draw not nigh hither: put off thy shoes from off thy feet, for the place whereon thou standest is holy ground." Frank Lloyd Wright was no stranger to this idea and applied it to some of his religious projects. For example, in his master plan for Florida

Southern Methodist College, he positioned the Annie Pfeiffer Chapel in the center and on the highest spot of the campus. This placement helps the chapel to present itself as a spiritual symbol of the campus and to radiate the Methodist mission of the college. Furthermore, to accentuate the importance of the Chapel, "Speakers atop each corner were connected to the chapel's organ so that music could be heard across the campus" (MacDonald et al. 2007: 19). In this context even "music transforms ordinary action into ritual action" with a sense of timelessness that enhances the separation from daily life (Kieckhefer 2004: 110). The location of Unity Temple is another example of the separation of holy from secular. Wright faced the Temple to the side street rather than the main one. There are several reasons for the Temple's position, which are described in Parts 3 and 4 of this book (Form and Building Technology, respectively). Yet, in this context, I argue that this orientation creates a separation from the noisy street that represents day-to-day life.

In summary, the scholarly work on faith commonalities and shared universal features highlights the similarities of religious expression through sacred architecture across faith. Frank Lloyd Wright's sacred architecture addresses these commonalities and illuminates their enhancement of the sacred space. Still, "each [faith] seeks its own relationship with the divine" (Wright 1958b/1997: 8) and therefore in the next section I discuss the relationship between diverse and specific faith programmatic/functional needs and the sacred form.

Faith Programmatic/Functional Needs and Form

The particular needs of each faith and their impact on sacred architecture (e.g., shape, size, procession, inclusion of secular activities, etc.) are specified in various religious manifests (such as the Bible, Roman Catholic Canon Laws, etc.), as well as in some design guidelines (e.g., Cram 1924; Conover 1948; Schwarz 1958; Roberts 2004 among others). For example, the Roman Catholic longitudinal cross serves as the blueprint for Catholic cathedral and church plans. This shape not only contains the spiritual symbol of the faith, but caters to the faith-based programmatic needs and rituals of a relatively long procession path.[8] Throughout history, the square cross of the Eastern Orthodox Church is expressed through central domical structures. This cross was the basis for Frank Lloyd Wright's design of the domical structure of the Annunciation Greek Orthodox Church in Wisconsin (see Part 3 on Form, this volume). Another example of specific faith requirements is the seating arrangements in a house of worship. Some religions require separate seating areas for women and men. This may be accomplished by the use of different levels in the building such as a gallery or a balcony (for examples see orthodox synagogues, or Wendish churches), or through interior partitions. In synagogues, the origin of a congregation influences the seating arrangements. The tradition of the

Ashkenazi Jews[9] has the stage (*Bima*) placed in front of the congregation. Thus, all seats face the front (see Frank Lloyd Wright's Beth Sholom Synagogue in Pennsylvania). The *Bima* in Sephardic[10] synagogues is located in the center. Thus, the seats are arranged on both sides of the stage. Another example of faith requirements that influence the form of the sacred place is the call for multi-functional spaces as in Unitarian churches. In this case, some churches include one multi-functional space, while others include interior moveable partitions. A good example of the latter solution is the woven partition in the Unitarian Meeting House designed by Frank Lloyd Wright.[11]

Throughout history the orientation/alignment of a house of God was one of the most common aspects associated with specific religion's interpretations. The orientation/alignment of a building reflects people's perception of the universe and influences the shape of the house of worship. Most ancient religious monuments were aligned to "the luminary, planet or star corresponding to the deity to be worshipped" (Mann 1993: 31). Stone circles erected during the Bronze Age (~2000–1000 BC) demonstrate how the rings of stones and burial mounds were aligned along the celestial order. Figure 1.9 illustrates a replica of such a circle as found in Gurteen, County Kerry, Ireland. An axis line joining the entrance and the axial stone, which is laid on its side, points to the setting sun in midwinter. If viewed from the opposite direction, this axis points toward the rising sun in midsummer. These circles contained a burial space and an internal stone called a monolith. Stonehenge in the United Kingdom (2550–1600 BC) is a famous example of such stone circles. Its primary alignment axis also follows the sun's rays at solstice sunrise, and the lunar alignment (Mann 1993: 68–69).

1.9
A Replica of Stone Circle in Ireland as Found in Gurteen, County Kerry.

In ancient Egypt, the identification of north determined the orientation of religious monuments (e.g., pyramids and temples). This delineation served as the first step in the construction of these monuments. The north–south axis is the direction of the Nile River and represents life; while the east–west axis follows the path of the sun, where sunrise symbolizes life and sunset is associated with death.

Historically, sunrise light is also an important aspect in the orientation of most Christian churches. The churches' altars were placed at the east where they were washed by the light of sunrise. The Apostolic Constitutions from the third to fifth centuries prescribed that church edifices should face toward the East (Apostolic Constitutions II, 7) and the propriety of the eastern apse was universally accepted from the eighth century onward (The Catholic Encyclopedia). This orientation continues to be used today and sunrise light is manipulated to enhance the spiritual ambience of churches (see, for example, The Cathedral of Christ the Light in Oakland, California designed by Skidmore, Owings & Merrill, and built in 2008). Vincent Scully (1991) described the east orientation of churches in history as capturing the light from the heavens, while the western entry is the connection to earth and represents glorification of the king. The notion of combining the spiritual and political realms under one roof was already implemented in the Roman Pantheon of the second century BC. The Pantheon's circular form (e.g., the dome, the oculus, the patterns of the floor) was used to symbolize heaven – the Gods; while the square shape (e.g., coffers in the dome, patterns of the floor) was used to represent the earthly realm – the glory of the Roman Empire (Licht 1966: 199; MacDonald 1976: 87; Kultermann 1979: 84).

The orientation of Muslim mosques and Jewish synagogues is based on the geographical location of the center of their religions rather than the sun. The orientation of mosques toward Mecca – one of the most sacred sites of Islam – is based on the traditional story that Muhammad, the prophet, turned and prayed toward Mecca during a divine service in Medina (Enderlein 2004: 64). With this act he established prayer orientation and determined the layout of the mosque. After the conquest of Jerusalem in 638 AD, the city became a religious center for Islam (Enderlein 2004: 64). The Koran (Sura 17: 1) describes Muhammad being taken from the "Holy Mosque" (the *Kaaba*) to the "Further Mosque" in Jerusalem. Since the *Kaaba* in Mecca and the site of the Temple in Jerusalem are both associated with Muhammad's ascension into heaven, researchers still discuss the exact orientation of a mosque, toward Mecca or toward Jerusalem (see, e.g., Saifullah et al. 2001).

Following the destruction of the Jewish Temple in Jerusalem by the Romans in 70 AD, the orientation of Jewish synagogues toward Jerusalem, the most sacred site to the Jewish faith, became the norm. Synagogues are built facing Jerusalem, pointing to the absent Temple and linking the synagogue with the center of the Jewish world – Jerusalem. Moreover, directing the synagogue toward Jerusalem means facing "the site of the ultimate Messianic fulfillment with the re-building of Solomon's temple and the resurrection from the dead" (Gutmann 1983: 12).

Frank Lloyd Wright understood the notion that "perpetuation of tradition is a function of religious buildings" (Stanton 1985: 139). Therefore, he carefully considered each congregation's beliefs, while abstracting symbolism of faith and integrating it as part of his design. For example, in his design for Beth Sholom Synagogue in Pennsylvania, "Every aspect of the building has intrinsic religious significance, so that meaning is embedded in its very fabric" (Humphrey and Vitebsky 2005: 110). The sanctuary of the Synagogue is directed toward Jerusalem. It is lit with an even distributed light to accommodate the faith requirement of enabling the whole congregation to read during services. Other examples of Wright's abstraction of faith symbols and meanings include the plan of the Pettit Chapel in Illinois, which was designed in a crucifix form (Fig. 1.10); the main elevation of the Unitarian Meeting House in Wisconsin, which was shaped to express the hands, folded in prayer (Fig. 1.11);[12] and the plan of Annie Pfeiffer Chapel in Florida, which represents a balance between the formal centralized and the longitudinal sacred plans with a skylight above their intersection (Fig. 1.12). For more details on these examples please refer to Part 3, Form (this volume).

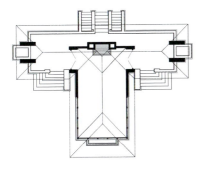

PETTIT MEMORIAL CHAPEL

1.10
The Crucifix Plan of the Pettit Chapel, Illinois (redrawn under author's supervision).

1.11
The 1947 Elevation of the Unitarian Meeting House, Wisconsin: a Symbol of Hands, Folded in Prayer.

Despite Wright's attentiveness to the programmatic and spiritual requirements of each faith, his church designs do not necessarily position the sanctuary to the traditional east orientation. Three aspects of his design can explain this decision. Some of his church designs were faced inward and lit by skylights or upper windows (see, for example, Unity Temple in

Illinois, Annie Pfeiffer Chapel in Florida). Therefore, there was no need to manipulate the light of sunrise. In other cases, where Wright introduced a glass wall at the prow (e.g., the Unitarian Meeting House in Wisconsin and the Minor Chapel in Florida), Wright oriented the church to capture either the outside view of nature or the sunset light. He related the sanctuary of the Unitarian Meeting House to the outside surroundings, believing that this would bring God/Nature into the sacred place. Wright oriented the prow of the Minor Chapel toward the sunset to capture its special light effect on the color of the glass and to enhance the spiritual ambience of the sacred space. One additional plausible explanation can address Wright's departure from the conventional church design of his time – his search for a unique American style that would untie the links to European styles of church design, and would express the American landscape.

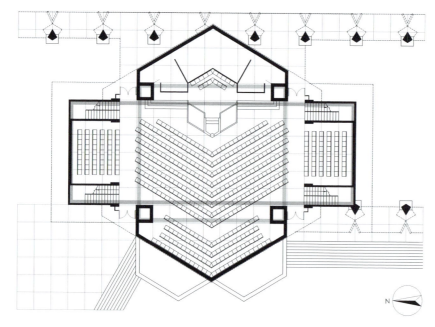

1.12

The 1938 Plan of Annie Pfeiffer Chapel in Florida: an Integration of Centralized and Longitudinal Plans (redrawn under author's supervision).

The above section on faith and form describes the first set of relationships in the conceptual model. As such, it captures some of the literature on the relation between faith and form in sacred architecture. The first part of this scholarly work focuses on the commonalities and shared features of sacred places across faith and how their fundamental spiritual and physical ideas influence the sacred form. The second part of this scholarly inquiry addresses examples of specific programmatic/functional faith requirements and how they impact on the sacred form.

Faith, Ambience Factors, and Form

Ambience is defined in the dictionary as *atmosphere*: "a feeling or mood associated with a particular place, person, or thing" (Merriam-Webster

Dictionary). Three major ambience factors enhance the sacredness of form and influence the atmosphere of a sacred space: light, sound/silence, and thermal comfort.

Light and sound are special aspects of the sacred ambience. They also serve as a reflection of building technology in religious projects (Plummer 1987; Cirillo and Martellota 2006; Andrews 2007).[13] Scholars consider the "holy" light and the "divine" sound/silence (voice and music) as an integral part of the *axis mundi*. This sacred verticality enhances the link between the worshiper and God (Plummer 1987; Hale 2007). Thus, these factors of the sacred ambience create a more profound spiritual experience: "If height evokes aspiration, and light mystery, the live acoustics . . . can be the most important element in creating a sense of timelessness" (Kieckhefer 2004: 110).

A description of the relation between light and cosmic forces is found early in the Old Testament: "Then God said let there be light and there was light – God saw how good the light was . . . evening came and morning followed – the first day" (Genesis 1: 35). This relation between light and cosmos also stems from the earliest light deities of dynamic celestial bodies: the sun and moon, stars and planets. These sky gods occupied the vault of heaven and their luminescence was seen as an entry of the Godhead into an otherwise dark and anemic material (Plummer 1987). As such, sky is considered the connection to divine light: "Even before any religious values have been set upon the sky it reveals its transcendence. The sky symbolizes transcendence, power and changelessness simply by being there. It exists because it is high, infinite, immovable, powerful" (Eliade 1958/1996: 39). Divine light, in turn, is a special aspect of symbolic light that represents the deity. The use of daylight in sacred buildings as symbolic and synonymous with heavenly light illustrates the association of light with cleanliness, purity, knowledge, and cosmic powers. Plummer (1987) claims that every nocturnal light offers a hopeful sanctuary, a safe-haven, and a friendly harbor in the cosmic sea.

Other studies suggest that light provides premonitions and points of departure for spiritual and mystical transcendence, creating a bridge from the profane (the earthly world) to the sacred (a state of pure light), and puts humans in touch with the eternal (Eliade 1958/1996; Arnold 1975; Hayes 1983; Gelfenbien 1987; Plummer 1987; Millet 1996; Geva and Garst 2005; Geva and Mukherji 2007). The divine response "comes back as streaming light out of the direction into which people have surrendered themselves" (Schwarz 1958: 76–78). Humans need to be given a glimpse of fire/light descending from above showing the presence of God illuminating their sacred place.

Light and its spiritual meanings create a space where heaven and earth melt into one another (Schwarz 1958: 180–181). Thus, light accentuates the *axis mundi* of the sacred space, and together with darkness creates one of the most dramatic visual effects. The completeness of light and darkness "symbolizes at once the day and night of nature, the appearance and disappearance of any sort of form, death and resurrection, the creation and dissolution of the cosmos, the potential and the actual" (Eliade 1958/ 1996: 450). The visual experiences in sacred settings enhance the spiritual experiences and contribute to the connection of the worshipers with a higher order of things, with the essential, with the immutable truth. The form of the sacred place and its sacred verticality influence these visual experiences, while faith-based programmatic and spiritual requirements of light impact on the form and its ambience. This in turn brings us back to the relationship between faith and form as described in the conceptual model. Faith commonalities such as the perception of light as the Divine in a religious building influence the form of sacred architecture; while specific faith requirements for the role of light in the religious building (e.g., orientation of the building to the light of sunrise) shape the form of a particular house of God.

A good example of light design that illustrates the relation between faith, ambience, and form is Frank Lloyd Wright's design of Beth Sholom Synagogue as "a mountain of light." On the one hand, he satisfied a faith requirement by providing an evenly distributed light for the congregation's reading needs; on the other hand, he created a beacon of light that would shine inward as well as outward to the community (Figs 1.3, 1.13, and 1.14).

1.13
An Interior View of the Translucent Roof in Beth Sholom Synagogue, Pennsylvania.

1.14

Frank Lloyd Wright's Sketch of Beth Sholom Synagogue in Pennsylvania as "A Beacon of Light" (© 2009 Frank Lloyd Wright Foundation, Scottsdale, AZ/Artists Rights Society (ARS), New York).

As light and darkness add to the holy experience in a sacred place, so sound and silence are believed to contribute to this spiritual experience and to have an important role in religious projects (Cirillo and Martellota 2006; Andrews 2007; Hale 2007).

Silence is considered because it is "separated only by the air's breath" from sound (Osmen 1990: 31). Sound produced by voices and music is considered to be a direct link between humans and the Divine, as mentioned in the Bible that God spoke to some people directly, in a voice they could hear (Genesis 3: 8), or in a whisper (I Kings 19: 11–13).

Similar to the way in which pure geometrical forms were associated with nature and with the sacredness of ancient civilizations, sound was always considered to be a part of nature and was included in early teachings (Andrews 2007: 3). Nature in its core is music: "Nature is a living music scroll, continuously changing and revealing itself. Its patterns are like notes on a page revealing the music within" (Hale 2007: 49–50). Ancient civilizations including the Egyptians, Greeks, East Indians, Chinese, Native Americans, and Pre-Columbian Indians all recognized that chant and music represent the voice of their land. They found that sound could elevate individual and communal spirits to new heights – creating a separation from the mundane (Andrews 2007: 6–7; Hale 2007: 135). This separation, as described before, is one of the fundamental definitions of a sacred place.

In his sacred architecture, Wright demonstrates sensitivity to light design and good acoustics. He provides the balance required for the functional tasks of these design elements as well as the spiritual ambience they create. For Wright, light was the beautifier of the building. Therefore, he utilized various techniques of light and shadow to highlight the sanctuary (see Chapter 12, this volume). Acoustics also played an integral part in Wright's sacred architecture. Wright worked with all of the elements of the sacred place in harmony rather than in dissonance (see Chapter 13, this volume). These harmonies, similar to lighting design, not only fulfilled acoustic tasks (e.g., echo or vibration of the sound), but helped in lifting the congregant's spirit. Listening to spiritual sounds links the worshiper to the Divine: "I heard the echo of faded chanting. In spite of its peaceful emptiness the temple seemed inhabited by a presence" (Eng 2008: 128).

Climate consideration is also a factor that influences the ambience of sacred spaces. Thermal comfort affects the condition of the mind, which reflects satisfaction with the ambience's climate conditions. Islam and Eastern religions such as Hinduism and Buddhism exhibit a strong consideration for thermal comfort in their sacred buildings. These religions aim to provide an all-around comfort level in order to free the worshipers from daily concerns and conditions and to enhance their spiritual experiences (Mukherji 2001). Thus, the faith concept of comfort impacts on both the sacred form of the house of worship and its building technology, while the form and building technology determine the achievement of the required comfort. In Western religious traditions (i.e., Judaism and Christianity), environmental forces such as climate comfort were not necessarily considered to be influential factors in design (Geva and Morris 2010). Although issues of thermal comfort in the history of church design were not fully researched, three plausible explanations can be stipulated: (a) Ancient pagans worshiped the sun and other environmental forces. Resenting any association with pagan worship, Western religions chose to ignore climate issues in their houses of worship; (b) It is plausible that during the Middle Ages, fear of God and trembling before the Divine were intensified by cold conditions in cathedrals; and (c) Sacrifice is fundamental to the Christian faith (especially Roman Catholic). Although it is not specified as such, it may be assumed that uncomfortable conditions in the church are part of the faith requirements.

Frank Lloyd Wright's innovative introduction of organic architecture highlighted the importance of design with Nature. It focused on the synthesis of habitation features with the environment (Kaufmann and Raeburn 1960). Wright acknowledged the impact of climate on design in his writing and described architecture as a refuge from sun and rain: "In our vast country alternate violent extremes of heat and cold, of sun and storm have to be considered . . . Umbrageous architecture is therefore desirable – almost a necessity both to shade the building from the sun and protect the walls from alternate freezing and thawing" (Wright in Kaufmann and Raeburn 1960: 103). He believed that climate influences people and their life and therefore cannot be ignored (Wright 1954). Consequently, his sacred architecture was part of his environmentally conscious design (see Chapter 14 on Thermal Comfort, this volume). As such, his religious projects were more in line with the Eastern religions' idea of comfort level rather than the traditional European church design, which tended to ignore climate comfort. It is not surprising that Wright followed the Eastern religions' attitude toward thermal comfort as he was fascinated with some of this religious philosophy and its temples (see Parts 2 and 3, this volume, on Faith and Form respectively). Wright's climate considerations may also be attributed to his departure from historic European church design. Moreover, catering to thermal comfort triggered Wright's continuous exploration of new building technologies (see Part 4, this volume).

The nature of a sacred building's context of time and environmental conditions directly influences its form and its ambience. Temporal changes and a variety of environmental conditions influence the quality of light, sound, and thermal comfort. Time and environmental conditions are major factors in the development of building technology. As mentioned before, as time progresses, so do developments in building technology. Different environments' conditions impact on the development of building technology, or on the selection of a specific technology to be utilized in the construction of a religious building.

Form and Building Technology

The other major part of the conceptual model highlights the role of building technology in relation to the sacred built form (Fig. 1.1). This relationship is indirectly influenced by the faith requirements and in turn helps in creating the built form as "solid and enduring temples" (Cram 1924: 7). In most conventional design processes, form directs the selection of building technology. However, often building technology serves as the major factor in determining the built form. For example, Frank Lloyd Wright's first idea in the design of Unity Temple was to keep a noble room for worship that would shape the edifice. His use of concrete determined the shape of this room to become almost a cube[14], which in Wright's eyes was "a noble form in masonry" – that portrays integrity (Wright 1932a/1977: 179). Concrete also shaped the flat roof of Unity Temple as Wright expressed: "What had concrete to offer as a cover shelter? The concrete slab – of course" (Wright 1932a/1977: 178). In his autobiography Wright explained how using concrete as the main material in the construction of Unity Temple shaped the church's form: "Nothing else of the building was to be thoroughbred, meaning built in character out of one material" (Wright 1932a/1977: 178).

Numerous scholars discuss the relation of building technology and the sacred form. For example, Kenneth Frampton (2001) demonstrates how material characteristics, construction methods, and constructional form were integral in architectural expression. He examines this premise throughout history, starting with a tectonic analysis of Gothic cathedrals and continuing with examples of tectonics from modern forms (i.e., Frank Lloyd Wright's text-tile; Auguste Perrer's rationalism; Mies van der Rohe's avant-garde; Louis Kahn's modernism, and more). In their respective books, Heather Martienssen (1976) , Robert Mark (1990), and Rowland J. Mainstone (2001) focus on developments in structural forms and how these shaped major religious buildings through history. Cecil Elliott (1992), John Fitchen (1994) and Norbert Lechner (2001) describe building environmental systems in general and as affected by religion. Cirillo and Martellota (2006), and Hale (2007) analyze sounds' spiritual meanings and acoustical techniques in sacred places.

Other scholars, such as Caroline Humphrey and Piers Vitebsky (2005), point out that the construction of sacred buildings is a truly universal human activity where the use of high-quality and long-lasting materials reflects "human longings for eternity." In Catholicism, the need for a permanent sacred building is expressed by allowing only stone houses of worship to be consecrated by the higher levels of clergy (such as a bishop). It should be noted that Wright designed most of his religious projects using masonry construction (stone and concrete), and thus his sacred architecture exhibits permanence.

Wright believed that building technology was part of his search for truth and beauty in design, and that the creation of truth and beauty would enhance spiritual experiences. He believed that this approach, with advancement in building technology, was "superior in harmony and beauty to any architecture" (Wright 1954: 19). More so, he emphasized that developments in building technology such as using steel, concrete, glass, and other modern materials would free design and construction from traditional constraints and help the church design of his time to depart from the era's conventional styles (Wright 1958b/1997: 8). In his eyes, truth was a divinity in architecture and beauty was the shining of man's light (Wright 1953a: 344–351). Wright interpreted the scriptures of the "Lord is the Light" (Revelation 22: 5; Isaiah 60: 19) as the inner light of man, or as he called it: "Manlight." He saw the inner illumination as an expression of the spirits, which grow upward from within and outward (Wright 1953a: 344–351).

In Part 4 on Building Technology (Chapters 12 and 14, this volume) I detail my study of Wright's treatment of light and thermal comfort design in some of his religious buildings (Geva 1999, 2000, 2002a; Geva and Mukherji 2009). The evaluation includes morphological analyses along accepted lighting design guidelines (Illuminating Engineering Society (IES) standards for religious projects), and along accepted "design with climate" strategies as developed by Victor Olgyay (1963), Baruch Givoni (1976), and Norbert Lechner (2001). I also utilized digital simulations that assess light design in the sacred space and analyze the level of thermal comfort and energy consumption in the target buildings. Specifically, I ran computerized light simulations on Unity Temple, Illinois to illustrate Wright's manipulation of natural and artificial light in creating the "holy" light ambience in the temple. In other studies, I used computerized energy simulations to evaluate Wright's environmentally conscious design of Unity Temple in Illinois and of Annie Pfeiffer Chapel in Florida. These empirical studies show how Wright's environmental management influenced the design of his sacred architecture, and how the use of his era's building technology shaped his sacred form and its ambience.

Advances in building technology are directly influenced by the context of time and environmental conditions. As mentioned before, Wright believed that sacred architecture "should be expressed in new styles attuned to the new day" (Wright 1958b/1997: 8). More so, he emphasized the relations between time, place, humans, design, and building technology (Wright 1958a/1995: 260). Place determines the environmental conditions such as site conditions and landscape, regional construction materials, light quality, surroundings sounds, and local climate. Temporal changes during a day, season, or year and specific environments influence light and sound quality, and thermal comfort. These conditions affect the development of building technology and its usage in the sacred built form. The conceptual model depicts this impact as an arrow pointing out from context to building technology and form (Fig. 1.1).

Summary of Part 1 (Conceptual Model of Sacred Architecture)

Part 1 introduces a conceptual model that focuses on sacred architecture. It demonstrates the relations between faith, form, and building technology as the major aspects of the sacred built form. It also serves as the framework for my analyses of Frank Lloyd Wright's sacred architecture. The first major part of the conceptual model looks at the relation between faith and form. Shared faith perceptions, definitions, and requirements across faith, as well as specific faith needs directly influence the sacred form. Faith also directly influences the sacred ambience, which in turn sets requirements for the sacred form. On the other hand, form impacts on the sacred ambience, which includes light, sound, and climate comfort. The other major part of the conceptual model examines the mutual relations of form, its ambience, and building technology. Building technology helps achieve the required form and highlights the sacred ambience. The projects' context of time and environmental conditions are illustrated as influencing both building technology and form and its sacred ambience.

Numerous scholars show that religion (faith) is an integral component of culture and constitutes a major part of society's socio-cultural structure (Rapoport 1969; Wagner 1972; Yi-Fu 1974; Altman and Chemers 1980; Upton 1986; Robinson 1989; Mann 1993; Geva 1995, 2002b). Its imprint on the physical landscape echoes faith rituals and symbolism (Cohn 1981; Geva 1995). As mentioned in this part of the book, each faith's specific requirements reflect cultural and historical differences, as well as a diversity of specific rituals. This in turn leads to different forms of houses of worship.

Furthermore, since culture embodies the enduring values and deepest cognitive structures of a social group (Upton 1986; Dubbelde 2006), faith may be considered as a cultural value that is expressed in the collective memory of a congregation. Cultural geographers and folklorists who examined architecture as a material expression of culture took this notion even further. They stated that architectural form serves as a reflection of culture in general terms and of religion as the specifics (Kniffen 1936; Rickert 1967; Glassie 1966, 1968, 1974, 1975; Collier 1979; Robinson 1989; Vlach 1991, 1993). The American Institute of Architects (AIA) acknowledged the relation between culture and religion in Frank Lloyd Wright's sacred architecture. The AIA designated Wright's religious projects of the Unitarian Meeting House in Wisconsin and Beth Sholom Synagogue in Pennsylvania as American cultural icons (Storrer 1993: 301, 401) (see Part 5, Conclusion in this volume).

As such, I consider the introduced conceptual model that focuses on the relation between faith and form as a more specific model of the relation between culture and built form.

In all his built and unbuilt religious projects, Wright believed that the design should stem out of the faith's programmatic and spiritual requirements. This notion manifests the strong relationship between faith and form in Wright's sacred architecture. Moreover, Wright's use of the innovative building technologies of his time and his renewal of old technologies accommodated and often influenced the built form to achieve the faith requirements.

As described in the Introduction to this book, the relationships among faith, form, and building technology serve as the basic layout of the book. Each of the major components of the conceptual model (faith, form, and building technology) heads a separate section of the book. Each of these parts includes analyses of Wright's sacred architecture along his three major design concepts: nature, democracy and freedom, and the whole is the equilibrium of its parts.

Notes

1 The book *One Song A New Illuminated Rumi* (2005) is by Michael Green. The poem "One Song" was translated by Coleman Barks.

2 Some scholars believe that Wright's attitude to geometry stems from his Froebel's kindergarten training (see, e.g., MacCormarc 2005: 124–143).

3 The poem is quoted from the web: http://www.panhala.net/Archive/Earth_Verse.html.

4 McNally (1985) claims that Nature archetypes, such as stone, tree, sky, water, earth, are repeated in sacred architecture.

5 In Wright's view fire was represented by color and light, and music expressed sound. He referred to water as an essential element, and to pageantry as the celebration of all elements.

6 Frank Lloyd Wright designed the Southwest Christian Seminary in Phoenix Arizona (1950), which was built in 1973 as the First Christian Church.

7 Antonio Alofsin (1993: 280) claims that Wright's proposal for the Johnson Desert Compound is from 1921; while Neil Levine (1996: 509, caption to fig. 133) questions the 1923 date and marks 1924 to 1925 as the year of the design.

8 The Second Vatican Council and its consequential liturgical reform impacted on Roman Catholic Church design. The idea that worship is now an act of the whole congregation, instead of being conducted by the clergy for the people, calls for a different church plan. For example, the idea that the alter can be placed more in the middle of the church rather than at the end of the longitudinal plan encourages more intimate and central design plans for Roman Catholic churches.

9 Ashkenazi Jews are those whose origin is West and East Europe.

10 Sephardic Jews are those descendent from Spain and the Arab world.

11 Members of the Unitarian Meeting House in Wisconsin used Wright's design in weaving a curtain to serve as a partition in the church's multi-function edifice (Hamilton 1991).

12 For more details about the image of the main elevation of the Unitarian Meeting House in Wisconsin see Chapter 4 (Nature) in Part 3, Form (this volume).

13 Light and sound as two aspects of ambience are described in two separate chapters in Part 4, Building Technology.

14 Please note that Unity Temple's "cube" volume is actually measured: 64'x64'x47' (height).

Part 2
FAITH

2
FAITH

[T]he noble room in the service of man for the worship of God.
(Wright 1945: 139)

In this section of the book, I discuss Frank Lloyd Wright's interpretation of Faith as well as its impact on his design concepts. This interpretation serves as the framework for the relationship between faith and Wright's sacred form. Following the book's conceptual model (Fig. 1.1), this relationship includes both the fundamental shared commonalities across faith, and the specific physical and spiritual requirements of each faith. The first aspect is addressed by Wright's design concepts of Nature and his American contextualized notion of Democracy and Freedom. The second connection of faith and form is explored through Wright's holistic approach to his design of sacred architecture.

Frank Lloyd Wright's faith, in the traditional sense, was Unitarian and he considered himself a deeply religious man (from Mike Wallace TV interview with Wright, September 1957). He was raised in a Unitarian family: "Myself the son of a minister who came down a long line of ministers extending back to the days of the Reformation in England" (Wright 1943b/1994). In another instance Wright said: "I am a son, a grandson – and a great grandson – of preachers" (Wright 1958b/1997: 8).

Wright's uncle, Jenkin Lloyd Jones, a pioneering Unitarian minister and a prominent figure in the Unitarian Church in the Chicago area, tried to move Unitarianism away from a Christian focus and towards non-sectarian engagement with world religions. This attempt by Wright's uncle was based on the concepts of freedom, fellowship, and character. Jones and the group known as the "Unity men[1]" defined Unitarian fellowship as a common effort to improve human life rather than a faith based on specific Christian doctrine (Tauscher and Hughes: online). Indeed, the Unitarian faith focuses on "unity through simplicity and solidarity" (Pfeiffer 1990: 88). Jones envisioned the construction of a church that would express these ideals. In his sermon entitled "The New Cathedral" (1902), Jones emphasized that the new modern church should portray honesty, simplicity, and unity (Siry 1991a: 265). These Unitarian ideals strongly influenced Frank Lloyd Wright's view on the role of religion in the life of the individual and of society. Joseph Siry (1996: 217) claims that Wright was attentive to the "theological debates of the Western Unitarian Conference in [the] 1880s on the distinction between principle and belief in the history of human religions." Despite this experience, Frank Lloyd Wright's belief was that philosophy, religious values, and architectural ideology were inseparable (Joncas 1998a: 105). In his correspondence with Dr. L.M. Spivey, his client and the president of Florida Southern College, Frank Lloyd Wright repeated his ideology that "Philosophy and Architecture" are inseparable. In his paper 'Is It Good-Bye To Gothic?' (1958b/1997: 8) Wright expressed this notion as related to religion: "All religions must hold a love of what is beautiful and true – in life and in conduct, but also in building" (Wright 1958b/1992: 227).

Frank Lloyd Wright's design of Unity Temple is an example of his implementation of the concept of unity of philosophy, religion, and architecture. The Temple's special form stands for "the unity of divinity central to Unitarian thought and the Universalist view of the unity of humanity" (Siry 1996: 196).

In addition to Wright's personal faith, the influence of religious trends during his time may be traced in his religious ideology. As in the case of Unity Temple, this ideology served as the basis for his design of sacred architecture. As a young man, Wright witnessed the American search for more liberal theological ideas, which was part of Chicago's cultural religious context in the late nineteenth century. The World's Parliament of Religions was held in Chicago in conjunction with the 1893 Columbian Exposition World Exhibition. This event was a milestone in the history of inter-religious dialogue, the study of world religions, and the impact of Eastern religious traditions on American culture. In his welcome address to the World's Parliament of Religions, the liberal Presbyterian minister John Henry Barrows introduced the goal of the gathering (Barrows 1893: Chapter III, 'The Assembling of the Parliament – Words of Welcome and Fellowship'). He emphasized that the aim of this meeting was the establishment of a dialogue between representatives of religions and denominations from around the world. Although Barrows saw the occasion as an opportunity to liberalize Christianity and to show the splendors of Jesus and the Christian faith, the success of the World's Parliament was mainly due to the introduction of Eastern (Oriental) faiths as liberal, gentle, and charitable religions. In his article 'The Great Parliament of Religions', Pringle (1893: 3857) states: "these representatives of the Orient triumphed over the audience by telling them unexpected truth." The Orient (specifically, Japanese) presence at the London (1862), Paris (1867), and Vienna (1873) Exhibitions spurred a European romantic interest in the East and in the "exotic".[2] The American exposure to and fascination with the Orient followed this trend as American attention to Eastern spirituality increased after the World's Parliament. Furthermore, it elevated the existing interest in the studies of the Orient by New England's (mainly Boston's) Transcendentalists (1830s–1850s) and New York's Theosophical Society (founded in 1875). The Boston Transcendentalists included among others some of the most influential contemporary cultural figures such as Ralph Waldo Emerson, Henry David Thoreau, and Walt Whitman. This group believed that the spiritual state transcends the physical through the individual, rather than through the doctrines of established religions (Gura 2007). The New York Theosophical Society included the study of Eastern religions in their agenda as part of their mission to encourage understanding and brotherhood among people of all races, nationalities, philosophies, and religions.

This cultural religious context and the open-minded Unitarian faith with its "leave thought free" philosophy served as the framework of Wright's faith ideology and defined the identity of his houses of worship. This framework consisted of two concepts. First, Wright searched for the common denominator in human spirituality and faith. He believed that there are spiritual needs in human character that can be served by the sacred building (Wright 1900/1992: 40). Second, Wright was attentive to the particulars of different religions and cultures, and considered them to be an integral part of his design. Wright believed in James Clark's idea (1871: 269) that "every great religion had produced its own special type of architecture".

Under the first concept, the commonalities shared by all faiths and humanity's spiritual experiences, Wright expressed the ideas of a universal, free, liberal, and humane religion. He asked, "Cannot religion be brought into human scale? Can it not be humanized and natural?" and "What is a church? Isn't it a gratifying home for the spirit of human love and kindness?" (Wright 1946a/1997: 6; Wright 1958b/1997: 8). He believed that "Human dignity [is] based upon [the] union of man's physical nature with his spiritual sensibilities" (Wright 1957: 129). Wright advocated focusing on human existence on Earth rather than human aspiration toward heaven (Wright 1932b/1992: 212; Kaufman and Raeburn 1960: 75). With this notion in mind, Wright's designs of houses of worship were aimed at the congregant rather than God or clergy.[3] Thus, his religious projects were based on human scale and proportions. Still, his goal was to create a physical space that would evoke the "high stage of any line of human development" (Wilber 2006: 101). As such, he created the physical journey to enter the sacred plan, and designed the three-dimensional experience by highlighting vertical axis, light, and sound. In his February 1951 speech, 'To Own or Be Owned', Max Otto[4] elaborated on the functional realm of Wright's Unitarian Meeting House in Wisconsin and the spirit it evokes. In his view, the building expressed the architectural beauty as "transformed and glorified by the religious life in it" (Hamilton 1991: 30, n. 30). This notion may be interpreted as a design that embodies the physical and spiritual elements, which endeavors to connect the congregation with their deity (Dubbelde 2006). Thus, the building becomes both *domus ecclesiae* (house church – the house of those who are called) and *domus dei* (the house of God) (Mannion 1997).

The second concept of Wright's religious ideology framework asserts that all forms of religion have a basic desire to function in harmony with their beliefs since "religion is not something you profess, but what you do, and that means what you are, and how you do it" (Wright in Hamilton 1990: 183; Hamilton 1991: 16). As such, Wright was attentive to each faith's symbolism, philosophy, and emotions (Pfeiffer 1990: 87). In his correspondence with the Building Committee of the Pilgrim Congregational Church in California, Wright wrote: "Now your faith has emotion in it and so does your building."[5]

Wright designed the Unitarian Meeting House in Wisconsin as "a structure preaching what the congregation professes to believe. In concrete form – the Unitarian ideal" (Wright quoted by Pfeiffer 1990: 94). This Unitarian ideal was in Wright's eyes leading "the ethical thought of humanity" (Wright 1946c/1994: 296). Thus, the wholeness of the Christian assembly and its sacred building are not oppositional, but rather harmonious and mutually constitutive.

The influence of the Unitarian faith and the religious ideologies of his time played a major part in Frank Lloyd Wright's development of three fundamental design concepts, which influenced his architecture throughout his career. His belief in Nature as God; his continuous search for an architectural style that would express American Democracy and Freedom; and his Holistic approach to design where the whole is a balanced equilibrium of its mutual parts. The significance of these concepts is especially pertinent to his sacred architecture, since Wright believed his religious projects to be basic and fundamental in design, and that consequently he could build a place of worship for any faith (from Mike Wallace's TV interview with Frank Lloyd Wright, September 1957; Meehan 1984: 292, 307; Pfeiffer 1990: 87). Moreover, Wright's basic ideas of a sacred place echo the shared universal symbols (elements) of the sacred spaces (earth, water, air [sky], and fire) as specified in Part 1 of this book. In his sacred architecture, earth, water, and sky represent his design concept of Nature; fire and sky express Freedom; and all four elements represent the universe as a whole from where nature draws its order, rhythm, and geometry. Wright's design concepts and their applications in his sacred architecture express the relation of the commonalities across faith with the built sacred form. Still, and as mentioned before, Wright was attentive to the specific functional and spiritual requirements of each faith. He abstracted these needs in his sacred architecture through his main design concepts of Nature, Democracy, and Freedom, and his Holistic approach to design.

The following chapters are organized along these three fundamental design concepts and beliefs. In these chapters I attempt to illustrate how Frank Lloyd Wright expressed these concepts through his religious ideology and his designs of sacred architecture. Through these analyses I show the relation of faith and form as manifested in Wright's houses of worship.

Chapter 1

Nature

*[B]ecause I study Nature do I revere God, because Nature is all the body
of God we will ever know.*

(Wright quoted in Pfeiffer 1990: 87)

Wright was often quoted saying that for him nature is spelled with a capital
N, the same way we spell God with a capital G: "Nature is of God" (Wright
1958b/1992: 231). In a way, Nature had become his Bible (Wright 1957: 21).
In Mike Wallace's 1957 interview with Frank Lloyd Wright, Wright stated
that his church is Nature with a capital N. He explained that this is the place
he goes to worship. In a talk he delivered to the Taliesin Fellowship on
December 30, 1956, he repeated, "I am fond of saying, and I feel when I use
the word 'Nature', that nature is all the body God has by which we may
become aware of Him, understand His processes, and justify the capital we
put on the word God" (Wright 1900/1992: 39). It seems that for Wright, the
terms God and Nature were interchangeable.

The idea of the relation between God and Nature became common in the
late eighteenth century and the beginning of the nineteenth century in the
West as well as in the East (Brauer 2007: 47) – Nature was perceived as the
whole universe (Frampton and Kudo 1997: 3). This notion is best expressed
by Lord Alfred Tennyson's (1809–1892) nineteenth century poem:

> *Little flower – but if I could understand*
> *What you are, root and all, and all in all,*
> *I should know what God and man is.*

Wright advanced the notion of the "holy" being present in natural objects.
He showed the relationship between architecture and Nature as derived
from the realm of Nature's beauty rather than being a physical imposition
of buildings upon it. Nature was, in Wright's eyes, the "secret of aesthetic
beauty . . . So if you will carefully study nature in this interior sense, you
will soon see how simply true Jesus was to 'the lilies of the field': to Beauty"
(Wright 1946b/1994: 289). He believed that "the new church would be a
rendezvous with the very heart of great Nature" (Wright 1958a/1995: 323).

The notion of beauty and truth was also part of the Transcendental philosophy (1830s–1850s), which was based on the theory that truth is innate in all of creation and that knowledge of it is intuitive rather than rational. Ralph Waldo Emerson (1841), a Transcendentalist, expressed the relation of Nature to the Divine and truth in his essay 'The Over-Soul'. He stated that the "presence of the divine spirit in both nature and the human soul made a direct understanding of God and an openness to the natural world avenues to self-understanding as well as to the perception of broader truth." Wright elaborated on these ideas to include the cosmos's rhythm as well as order and geometry, which in his point of view reveal beauty and consequently truth: "It [Nature] has a reverence for the beautiful and the true. It senses the cosmic order as clean integrity in the terms of living" (Wright 1958b/1997: 8). Thus, for Wright, the cosmos's order and geometry only enhanced the relation of Nature and the Divine.

As such, he looked at Nature for its adherence to consistent principles of the fundamental order and form of the universe. This sense of beauty and truth was fundamental in Wright's theory of organic architecture and served as the framework of his design concepts. It is not surprising to find the development of these ideas in Wright's sacred architecture where he attempted to evoke the "feeling toward a spiritual presence manifesting itself in Truth, Goodness and Beauty" (Everett 1909: 484).

Wright repeatedly referred to Nature as the ultimate sacred place: "I attend the greatest of all churches. And I put a capital N on Nature and call it my church" (Wright in Wallace Mike's TV interview, September 1957). His consideration of nature can also be perceived as an inspiration for his continuous search for an American style that would express or grow out of the local landscape. He believed that the study of the relation of Nature to God would help him to find beauty and truth and teach him how to evoke a spiritual awakening of an "America more in tune with the principles of nature and the creator" (Owings Jr. 2003: 11). In this respect, it is interesting to note that studies by cultural geographers suggest that the architectural messages of dominant cultural values (human experiences) should be analyzed in their environmental context (Rickert 1967). Still, studies in phenomenology believe that the relation to Nature is not necessarily geographical, but rather provides more universal symbols and meanings of human existence (Heidegger 1985: 229).

To enhance the relationship between Nature and Church, Wright positioned the house of worship within its environmental context, and created a connection between its indoor space and outdoor site. In his attempt to position these buildings as part of their environment, he was attentive to the site and its environmental constraints (e.g., topography, climate, noise, vistas), and to the nature of local materials (see Chapter 9 on Nature in Part 4, Building Technology). For example, Wright located Unity Temple on a secondary street to avoid the main street's noise, and in an orientation of east to west to capture the prevailing winds for summer cooling (see Chapter 14 on Thermal Comfort in Part 4, Building Technology). Another example is Wright's Minor Chapel in Florida, where he positioned the building on a northeast–southwest axis to capture the sunset light that enriches the effect of the stained glass wall situated behind the Chapel's rostrum (Fig. 2.1.1).

2.1.1
The Minor Chapel, Florida: a Stained Glass Wall Situated Behind the Chapel's Rostrum.

Wright's exploration of local materials and the study of their nature can be demonstrated in his design of the Unitarian Meeting House in Wisconsin. For this project, Wright employed local limestone that was quarried thirty miles from the site, and indigenous oak as the primary construction materials (Fig. 2.1.2). Similarly he used regional stone and wood for the Pilgrim Congregational Church in California (Fig. 2.1.3) (see more details in Chapter 9 on Nature in Part 4, Building Technology).

2.1.2
Primary Construction Materials of the Unitarian Meeting House, Wisconsin.

2.1.3

Primary Construction Materials of
Pilgrim Congregational Church,
California.

Wright provided vistas of the outdoors as part of the buildings' positioning within their environment. He believed that an open dialogue with the buildings' outdoor environment would enhance the relationship of the architecture with Nature. He also felt that this dialogue would enhance the buildings' spiritual feel by bringing God/Nature inside. Examples include Wright's Unitarian Meeting House in Wisconsin, Minor Chapel in Florida, his proposal for Trinity Church in Oklahoma, and the Pettit Chapel in Illinois. In the first example, Wright installed glass walls behind the rostrum to capture a view of the landscape around the building, as well as a glimpse of Lake Monona before this area was built up. In the Minor Chapel in Florida, Wright created a dialogue with nature, which was enhanced by red and gold stained glass. In his proposal for the Trinity Church in Oklahoma, the diamond stained glass walls would diffuse the outdoor light into the holy space, and add to the spiritual ambience of the building (Fig. 2.1.4). Wright used clear thick glass modules in the Pettit Chapel in Illinois, forming a mysteriously lit relationship with the building's outdoor surroundings (Fig. 2.1.5).

In other houses of worship, such as Unity Temple in Illinois and Annie Pfeiffer Chapel in Florida, Wright created a dialogue with God/Nature through a skylight, which provides a link between earth and sky (Figs 1.4, 1.5, and 2.1.6). This in turn creates the *axis mundi* (the axis of the world) for the house of worship and caters to humanity's religious desire to reach the sky – heaven. Moreover, worshipers can witness the cosmic order through temporal changes during the day and throughout the seasons: "Sunlit space becomes the servant of . . . the human spirit" (Kaufman 1978: 38).

2.1.4
The Diamond Stained Glass in Frank Lloyd Wright's Proposal for Trinity Church in Oklahoma (© 2009 Frank Lloyd Wright Foundation, Scottsdale, AZ/Artists Rights Society (ARS), New York).

2.1.5
The Clear Thick Glass Modules of the Windows of The Pettit Chapel, Illinois.

Wright acknowledged that the relationship between sacred architecture and Nature could be traced in history to ancient religions all over the world (see Part 3, Form, this volume). Moreover, he believed in a Welsh triad that originated during the time of King Arthur and emphasized the relationship of humans and Nature as the basic tenant for thought and creativity (Wright 1958a/1995: 231). Wright claimed that freedom of spirit can be achieved through harmony with Nature, and therefore humans should strive to live in agreement with Nature (Wright 1958a/1995: 260). This harmony with Nature became the core of Wright's organic architecture theory, and led him to search for a unique American style in his work. He alleged that this style would express the American landscape and values. Moreover, Wright believed that democracy in America could be represented by the integration of the individual spirit and groups' collective memory with Nature. This notion is further discussed in Chapter 2 on Democracy and Freedom.

2.1.6

The Skylight of Unity Temple, Illinois.

As described in this chapter, Frank Lloyd Wright's ideas of the relationship between Nature and sacred architecture can be linked to the book's conceptual model where faith directly influences the sacred form. The common and universal shared aspects of faith as related to the perception of the cosmos/universe are expressed by Wright's belief that Nature is the universe and represents God's creation. In addition, Wright related Nature to faith by his holistic approach to design where he linked the interior sacred space with the exterior of the building and its surroundings. One may argue that this relation of the building to nature may take away from the notion of setting apart the sacred place from the mundane. Still, Wright managed to develop archetypal sacred-style architectural features such as the sacred path and plan, the vertical axis, as well as creating the ambience factors (light, acoustics, and thermal comfort). In his belief these elements enhanced the spiritual experience in his religious buildings, brought God into the sacred space, and separated the house of worship from the mundane.

Chapter 2

Democracy and Freedom

Religion should promote firmer faith in the nobility and beauty of which human nature is divinely capable when once men are truly Free.

(Wright 1945: 27)

Frank Lloyd Wright saw Democracy as an American ideal and as the ultimate opportunity for freedom and individualism. He believed that Freedom in America was based on democracy and on the creative, unique, and free individual (Wright 1932a/1977: 402; Wright 1958b/1992: 229). "This dream of freedom, as voiced by the Declaration of Independence, is dear to the heart of every man who has caught the spirit of American institutions . . . Individuality is a national ideal" (Wright 1910/1992: 107; Wright 1953a: 350). Wright acknowledged that these ideas also corresponded with the philosophy of the Chinese philosopher Lao-tze who believed that: "Democracy was conceived as the free growth of human individuality, mankind free to function together in unity of spirit" (Wright 1958a/1963: 48).

This notion guided Wright in his continuous search for an architectural expression of democracy, which would in turn become a unique American style. This search was also influenced by Wright's Unitarian faith, which advocates providing complete freedom in the governing of the Church (Elgin 1971). This freedom would stem out of an independent church with no Supreme authority to dictate. As such, Frank Lloyd Wright's idea was to build a modern church as "truly free" from the conventional constraints of religious building design. He believed a new church should serve the "depths and breadths of the universal spirit belonging to democracy" (Wright 1958a/1995: 322–323). He saw democracy as faith and wanted "to build this faith – life long" and to express freedom (Wright 1957: 88; Wright 1932a/1977: 402). He saw the institution of the Church as the leader in teaching freedom to the people: "The Church by its acts should say *Liberate*" (Wright 1946c/1994: 296). Wright considered the role of the Church to be a less sectarian institution, one that expresses more humility. With this fundamental architectural concept of individuality and humility, Wright could face the challenge of finding an American architectural style for the design of other, less egalitarian houses of God (e.g., his 1950s design for the Southwest Christian Seminary in Arizona was later built as the First Christian Church).

The notion of sacred humility guided Wright's designs of religious architecture to be based on human scale and serve the individual (Wright 1932a/1977: 178). These ideas gave room to church design and construction such as Wright's Unity Temple, which was built for the worship of God and for the service of man (Johonnot 1906: 2–3). This statement was so important that it is engraved in the concrete lintel over the main entrance to the Temple (Fig 2.2.1). More so, it became a symbol of some modern religions (Scully 1996: 20).

2.2.1

Main Entrance to Unity Temple, Illinois.

Wright also expressed his idea of modern religion in the design for the Unitarian Meeting House in Wisconsin. As Max Gaebler, the minister of the Unitarian Meeting House, declared: "Mr. Wright has caught the spirit of liberal religion and has given it architectural embodiment, and created a feeling of unity and elevation which surpass description" (Gaebler et al. 1952: 86). In his article 'The Church of Tomorrow' (1947), Reverend Kenneth Patton of the Unitarian Meeting House also praised Wright's departure from traditional church design to exemplify modern religion. Patton saw Wright's design as an organic unit of function and symbolism: "Frank Lloyd Wright asked a fundamental question. What was the building supposed to express? It must express 'unity' was his conclusion" (Patton 1947: 241, 268).

In his search for a unique American style for sacred architecture, Wright faced traditional church design that expressed the collective memory of the European immigrants in America (e.g., Gothic Revival Church or Classic Temple façades). The traditional architectural styles reflected not only the community's collective memory, but their desire to preserve one's lifestyle, heritage, and shared experiences. In fact, this tendency has such a dominant force that it has been shown that when immigrants leave their homelands for new locations, they attempt to perpetuate the built form of their origin (Rapoport 1969; Fitch 1982: Upton 1986; Geva 1995, 2002b, 2009a; Dubbelde 2006). "Our memories are localized within a social group, situated in the mental and material spaces provided by that group" (Halbwachs 1980: 52–55; Connerton 1989: 36–37). While the new settlers modified their homes to accommodate changes in environmental conditions, their houses of worship retained the original form of the churches left behind in their homeland (Fitch 1982; Upton 1986; Geva 1995, 2002b, 2009a). This may be attributed to the profound role of our collective memory in defining a sacred place (Barthel 1996; Halbwachs 1980; Connerton 1989; Bastea 2004; Cubitt 2007; Moore and Whelan 2007). "We are all carrying our memories around, looking for a new home for them to rest" (Bastea 2004: 8).

Frank Lloyd Wright acknowledged the power of collective memory in relation to immigrants' architecture, but gave this more traditional architecture a negative connotation. In his eyes this architecture imitated historic European styles and did not represent American landscape and democracy or the ideals of "the land of the free" (Wright 1955). Wright believed that the traditional European church design constrained the efforts of establishing an American style free from the "old world." Therefore, he looked for local indigenous symbols and traditions of Native American rituals, which he considered to be a "pure" American religion.

Many of the Native American tribes believed in their cosmic purpose and held religious ceremonies to benefit individual life and the community/ society as a whole. Guthrie (1927) elaborated on this spiritual context in his book *Offices of Mystical Religion,* where he described the spiritual rituals of the Native tribes as the sources for American religions.[6]

Frank Lloyd Wright interpreted and abstracted Native American symbols such as the tippi shape and other triangle details in his design of Beth Sholom Synagogue in Pennsylvania. The tippi became the light pyramid of the Synagogue, which in the Jewish faith is associated with Mount Sinai. Its decoration on the three sides of the tripod consists of a *menorah* – a Jewish symbol of light and freedom (Fig. 1.3). The pattern of each of the *menorah*'s seven "candle holders" is an abstraction of a Native American motif. This pattern appears again as light fixtures at the entrance hall of the synagogue (Fig. 2.2.2). This combination of Native American features with traditional Jewish symbols aimed to express the link of the building to its place and local history, and in turn to create an American synagogue.

2.2.2

Light Fixtures in Beth Sholom
Synagogue, Pennsylvania.

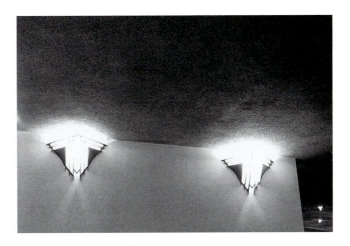

Ancient civilizations' religious monuments (such as Egyptian, Pre-Columbian, Japanese) also served as an inspiration to Wright's sacred architecture and helped free his work from the European trends of church design in America.[7] It is interesting to note that these monuments represent not only God's power but the dominance of the supreme power of these particular people's rulers. It is hard to associate the ideas of freedom and democracy with this type of tyrannical power and force. Still, ancient monuments appealed to Wright because their shapes expressed spiritual roots and reflected the cosmos and their order (see Chapter 7, Sacred Path/Plan in Part 3, Form). In addition, Wright believed that the vital power and superiority of Christianity was based on all preceding religious forms and that ancient sacred architecture served as God-makers. In Wright's eyes, the ancient civilizations created God through their monuments: the Egyptians were God-makers through myth and astrology, the Mayans through force, and the ancient Oriental shrines harmonized with nature around them (Wright and Brownell 1937/1993: 228, 232).

An additional aspect of the ancient religious monuments of the Maya, Mesopotamia, Egypt, and Byzantine is their use of pure geometry (Scully 1988, 1996; Alofsin 1993). Pure geometry became part of Wright's architectural language as he associated it with symbols derived from sacred architecture (Alofsin 1993: 158). For Wright, the square signified integrity and the cube was a noble form; the circle represented the universe and the sphere expressed universality; and the triangle stood for aspiration. It is interesting to note that at the turn of the twentieth century, Japanese aesthetics contributed to the trend of geometric abstraction. Thus, it may be concluded that the study of Wright's ideas for sacred architecture may be considered as the juxtaposition of the two modes: the analyses of his pure geometric language as influenced by ancient religious monuments, and the comparison of Wright's design to Japanese temples.

Typically, a temple is associated with ancient sacred monuments and is understood in religious history as the earthly dwelling place of the gods.

As such the temple is separated from the mundane, becoming a sacred place.[8] Since a Christian church cannot be regarded as the residence of the gods, the European Christian tradition used the words basilica, cathedral, and church in describing their houses of worship, rather than the word "temple". Since Wright broke from the European tradition of church design and referred to ancient preceding religious forms, some scholars analyze the use of "ancient temple" in Wright's sacred architecture. Most of this research posits the relation of Wright's religious buildings to ancient Japanese temples (Siry 1996; McCarter 1997; Nute 2000: 167–170). This notion is exemplified by the analysis of Wright's Unity Temple in Illinois as inspired by seventeenth century Japanese temples of the *Gongen* style. Specifically, these scholars demonstrate the influence of a Buddhist temple from 1653 – the Taiyu-in-byo in Nikki, and a 1634 Shinto shrine – the Tosho-gu in Nikki (Siry 1996; McCarter 1997; Nute 2000: Figs 8.18–8.20). Both temples share a similar floor plan, which includes three main elements: the *Honden*, the holy sanctuary; the *Baiden*, worship area; and the *Ainoma*, a corridor connecting the two. Similarly, Wright's Unity Temple consists of three elements: the worship space, the house, and the entrance foyer connecting the two main areas. Scholars such as Joseph Siry (1996), Robert McCarter (1997), and Kevin Nute (2000) describe additional similarities, such as entrance details and steps toward the worship area. However, one may also consider the monumentality of Unity Temple's concrete "cube"[9] and its pure geometry to resemble the ancient temples of the Maya.

Unity Temple portrays the "aura of an ancient temple" while becoming a symbol of a modern liberal religion, representing democracy and freedom. Rodney J. Johonnot, Unity Temple's pastor, strongly believed that Unity Temple was the true expression of the spirit of the Christian faith: "This building which is to be dedicated to the worship of one true and living God in the spirit of Christian faith may then very properly be called a temple". The term is further made especially fitting here because the building has the feeling and to some extent the form of an *ancient temple*" (Johonnot 1906: 3, 16).[10] Joseph Siry (1996: 202) mentions that Ralph Waldo Emerson's 1841 essay on History, where he published his idea of unity as related to nature and history, served as the context for Pastor Johonnot's discussion of Unity Temple's design.

Frank Lloyd Wright looked at houses of worship as temples that can free the Church from its doctrine and reach closer to democracy. This point of view was part of his ideas that sacred architecture should manifest the "democratization" of the church institution: "I believe religious experience is outgrowing the church – not outgrowing religion but outgrowing the church as an institution" (Wright 1932a/1977: 184). In his eyes, the temple served both as a forum and as a good-time place rather than as a religious edifice imitating old European churches. He referred to the latter: "I cannot see it at all as living. It is no longer free" (Wright 1932a/1977: 184).

The idea of the sacred place as a combination of sacred and secular spaces also refers to the definition of the word "temple." The word is associated with the ancient Temple of Jerusalem, which represented a complex of sacred buildings related to the functional tasks of spiritual activities (Wordnet online; Merriam-Webster online). The sacred complex of this definition of temple was developed through history into the words "synagogue" or "meeting house" (*Beth Kneset* in Hebrew). These buildings are defined as assembly places that determine tradition and identity (Humphrey and Vitebsky 2005: 42). As such, the meeting houses may include a mixture of sacred and secular buildings. Alternatively, one hall can be designed as multi-functional, as in the case of Wright's Unitarian Meeting House in Wisconsin, Annie Pfeiffer Chapel, and the Minor Chapel in Florida. Wright designed the sanctuaries of each of these buildings to also serve as an auditorium for secular activities such as music performances, lectures, and meeting spaces. In houses of worship such as Unity Temple in Illinois, Unitarian Meeting House in Wisconsin, Beth Sholom Synagogue in Pennsylvania, and the Pilgrim Congregational Church in California, Wright created complexes which accommodated sacred and secular activities (such as education wings, celebration assembly spaces, kitchen, etc.). It is interesting to note that the combination of the sacred and the secular in one "temple" was also a response to the twentieth century reformation in liturgy where man's place within the world and his relationship to God was reassessed (Cartledge 2007). Wright expressed this reassessment in his departure from traditional church design, where his idea of a temple represented Freedom and American Democracy (Wright 1932a/1992: 218). The expression of freedom in his sacred architecture lifted one to a transcendental place where "the structure and distinctions necessary to the ordering of life in this world do not apply" (Yi-Fu 1978: 90).

In his sermons entitled 'The Ideal Church' (1882) and 'The New Cathedral' (1902), Jenkin Lloyd Jones, Frank Lloyd Wright's uncle and a prominent leader of the Unitarian church in Chicago, preached on "a free congress of independent souls" (Jones 1882: 4–6 quoted by Siry 1991a: 257). Jones envisioned an innovative church building, which would express the idea of freedom and independence and depart from the conventional cathedral setting (Jones 1882: 202 in Siry 1991a: 258). It is no surprise that even the liberal religion of American Unitarian and Universalistic churches viewed Unity Temple as a "most radical departure from traditional church architecture" (Siry 1996: 198). Unity Temple's Pastor, Johonnot, preached that the modern American democratic ideals of worship proposed a religion of the people, by the people, and for the people. He strongly believed that architecture typified the faith of the Church as well as the Unitarian movement (Johonnot 1906). For him Unity Temple was a true expression of this movement (Siry 1996: 195–196), and he could not imagine building a church in the Gothic style since that would be "unjustifiable by any canon of art" (Johonnot 1906).

Other congregations and their religious leaders that supported Wright's philosophical and architectural ideas of expressing democracy and freedom include Pastor Kenneth L. Patton of the Unitarian Meeting House in Wisconsin, Dr. Ludd Myrl Spivey, President of Florida Southern College, and Rabbi Mortimer Cohen of Beth Sholom Synagogue in Pennsylvania. All three supported Wright's departure from the times' conventional church design.

Pastor Patton was a liberal minister who envisioned the church as a multi-use facility that is open and operating seven days a week (Hamilton 1991: 6). Wright shared this vision and designed a multi-functional sanctuary, which holds services, as well as meetings, lectures and music performances.[11] The space includes a fireplace to create the feeling of a large multi-functional living room (Figs 3.8.4 and 4.14.7).

Dr. Spivey of Florida Southern College commissioned Wright to design a modern house of worship, which would express the Methodist faith (Christ-Janer and Foley 1962: 191–192). Indeed, Wright's design of the two Methodist chapels for Florida Southern College (e.g., Annie Pfeiffer Chapel and the Minor Chapel) illustrated the departure of Methodism from the mystic and unquestioning faithful Gothic style.

Rabbi Cohen wrote in his correspondence with Wright: "you have translated that moment [the revelation of God to Moses on Mt. Sinai] with all it signifies into a design of beauty and reverence" (Wright 1986: 306). The Rabbi hoped that the synagogue would be regarded as a religious shrine, commemorating the 300th anniversary of the arrival of the first Jewish settlers to the United States (Wright 1986: 312).

In summary, Frank Lloyd Wright saw Democracy and Freedom as the main characteristics of the American spirit. He related this spirit as a common aspect of faith to his search for an American style of sacred architecture. This relation stemmed out of nature and its regional conditions, which in Wright's view linked the indigenous spiritual roots and forms to his design. Ancient religious monuments, which represent monumentality and religious and political powers/force, also inspired Wright's design. This is in obvious contrast to his ideas on democracy and freedom and his preaching on the democratization of the church institution. Still, Wright claimed that these monuments were built with an understanding of the cosmic order and the power of Nature, and therefore their pure geometrical shapes represent God's creation. He abstracted the ancient geometry and motifs and adjusted them to human scale. As such, he reduced the monumentality effect of expressing political power in order to express the human spirit of democracy and freedom. Wright's major mark on American sacred architecture was his departure from the traditional European church design of his time, which freed modern religions from these constraints.

This chapter focuses on the common idea of humanity's aspiration for freedom, which exists in all faiths. Chapter 3 illustrates the more specific needs of each faith. It illustrates how Frank Lloyd Wright's holistic approach to design expressed faith spiritual and programmatic requirements.

Chapter 3

The Whole as the Equilibrium of its Parts

[T]he free growth of many individuals as units free in themselves, functioning together in a unity of their own making.

(Wright 1932b/1993: 77)

Frank Lloyd Wright's religious ideology and its impact on his design concepts of Nature and Democracy and Freedom exhibit his general interpretation of the relation of faith and sacred architecture. In his interpretation he strived for unity and harmony. This is demonstrated in his design of the New York Steel Cathedral. In this proposal Wright tried to unite all religions under a humongous vertical roof of light. The roof would reach 756 feet with an additional tripod on top to serve as a steeple. He used the *axis mundi*, one of the common shared ambience factors across faith, and combined it with light to create a design able to host 500 galleries and 220 balconies connected by spiral ramps (Fig. 2.3.1). This approach was used by Wright to achieve a design that integrated all faith symbols and details into one holistic project. In addition, this approach linked the building with its surroundings and merged the interior and exterior of the structure into one project.

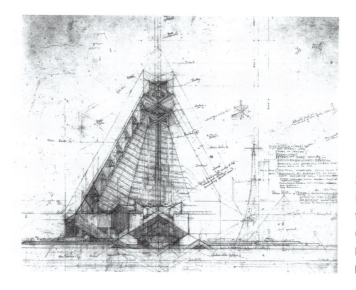

2.3.1

Frank Lloyd Wright's 1926 Proposal for the Steel Cathedral in New York (© 2009 Frank Lloyd Wright Foundation, Scottsdale, AZ/Artists Rights Society (ARS), New York).

Although Wright's holistic approach to design served as one of his basic design concepts in all of his projects, it was especially emphasized in his sacred architecture. In this unique building type Wright was able to highlight his method of showcasing the whole as the equilibrium of its mutual parts by linking all specific faith requirements with the common factors that are shared across faith.

Wright's holistic approach to design may be viewed in the context of the *Gestalt* theory. It was developed at the beginning of the twentieth century. Max Wertheimer, one of the three founders of *Gestalt* psychology, articulated the credo of the *Gestalt* theory, which manifested that the structural laws of the whole govern the properties of any of its mutual parts, and that the whole is not simply the sum of its parts (Behrens 1986). In the literature on the influence of *Gestalt* concepts on art and design, Kurt Gottschaldt's work on the "Embedded Figure" is often mentioned. This line of research focuses on the perception of geometric figures. In his experiments Gottschaldt used patterns based on puzzles in which smaller and simpler forms were hidden within larger and more complex designs (Behrens 2000: 97). The goal of these puzzles was to "'take things apart' to unearth a detail from a larger *Gestalt*" and to "create new wholes by repositioning the same set of parts" (Behrens 2000: 99). It is interesting to note that the same goal governed the 1830s Froebel kindergarten wooden building blocks educational method. It should also be noted that Frank Lloyd Wright attested in his *Autobiography* (1932a) to the influence of the Froebel blocks on his work. Indeed, some scholars find this influence particularly fascinating and attempt to analyze Wright's architecture along the Froebel blocks method (see, as an example, MacCormac 2005: 124–143).

More so, the puzzles in Gottschaldt's "Embedded Figure" theory include the oldest *tangram* – a puzzle that was introduced into Europe from Asia in the early nineteenth century and which is related to the traditional Japanese floor mat, the *tatami*. The measurements of the *tatami* (three feet by six feet) serve as the module for traditional Japanese house and shrine design. The module of six feet also served as one of the major basic grids of Wright's sacred architecture (see Part 3 on Form, this volume). In his book *The Japanese Print*, Wright illustrated how this form of art is organized in "a very definite manner of parts or elements into larger unity – a vital whole" (Wright 1967: 15). Others such as Melanie Birk (1996), Kevin Nute (2000), and Robert McCarter (1997, 2005a) write that the Japanese aesthetic theories of that time inspired Wright's design (see Part 3 on Form, this volume).

This cultural context was the basis for Wright's holistic approach to design, where all parts belong together and "speak" the same language, and where the whole is the equilibrium of its mutual parts. Wright's holistic approach influenced his interpretations of the rituals, myths, and symbols of the different faiths. He understood the importance of each faith's rituals and symbols as spiritual elements and believed that they should be integrated into the design as part of the whole project. The basic shapes of Wright's houses of worship include symbols such as the Christian cross (crucifix form); the triangle representing the Trinity in Christianity or the three fathers in Judaism; the dome as part of the central plan of Orthodox Christianity; and lions at the entrance following the Chinese and ancient civilizations' traditions expressing power and security.

Wright's interpretation of these symbols unfolds in two ways. First, he abstracted each faith's historic traditional aspects: "Abstract form is the pattern of the essential. It is, we may see, spirit in objectified forms" (Wright and Brownell 1937/1993: 231). Second, he embedded the abstracted elements in his designs as part of the whole project. For example, as mentioned before, the plan of Annie Pfeiffer Chapel in Florida is a juxta-position of hexagonal (central plan) and rectangular (longitudinal plan) forms (Fig. 1.12). The plan's geometry creates an abstract balance between the formal traditional centralized plan and the longitudinal sacred plan (Doremus 1985: 150). A bell tower rises into a breezeway-shaped skylight above the congregation, accentuating the intersection of the two plans and emphasizing the abstracted crucifix form. Although the tower was designed and built for the functional purposes of accommodating bells and bringing light into the chapel, it can easily be linked to the religious tradition of steeple construction (see Chapter 8 on Verticality in Part 3, Form, this volume). The relationship between these geometries, which abstract the symbols, the rituals, and myth generates drama and unity in the sacred space (Hertz 1995: 110).

The cross is also seen in the plan of Unity Temple, where the Temple may be seen as a symbol of the square cross, while the whole complex of the Temple and the house creates a longitudinal cross with its intersection placed at the entrance hall (Fig. 2.3.2). The latter configuration is also expressed in the plan of the Unitarian Meeting House complex where the entrance, the auditorium, and the school create a longitudinal cross (Fig. 2.3.3).

It is interesting to note that in both cases the sacred (the religious space) and the secular (the community center) are combined in a traditional religious symbol. This brings us back to the idea of the democratization of the Church to include secular activities under the same symbol as well as to the definition of a temple, which maintains sacred and secular functions in the same complex. In discussing the Unitarian Meeting House complex, Minister Patton wrote: "all the social and utilitarian functions of the church are equally 'holy' as are the services of Worship" (Patton 1947).

A crucifix is also apparent in the floor plan of the Pettit Chapel in Illinois (Fig. 1.10). William Storrer (1993) illustrates examples of Wright's use of crucifix configurations in some of the plans of his prairie-style residential projects. This fact strengthens the notion that Frank Lloyd Wright considered the house as a sacred building (see Chapter 6 in Part 3 on Form, this volume).

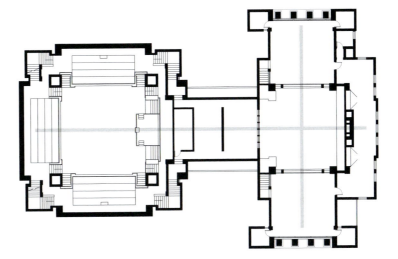

2.3.2
The Plan of Unity Temple, Illinois (redrawn under author's supervision).

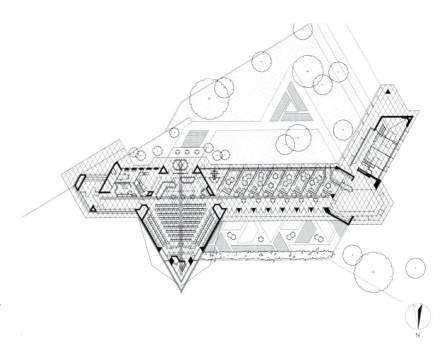

2.3.3
The Plan of Unitarian Meeting House, Wisconsin (redrawn under author's supervision).

Wright's holistic approach also included the triangle as another religious symbol and myth. He embedded it as a basic geometric unit in some of his houses of worship and their details. This triangular symbol of the Christian Trinity appears in Wright's design of the First Christian Church in Phoenix, Arizona. It includes not only a triangular plan, but a triangular spire and a freestanding triangular bell tower, which are detailed in Chapter 5, Part 3 on Form, this volume (Figs 2.3.4 and 3.1). More so, each detail of the building is derived from the triangle shape. For example, the patterns of the concrete columns (Fig. 2.3.5) and the shape of the skylight (Fig. 2.3.6) are triangular.

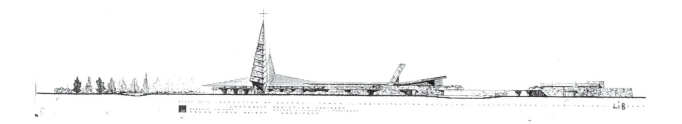

2.3.4 (above)
Frank Lloyd Wright's Elevation of the Southwest Christian Seminar, Arizona (1950), Built as the First Christian Church (1973) (© 2009 Frank Lloyd Wright Foundation, Scottsdale, AZ/Artists Rights Society (ARS), New York).

2.3.5
The Triangular Pattern of the Concrete Columns of the First Christian Church in Phoenix, Arizona.

2.3.6
The Triangular Module of the Skylight of the First Christian Church in Phoenix, Arizona.

Additional use of the triangle can be seen in Wright's proposal for the Steel Cathedral in New York and his design for Beth Sholom Synagogue in Pennsylvania. The first design shows how building technology (e.g., modern materials and innovative structural systems) accommodates spiritual needs and unites all religions under one roof as "religion is one" (Fig. 2.3.1) (see Part 4, Building Technology, this volume). The second example shows that in addition to innovations in building technology, "the American spirit [is] wedded to the ancient spirit of Israel" (Davis 1974: 33). Rabbi Cohen, who worked with Wright on the design of the synagogue, was quoted by William Weart in the *New York Times* (September 13, 1959: 16) saying that the design of the synagogue was "the desert peak that was transformed into a mountain of light at the time of God's communion with the people of Israel." In addition to the pyramidal structure of the synagogue, which represents Mount Sinai, Wright introduced a triangle concrete bastion to signify strength and stability (Fig. 2.3.7). He designed a triangle canopy at the synagogue's entrance in the belief that it would symbolize the outstretched hands of the Rabbi calling the congregation to join together under one roof (Fig. 2.3.8). The floor of Beth Sholom Synagogue was designed to gently slope inward in order to signify that the congregation is resting in the hands of God and to portray a symbol of spiritual unity.

2.3.7
The Triangle Concrete Bastion of Beth Sholom Synagogue, Pennsylvania.

The synagogue's triangular chandelier, also designed by Wright, expresses the belief that only through a series of colors may God reveal Himself to the worshippers. According to Jewish mysticism (*Kabala*), each color has a special meaning: blue represents wisdom; green represents insight and understanding; yellow/gold represents beauty; red shows strength, courage and justice; and cream/white shows mercy and loving kindness (Fig. 2.3.9). As illustrated above, Wright designed seven projecting lights in a triangular shape. These features are on the exterior of each of the three posts of the synagogue and resemble the Jewish symbol of the *Menorah* – the Jewish candelabra. The seven-candled *Menorah* is also part of the interior details of the synagogue. Wright designed these candelabras to be posted on each side of the major pulpit. Today, they stand on each side of the Sisterhood Chapel's pulpit (Fig. 2.3.10). The design of the whole synagogue, which includes the abstracted interpretation of the faith's symbols, made the building a visible form in which "the voices of God and Moses were called again to life" (O. Wright 1960: 192).

2.3.8
The Triangle Canopy Covering the Entrance of Beth Sholom Synagogue, Pennsylvania.

2.3.9
Frank Lloyd Wright's Design of the Triangular Chandelier in Beth Sholom Synagogue, Pennsylvania.

2.3.10
Frank Lloyd Wright's Design of the Seven-candled Menorah in Beth Sholom Synagogue, Pennsylvania.

Wright included additional religious and traditional symbols in his sacred architecture designs. These served as a motif for his holistic approach and are manifested in his attention to details. The Greek Orthodox square cross served as the basic motif in the design of the Annunciation Greek Orthodox Church in Wisconsin. This square cross is shown in the architectural plan (Fig. 2.3.11) as well as in the appointed details of the church: the cross on the major buttresses (Fig. 2.3.12); the metal gate (Fig. 2.3.13); and the sign of the church as designed by Wright (2.3.14).

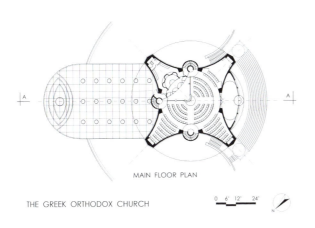

MAIN FLOOR PLAN

THE GREEK ORTHODOX CHURCH

0 6' 12' 24'

2.3.11
The Plan (Based on a Square Cross) of the Annunciation Greek Orthodox Church, Wisconsin (redrawn under author's supervision).

2.3.12
A Detail of a Cross as Part of the Major Buttresses of the Annunciation Greek Orthodox Church, Wisconsin.

2.3.13
A Detail of a Square Cross as Part of a Metal Gate of the Annunciation Greek Orthodox Church, Wisconsin.

2.3.14
The Square Cross in Frank Lloyd Wright's Design of the Sign of the Annunciation Greek Orthodox Church, Wisconsin.

The shallow 105-foot wide dome of this church is an interpretation of the traditional Greek Orthodox domical churches. Instead of locating the dome over the intersection of the cross, the dome covers the whole square cross resting on a wide and shallow bowl, which is supported by four concrete piers that symbolize the cross. "The building is therefore not a copy of Byzantine architecture – but better than a copy . . . [it] reflect[s] the beauty of the architectural heritage of that ancient period" (Wright quoted by Legler 1997: 5) (Fig. 3.2). Wright intended to have Guastavino's tile work on the dome, but due to budget constraints and a possible lack of communication with Guastavino's company, the concrete shell dome was surfaced with blue ceramic mosaic tiles (Storrer 1993: 428). Over time, due to the flaking of the tiles, the congregation replaced them with a blue synthetic plastic resin (Neolon). The blue color resembles the "wonderful [Persian] blue dome so simple in form – a heavenly thing" (Wright 1928c/ 1992: 289; Wright and Brownell 1937/1993: 229; Pfeiffer 1990) (Fig. 2.3.15). The dome represents the traditional domical churches of Orthodox Christianity. Inside, the gold luster domical ceiling resembles the gold leaf mosaic ceilings of Greek Orthodox and Byzantine churches.

2.3.15
The Annunciation Greek Orthodox Church, Wisconsin.

Wright's proposal for Trinity Chapel in Oklahoma exemplifies his integration of ritual, spirituality, and form in his design of a sacred place. In the proposed plan, the walls and stained glass panels continue in an uninterrupted line to rise and become the tower and steeple (Fig. 2.1.4 and the book's cover). This way, the whole project is one symbol of the vertical axis of the world (*axis mundi*), which connects earth, humans, and heaven. The chapel seems to float above the earth, creating an illusion that the building is reaching towards heaven. In addition, in this design proposal Wright included two stone lions at the entrance to each of the ramps leading to the chapel. These sculptures resemble ancient Chinese traditions and myth, where lions are perceived as the protectors of the entrance. Thus, Wright added a touch of "ancient China to his modern chapel" (Pfeiffer 1990: 103).

These examples not only express Wright's architectural interpretation of rituals, myth and symbols, but show how he incorporated them into the whole design as part of the sacred building. Its symbols, which refer to rituals, "carry living archetypal qualities and multiple layers of meaning" (Mann 1993: 14). Wright's inclusion of these symbols as an integral part of his sacred architecture enhanced both the individual's and the group's spiritual experience.

Summary of Part 2 (Faith)

As described in the book's conceptual model the relationship between faith and form encompasses two levels of interpretation. First, the more general approach where this relation is determined by shared fundamental aspects across faith. Second, the more specific level of each faith requirement. Applying this model to Frank Lloyd Wright's sacred architecture demonstrates that he incorporated religious ideology, faith symbolism, and core universal ideas into his religious projects as part of his holistic approach to design.

Wright's expression of faith in form was also part of his fundamental belief in beauty and truth in design and in life. This notion was reinforced by Wright's contextual design as related to nature and place. He believed that beauty and truth could be found in nature, since nature is God. This belief and the aspects of American values of Freedom and Democracy enabled Wright to depart from the constraints of European traditions of church design. His sacred architecture was rooted in these contextual concepts and still fulfilled the physical and spiritual requirements of each faith.

Notes

1 The "Unity men" group included William Channing Gannett, James Vila Blake, Henry Martin Simmons, John Learned, and Frederick L. Hosmer.
2 See Kevin Nute (2000: 10–33) and Anthony Alofsin (1996) for more on Japanese influence in Europe at the end of the nineteenth and beginning of the twentieth century.
3 One can raise the question whether such a perspective would limit Wright's designs to religious contexts that are more democratic, where religious leaders are less likely to intercede between the congregation and God. However, Frank Lloyd Wright did propose two alternative designs for the Christian Catholic Church in Zion Illinois (1911 and 1915) where the religious leaders intercede between

congregation and God. Still, these unbuilt designs are relatively more egalitarian than other Catholic churches of that era.

4   Max Otto was a distinguished philosophy professor at the University of Wisconsin in Madison, and a member of the Unitarian Church.

5   The quote was taken from a manifest of the Building Committee (March 1958) that hangs in the church administrative office.

6   Anthony Alfosin (1993: 231) assumes that since Wright owned many Guthrie texts, these descriptions may have served as a spiritual context for Wright's search for an American sacred architecture style.

7   Wright proclaimed that these ancient civilizations did not necessarily inspire his design, but rather confirmed it.

8   As mentioned before, the word "temple" follows the Latin word *templum,* which means to cut out. Thus, the temple expresses a separation of the sacred from the mundane (Yi-Fu 1978: 85).

9   See note 14 in Part 1.

10 Joseph Siry (1996: 197) also cites the quote from Johonnot's letter published in *Universalist Leader* 10 (December 21, 1907): 1617.

11 The Unitarian Meeting House in Wisconsin also has an education wing that is separated from the multi-functional sanctuary.

Part 3

FORM

3
FORM

[R]eligion is entitled to an architectural style of its own, expressing its searching for God.

(Wright 1958b/1992: 229)

Frank Lloyd Wright's sacred architecture represents "a vast spectrum of religious faith and a complex array of architectural form" (Legler 1997: 5). Indeed, Frank Lloyd Wright designed more than thirty houses of God for congregations of different faiths in various locations in the USA (see Appendix). Ten of these projects were built. The chronological organization of Frank Lloyd Wright's sacred architecture demonstrates the culmination of a series of design innovations and building technology experiments. Wright's design of various types of houses of worship shows the development steps in his holistic approach to design and the link of this type of architecture to nature and to American cultural values (democracy and freedom). Since these concepts dominated Wright's approach to his religious projects, I examine the form of his sacred architecture along these major design concepts rather than analyzing his projects chronologically.

The relationship between faith and form as illustrated in the conceptual model of this book may be examined along specific faith requirements. Consequently, this relation shows how Frank Lloyd Wright catered to each faith's architectural needs. Still, Wright's interpretation of faith as a universal construct relating to nature and democracy and freedom, rather than to specific religious doctrines (see Parts 1 and 2, this volume), serves as the framework of my analyses of his sacred architecture's form.

Wright's interpretation included the abstraction of each faith's symbols, rituals, and their relations to the fundamental meaning of the sacred place. He strongly believed that an abstract design of symbols could bring forward their significance and serve as religious inspiration. As mentioned in Part 2 of this book, Rabbi Mortimer Cohen from Beth Sholom Synagogue in Pennsylvania acknowledged Wright's ability to capture a historic moment and symbol of the Jewish faith in his design (Wright 1986: 306).

Wright also described some of his religious projects using metaphors related to faith traditions and myth. For example, he stated that the Pilgrim Congregational Church in California "has all the earmarks of Israel's 40 years of wandering in the wilderness" (Church brochure); and described the procession in his proposed design of the Wedding Chapel in the Claremont Hotel in Berkeley, California with these words: "wedding bells can ring and the population can go forward."[1] He believed that the traditional sound of the bells would express the spiritual experience of the procession from the secular hotel and into the sacred chapel.

As defined earlier (Part 1), "Form" is a three-dimensional composition that produces a coherent image (Ching 1996). In a sacred context these three-dimensional compositions express the *imago mundi* (the image of the world) and reflect the cosmos. As such, the sacred form is a dynamic space comprising the universe's sacred horizontal and vertical axes.

The Form's Axes

Frank Lloyd Wright articulated the sacred horizontal and vertical axes in his religious projects as horizontal lines parallel to the earth and the horizon, and vertical lines that illustrate Nature's depth, sky, and light. Wright's 1950 design of the Southwest Christian Seminary in Phoenix, Arizona, which was built in 1973 as the First Christian Church,[2] demonstrates his expression of the two sacred axes (Fig. 2.3.4). The horizontal lines project a building that is low and parallel to the earth, while the vertical lines of the spire and the independent bell tower soar to the sky, cutting the horizon (Fig. 3.1). Wright's intention in this design was to use these universal sacred axes in combination with the local stone (pierced into the church's concrete walls and ceiling) to express both the American landscape and to exploit his innovations in building technology. He used this approach to free his form from the conventional church design of his time (for more details on these axes see chapters 7 and 8 in this part of the book).

Three important sets of relationships emerged out of Wright's search for a democratic and free style, his attitude to nature, and mainly out of his holistic approach to design: Form and Function as One; Truth and Beauty as One; and God and Man as One. These major ideas influenced the form of his sacred architecture and are highlighted throughout his religious projects.

Form and Function as One

The first idea of "Form and Function as One" stresses the relation between faith requirements and tasks (function) with the sacred form (see conceptual model in Fig. 1.1). On the one hand, Wright attempted to express the

3.1

The Vertical Lines of the Spire and the Bell Tower of The First Christian Church in Phoenix, Arizona.

specifics of each faith (Wright 1958b: 8). He considered the functional program of each faith as an integral part of its built form, believing in a new concept of architecture where form and function are one (Wright 1931b: 89). On the other hand, his abstraction of form reflected his universal interpretation of faith. These interpretations allowed him to "recycle" some of his designs for a specific faith and to use them with different religions (e.g., the 1926 Steel Cathedral in New York inspired the 1954 Beth Sholom Synagogue in Pennsylvania; the 1954 Danforth Chapel (Minor Chapel) in Florida served as the basis for one of his 1956 alternative designs for the Christian Science Church in California; for more examples see Part 5, Conclusion, this volume).

Wright's proposition of "Form and Function as One" presented a very innovative school of thought that replaced the common architectural concept of the time: "Form Follows Function"[3] (Wright 1939/1970: 246; Wright 1953a: 348; Wright 1954: 31; Pfeiffer 1990: 88). Note that in this proposition, Wright included all architectural and construction features as part of the entire three-dimensional dynamic composition of a sacred place (Hertz 1995: 23) (see Chapters 6 and 11, this volume). The form and the structural system of Wright's Annunciation Greek Orthodox Church in Wisconsin exemplify his approach of "Form and Function as One" (Fig. 2.3.15). The section drawings of the church illustrate how the domical form and the structural bowl that supports the dome influence and create the seating arrangement in the church. Thus, form and function are incorporated into the church's plan, section, and structure (Figs 2.3.15 and 3.2). In his biography Wright explained this approach "it was inevitable that this esthetic ideal should be found to enter into the actual building of the building itself as a principle of construction" (Wright 1932a/1977: 171). As described before, the form of this church is based on the square cross of Eastern Orthodoxy (Fig. 2.3.11). Thus, sacred symbols were also embedded into the building's form and function.

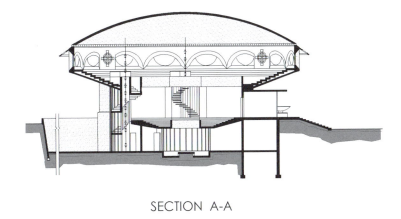

SECTION A-A

0 6' 12' 24'

3.2
A Section of the Annunciation Greek Orthodox Church, Wisconsin (redrawn under author's supervision).

Because Wright did not differentiate between function and form, his designs opened the space and enabled a continuous flow of one area into another, of one function into the next. David Hertz (1995: 23) describes Wright's architecture as a composition created from a continuous flow of sections and segments that clearly define spaces/functions. He shows that this movement within the space was a major contributor in defining the form of Wright's Unity Temple where visitors experience "a continuous process of human movement through the building" (Hertz 1995: 31). Moreover, since Wright emphasized the importance of all points of view rather than a fixed point of view, his continuous flow of three-dimensional spaces created "stability and aesthetic harmony" (Hertz 1995: 122) (see Fig 1.4 this volume illustrating the interior of Unity Temple). Robert McCarter (2005c: 307) claims that Wright created three-dimensional spiritual experiences in his sacred architecture by utilizing this harmony as a balance of interdependent volumes. These volumes include unfolding spaces, which comprise "four volumes that spin around a solid center" and projecting spaces that form a cruciform shape. McCarter (2005c: 309) adds that Wright often used a combination of volumes to create "opposite spatial forms (e.g., static and dynamic; unfolding and exfoliating)". These design shapes were part of Wright's abstraction of faith requirements.

Truth and Beauty as One

Wright's second idea of "Truth and Beauty as One" is especially evident in his sacred architecture design and construction.[4] Wright's projects were "all designed to enhance life – each to be a center of beauty and excellence"[5]. In this context, it is interesting to note that Wright's proposal for the Daphne Funeral Chapels in San Francisco, California (1945) was based on celebrating life rather than expressing death (Futagawa 1984: (7): 92).

Wright believed that the truth of form and its beauty could be found in nature (Wright 1943b/1994: 243). Similar to Ernest Fenollosa's 1896 Japanese aesthetic theory,[6] Wright's work explored the aesthetic values of architecture through universal ideas and a metaphysical interpretation of Nature (Nute 2000). Wright's expression of the fundamental relationship between architecture and nature marks an intersection in spirituality since he saw Nature as the creation of God. Nature for Wright expresses the universe, its laws, order, geometry, and sacredness. As such, Wright found his inspiration for truth and beauty in Nature, using its pure geometry as the grammar of his sacred form (Wright 1912). Although he saw this geometry as sacred, he did not offer much insight to his compositional methods associated with what scholars call "sacred geometry". He dismissed the idea of potential sacred geometrical derivations, saying: "it is worthy of note in this connection that 9×9 equals 81 is just as simple as $2 + 2$ equals 4" (Wright 1953a: 147).

Interestingly, most of the scholarly work on Wright's use of geometry relates more to the development of typologies (Laseau and Tice 1992; Storrer 1993; McCarter 2005a); or to the symbolic meanings associated with each form (Alofsin 1993; Siry 1996); or to the influence of Froebel's kindergarten training on Frank Lloyd Wright (Laseau and Tice 1992; MacCormac 2005), rather than examining the issue of "sacred geometry". The analysis that is closest to the idea of sacred geometry in Wright's religious architecture is Otto Antonia Graf's work on Wright's Steel Cathedral project in New York (Fig. 2.3.1) (Graf 2005: 144–169). Graf investigates Wright's use of pure geometry along the transposition and transformation of a sequence of geometry from four to six. Four represents the square/cube, while six is the basis for the hexagon or isometric version of the cube. Graf illustrates this sequence in a series of drawings/diagrams showing the consistent geometrical systems of the plan, section, and elevation of the proposed cathedral. Graf concludes that this sequence indicates a strong relation to ancient geometry, a geometry that represents an ancient civilization's view of the cosmos, its order, and its systems. Wright believed that ancient religious monuments were pure reflections of the ancient perception of Nature. In his mind they created "a reverential recognition of the elements that made its ancient letter in its time vital and beautiful" (Wright 1975: 53). His admiration of the ancient religious monuments was inspired by their beauty and truth of form (pure geometry). Wright's alternative design solutions for the Christian Catholic Church in Zion City, Illinois (c. 1915) demonstrate this approach since they resemble an ancient religious monument more than a traditional historic Catholic church (Fig. 3.3).

Wright's belief that truth and beauty are one served as a fundamental basis for his design in general, but was particularly accentuated in his sacred form where it became the motif of his design. He said, "if your church isn't beautiful tear it down" (Wright 1958b/1997: 11). In his design he said "NO!" to the Gothic Revival church style, but he acknowledged the Gothic spirit of beauty: "Yes, it's good-bye to Gothic as a style. But not to its spirit of reverence for beauty" (Wright 1958b/1992: 227).[7] Similarly, some scholars believe that the Gothic spirit stands as "an image of the unity of things material and things spiritual, things sensual and things of mind, or more properly, the movement from one to the other" (Bernier 2007: 82). Other scholars, such as Hans-Georg Gadamer (1986), looked at beauty in the sacred space across time and styles. They associate it with the experience of eternity and thus posit that beauty and truth in form serve as a transcendental quality of the spiritual world.

God and Man as One

Although Wright was inspired by the vastness and glory of Nature and ancient religious monuments, he believed that the worshiper should

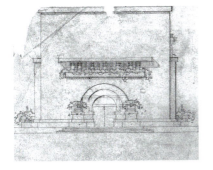

3.3
Front Elevation of Frank Lloyd Wright's Second Proposals for the Christian Catholic Church in Zion City, Illinois (ca 1915) (© 2009 Frank Lloyd Wright Foundation, Scottsdale AZ/Artists Rights Society (ARS), New York).

be placed in the center of the spiritual space. This concept was part of Wright's search for a church that would express democracy and freedom rather than a hierarchical doctrine. From his point of view, "God and Man are One" (Wright and Brownell 1937/1993: 238). As such, his design of the sacred form was based on human scale and proportions. For example, in most of his religious projects Wright used a grid based on a unit of six feet. This was inspired by the Japanese floor mat (*tatami*) which measures three feet by six feet. For centuries, the *tatami* mat has served and continues to serve as the basic module in Japanese dwellings and shrines. The Japanese sense of harmony in using this simple module may constitute a basis for understanding sacred spatial ambience and human connection to the Divine (Okakura 1906). Emphasizing the human scale, Wright envisioned the house of God becoming a "citizen's haven of refuge" where worship becomes "more profound and comprehensive" (Wright 1958a/1995: 322–323). As such, Wright asked: "Why not, then, build a temple, not for God in that way, but a temple to man, appropriate to his uses as a meeting place in which to study man himself for God's sake?" (Wright 1932a/1977: 178; Wright 1932a/1992: 212).

This question and his belief in the notion of "God and Man as One" exhibit Wright's departure from Gothic Revival church design where the building only glorifies God. As shown before, this divergence was reinforced by Wright's continuous search for an American style that would express the American landscape and its cultural values of democracy and freedom.

As explained in Part 2 of this book, this exploration was also part of Wright's belief in the democratization of the church (Wright 1932a/1977: 178; Wright 1932a/1992: 212). He claimed that we build temples "to the interior or spirit-power of manhood as released by American democracy and its science . . . A new light may shine from every edifice built by the human mind" (Wright 1957: 62). Similar to Walt Whitman and Ralph Waldo Emerson who emphasized the continuous search for an American culture free from European constraints, Wright preached a departure from traditional architecture's church forms. In his view, this departure would create a new unique style for America – a "Church of Democracy". He claimed that sacred architecture should be part of "the idea of democracy" and wished "to make a way for the return of worship to the life of the citizen as well as for the uplift and integrity of the nation" (Wright 1958a/1995: 322–323).

Wright's idea of the American style included the expression of the American landscape (Nature) and its democracy and freedom:

> So the church, by way of the ideal building in the free city, might be as a song without words, comprising minor churches grouped about a common meeting place. It is certain, in any case, that the new church would be a rendezvous with the very heart of great Nature.

> Thus will be served the depths and breadths of the universal spirit belonging to democracy.
>
> (Wright 1958a/1995: 322–323)

This quote summarizes Wright's major design concepts of Nature, Democracy and Freedom, and his Holistic approach to design where the whole is an equilibrium of its parts. In the next chapters of this part of the book I analyze the form of Wright's sacred architecture along these design concepts.

Chapter 4

Nature

Modern architecture – let us now say organic architecture – is a natural architecture – the architecture of nature, for nature.

(Wright 1939/1970: 245)

Frank Lloyd Wright believed that architecture should be developed in harmony with the environment rather than as an external imposition on nature (Wright 1914: 406). "I knew well that no house should ever be on a hill or on anything. It should be of the hill. Belonging to it" (Wright 1932a/ 1977: 192). Wright viewed nature as a place for free architecture: "I would like to have a free architecture. Architecture that belonged where you see it standing – and is a grace to the landscape" (Wright in Mike Wallace's TV interview September 1957).

Wright studied Nature by looking *in* it rather than *at* it and saw architecture as "following the principles that govern nature" (Pfeiffer 1995: 45). He thought that his buildings ought to respond to Nature and its specific characteristics (Hoffman 1986: 11). As such, Wright stated that architecture could make the landscape more beautiful than before the building was built (Green 1988: 135). Moreover, Wright believed that the integration of the building with its surroundings was essential to people's lives (Pfeiffer 1990: 89).

The relationship between architecture and nature was the core of Wright's theory of organic architecture, where he emphasized natural intrinsic harmony with the environment. Wright saw organic simplicity as part of Nature's harmonious order (Wright 1954). For example, when Wright wrote about the beauty of a flower he claimed it is "proof of the eternal harmony in the nature of a universe " (Wright 1912: 117). He analyzed nature through its geometric structure and rhythm, and observed, for example, that the Sahuaro cactus was "a perfect example of reinforced building construction" (Wright 1955: 196). Nature's order and laws became part of Wright's theory and design ideas. He claimed that a building's form should become an integral part of its structure and "take the character of an organism which existed according to its own complete and balanced laws" (Scully 1996: 13–14). In a public lecture delivered on August 14, 1951, Wright compared his design of the roof of the Unitarian Meeting House in Wisconsin to "the underside of the wing of a bird" (Hamilton 1991: 16; 1990: 183). This image expressed an abstraction of a natural organism, which is often associated with freedom and aspiration. This image was later described as symbolizing cupped praying hands, thus creating a spiritual meaning out of Wright's first idea of a natural living organism (Fig. 1.11). Another example is Wright's Beth Sholom Synagogue in Pennsylvania. Oligivanna Wright (1960: 189) compares it to a living, breathing organism in its reality. The congregation's Rabbi Cohen said that the synagogue lives and breathes, moving gracefully with the changes of light and shadow (Fig. 1.3; Fig. 3.6.19).

Wright was inspired to use pure geometry, proportions, modules, and patterns by Nature. He believed that design should not imitate Nature. Rather, design should be an "abstraction of nature-elements in purely geometric terms" (Wright 1932a/1977: 181). Wright interpreted the laws of Nature as guidelines for man in creating appropriate architectural forms and enhancing the human spirit (Wright 1958a/1995: 260). The 1948 *Forum* published Wright's design of Unity Meeting House in Wisconsin as well as several of his other 1940s secular projects, and highlighted their relation to Nature. Neil Levine (1996: 425) states that these examples "set the stage for the organic expressionism of architects like Le Corbusier and Sarrinen".

Diagonal Plans

The desert fauna and its "supple patterns of movement and repose" were one source of Wright's inspiration (Kaufmann 1978: 34). The engagement of this type of landscape in Wright's design allowed him to explore new spatial configurations and use non-rectilinear geometry. Wright's diagonal and non-square plans were developed as early as 1921[8] while working on the design of the Albert M. Johnson Compound and Shrine in California's Death Valley (Alofsin 1993: 280). In the desert landscape Wright discovered the combination degrees for his grid and module systems (30, 60, 120 degrees). This discovery "marked Wright's first contact with the desert . . . extraordinary for both its natural and its human history, so much so that it had already acquired a mythical place in the American mind" (Levine 1996: 174–175).

Frank Lloyd Wright used the diagonal plan again in his 1938 master plan for Florida Southern College, Lakeland, Florida. This plan was laid out on a six-foot grid that served as the common base for the various geometries used for the buildings on campus.[9] Entering the Florida Southern College campus on the west side, one walks to the circular library, then turns 30 degrees southeast toward Annie Pfeiffer Chapel, the center icon of the campus. This diagonal creates an interesting relationship between the sacred and the secular. Some scholars compare this campus plan and the relation between the chapel and the library to Thomas Jefferson's plan of the University of Virginia. For example, David Hertz (1995: 108) states that Wright's campus plan and buildings grow out of the land and relate to the site, while Jefferson's university crowns the land with a symmetrical plan. Jefferson conceived the library as the shrine of education and positioned it as the central point of the campus, while Wright situated the chapel as the focal point of the relation between the sacred and spiritual activities on campus. Indeed, Wright's master plan positioned Annie Pfeiffer Chapel at the center of the campus as growing "out of the ground into the light – a Child of the Sun" (Turner 1984; MacDonald et al. 2007: 7).

Growing Out of the Land

Wright's use of modules and a grid in his sacred architecture is discussed later in this part of the book. What should be emphasized here is the relation between Wright's primal geometrical forms to Nature and their association with sacred meanings across religious symbols. Wright argued: "A building should appear to grow easily from its site and be shaped to harmonize with its surroundings if Nature is manifested there" (Wright 1908/1992: 87). His proposal of a chapel for the Newman family in Cooksville, Wisconsin, known as the Memorial to the Soil Chapel (1936), exemplifies the idea of a building growing out of its site (Fig. 1.2). Wright designed earth berms to surround most of the exterior of the chapel's walls. He explained his use of berms in this design by describing the project as a "Memorial to the Tillers of the Ground. Making the earth a feature of the monument, or vice versa".[10] Donald Hoffman (1986: 9) wrote that Frank Lloyd Wright's architecture exhibits a form with a vital relation to earth. As stated before (Part 1), earth is considered as the sacred ground of the world: on the one hand it is stable and powerful, while on the other hand it is nurturing and receptive in its nature. As such, Wright's work with earth in the design of his various chapels may also be seen as his work with one of the fundamental elements of sacredness.

In his 1958 design of the Pilgrim Congregational Church, California, Wright proposed battered sides that gently rose from the grade toward the sanctuary in a slope of 30 degrees. This design gives the appearance that the church is growing out of the ground (Fig. 3.4.1). In his book on Wright's meaning of materials, Terry Patterson (1994: 74–75) demonstrates that the design of the earth battered sides of the Pilgrim Congregational Church "exaggerated stability [and was] not matched by the reality of design". Indeed, Wright's design of this church focused more on his concept of a building growing out of the earth, rather than on the issues of structure and construction. Unfortunately, only parts of this project were built and the battered sides design was left unbuilt (Fig. 3.4.2).

3.4.1

Frank Lloyd Wright's 1958 Proposal
for the Pilgrim Congregational
Church, California (© 2009 Frank
Lloyd Wright Foundation, Scottsdale,
AZ/Artists Rights Society (ARS),
New York).

3.4.2

The Built Part of the Pilgrim
Congregational Church, California.

The Horizontal Lines

The relation to earth was also exhibited by Wright's use of horizontal lines
parallel to the land as the horizontal axis of the universe. This approach
is illustrated in Frank Lloyd Wright's proposal for the Albert M. Johnson
Desert Compound and Shrine in California (1921? 1923? 1924–25?),[11]
where earthwork takes greater focus than building design. This project
included graceful horizontal lines blended into the desert landscape
emphasizing the building's continuous, low-lying horizontal forms. The

lines of this project expressed the ever-changing quality of the desert landscape as well as the forms and crafts of the local nomadic tribes of the region. These rooted local elements strongly dominated the design and became the major reason why client Albert Johnson rejected the project. Johnson claimed that Wright's proposal was more of an adobe Indian village than a ranch of his liking (Levine 1996: 181). It is interesting to note that Wright was already using the horizontal forms to express the Prairies lines in sacred buildings (see, e.g., his 1906 Pettit Chapel in Belvedere, Illinois: Fig. 3.7.6). He continued to explore theses lines/forms in other religious projects such as the Community Church (Church of the Future) in Kansas City, Missouri (1940) (Fig. 3.4.3), and the 1950 Southwest Christian Seminary in Phoenix, Arizona (built in 1973 as the First Christian Church: Fig. 2.3.4).

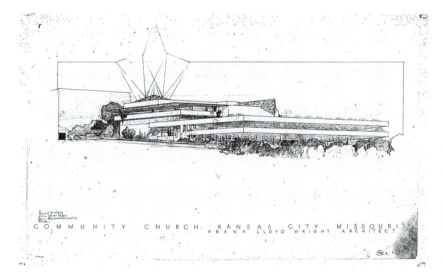

3.4.3
Frank Lloyd Wright's Community Church (Church of the Future) in Kansas City, Missouri (1940) (© 2009 Frank Lloyd Wright Foundation, Scottsdale, AZ/Artists Rights Society (ARS), New York).

Wright also used the horizontal parallel lines to the ground as parallel to the horizon. Thus, in his sacred architecture these lines were parallel to air and sky[12] becoming "humble horizontal line[s] as the line[s] of human life upon the earth"[13]. In other words, Wright's horizontal forms express "man in love with nature" (Blake 1969: 24). It should be noted that the relationship between man and Nature/land is rooted in the life, myth, and poetry of indigenous people. As an example, here is Aboriginal Australian poet, Oodgeroo Noonuccal, describing the human longing for a rainbow:

> *Perhaps she will come again*
> *when the spirits of men*
> *And the spirit of this land*
> *Are once more together as one.*

In his introduction to Wasmuth's 1910 book, Wright depicts ancient and vernacular architecture as the ultimate example of "simple conventions in harmony with nature", and as "most capable of cultural reaction". Similarly, studies in cultural geography and folklore also emphasize that architectural messages of cultural values should be analyzed in their environmental context (Rickert 1967; Glassie 1966, 1968, 1974, 1975; Vlach 1991, 1993).

Transparency to Nature

The dialogue between the sacred form and Nature appears in Wright's design of large glass walls, which face the direction of a major view or capture a special effect of natural light. As described in Chapter 1, this volume, these designs (The Unitarian Meeting House, Wisconsin; The Minor Chapel, Florida; Trinity Chapel, Oklahoma) show Wright's belief in Nature and in the fundamental and universal elements of the spiritual experience: "we ought to help the indoors to go outdoors and outdoors to come inside", and "to bring God's outdoors into man's indoor" (Wright quoted in Rogers 2001: 8).

The spiritual link to the sky, which represents Nature and heaven, may be observed in Wright's design of upper clear windows and skylights in such projects as Unity Temple in Illinois (Fig. 3.4.4), and Annie Pfeiffer Chapel in Florida (Fig. 3.4.5). Wright described the link to Nature through skylights and its connection to the Divine as driven by the "spirit [which] grows upward from within and outward" (Wright 1953a: 349). The strength of this link is based in its transcendence eternal power (see Part 1, this volume, and Eliade 1959/1987: 39).

3.4.4
Upper Windows and Skylight of Unity Temple, Illinois.

3.4.5
The Skylight of Annie Pfeiffer Chapel, Florida.

Surrounding Landscape and Vegetation

Robert Spencer Jr. (1865–1953), Wright's colleague and a Chicago architect, claims that Wright's inspiration was Nature, as well as the way Nature
was interpreted by Japanese art. Anthony Alofsin (1996: 9) reinforces
this idea when describing Frank Lloyd Wright's fascination with the
simplicity and purity of the aesthetics of Japanese art that allow the forms
of Nature to be abstracted. The abstractions in Wright's sacred forms were
components from rocks, shrubs, and trees. He paid attention to the land,
and attempted to "echo the shapes and dominant rhythms of the
landscapes in which his buildings were set" (Scully 1996: 12). In addition
to the previous example of the desert as an inspiration landscape for
Wright's design, mountains also influenced his site and building developments. As mentioned before, Wright created Beth Sholom Synagogue in
Pennsylvania resembling the sacred mountain – Mount Sinai. In another
case, the mountains in the background of the site of Wright's Pilgrim
Congregational Church in Ridding, California inspired the church design.
Long pre-cast concrete poles rise from a local stone base and convene
above the sanctuary in a triangular shape resembling the surrounding
mountains (Figs 3.4.6 and 3.4.2). In addition, the design took "its place
naturally and beautifully in a land of forests and stone, molded of materials
indigenous to the countryside and created into a design of strong quiet
aspiration".[14] Indeed, the building is situated on a crown of a small hill
surrounded by pine trees (Figure 3.4.2).

An additional example of Wright's attentiveness to the surrounding landscape is his design of the Annie Pfeiffer Chapel in Lakeland, Florida (1938).
He placed the chapel within an orange orchard (Fig. 4.14.3), and his design
called for planters to be hung in the chapel's tower (Figs 3.4.7 and 4.14.3).[15]

3.4.6
Pre-cast Concrete Poles During
Construction of the Pilgrim
Congregational Church, California
(1960) (picture taken at the church's
office).

Wright described the design of this building as "Floridian in character . . . southern and plastic in feeling, richly planted" (Wright 1957: 168).

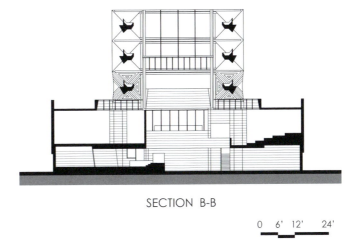

SECTION B-B

0   6' 12'   24'

3.4.7
A Section of Annie Pfeiffer Chapel, Florida (redrawn under author's supervision).

It is interesting to note that the idea of including external planters in his sacred architecture had already been explored by Wright in his design of Unity Temple in Oak Park, Illinois (1906). Concrete planters were designed as part of the exterior façades of the temple and located at the stairs on the entrance and rear paths of the house of worship (Fig. 3.4.8). Wright also built two large flower boxes on both sides of the Pettit Memorial Chapel in Illinois (1906) (Figs 1.10 and 3.6.25).[16]

3.4.8
Concrete Planters in Unity Temple, Illinois.

The use of local vegetation as an integral part of a religious building became a unique feature in Wright's designs. This idea was not an accepted common feature in houses of God, and thus expressed Wright's beliefs in the strong relation between Nature and faith. This belief was so dominant that Wright also introduced vegetation into some of the interiors of his houses of worship. For example, Wright designed two built-in planters on each side of the pulpit of Unity Temple (Fig. 3.4.9). He designed large planters that flanked the Annie Pfeiffer Chapel's original pulpit, and two planters on either side of the rostrum in the Minor Chapel in Florida (Fig. 3.4.10).

3.4.9 (left)
Interior Built-in Planters and Square-based Chairs on Both Sides of the Pulpit of Unity Temple, Illinois.

3.4.10 (right)
Interior Built-in Planters in The Minor Chapel, Florida.

When possible, Wright also abstracted vegetation motifs such as grain and plants in his decorative patterns of glass and concrete: "He imagined concrete columns as analogues of great trees that formed a forest cover" (Hoffman 1986: 22). These patterns bring us back in history to the columns of Egyptian and Greek Temples.

The Environment in Wright's Drawings

Frank Lloyd Wright's belief in the essential relationship between the environment and the built form was so important to him that he expressed it in all of his drawings. These include the whole context of the natural or urban setting of each of his buildings. For examples, see Wright's drawings for his 1953 proposal of the Kaufman Rhododendron Chapel in Mill Run, Pennsylvania (Fig. 3.4.11), and his second alternative design for the Christian Science Church in Bolinas, California in 1956 (Fig. 3.4.12). These drawings illustrate the natural setting for his sacred architecture, and depict how his designs blend with the surrounding natural environment. Kevin Nute (2000: 95, Figs 5.24 and 5.25) compares some of these drawings to some of the sketches of the American painter and art educator Arthur Dow (1857–1922). Dow emphasized that landscape composition should be based on lines "[l]ooking out from a grove we have trees as vertical straight lines, cutting lines horizontal or nearly so" (Dow 1899/1913: 25). This comparison illustrates the underlying aesthetic structure of Wright's landscape.

3.4.11
Frank Lloyd Wright's 1953 Proposal of
the Kaufman Rhododendron Chapel
in Mill Run, Pennsylvania (© 2009
Frank Lloyd Wright Foundation,
Scottsdale AZ/Artists Rights Society
(ARS), New York).

3.4.12
Frank Lloyd Wright's 1956 Second
Proposal for the Christian Science
Church in Bolinas, California (© 2009
Frank Lloyd Wright Foundation,
Scottsdale AZ/Artists Rights Society
(ARS), New York).

The examples above depict Wright's method of framing a building within
Nature. In 1945, Wright proposed a design for the Daphne Funeral Chapels
in San Francisco, California. This design is an example of his use of the
urban setting as the frame of a sacred project. Wright created a context
for the round chapels, where the urban setting serves as the boundaries
of the project. The chapels were developed inward as a cluster of five small,
round chapels, each for 100 people, surrounded by gardens (Fig. 3.4.13).
The cubical urban background helps to set apart and distinguish the
circular shapes of the sacred complex.

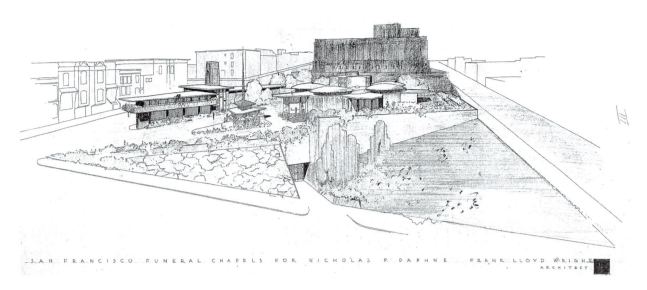

_S.A.N. F.R.A.N.C.I.S.C.O. F.U.N.E.R.A.L C.H.A.P.E.L.S F.O.R N.I.C.H.O.L.A.S. P. D.A.P.H.N.E. F.R.A.N.K L.L.O.Y.D W.R.I.G.H.T ARCHITECT

3.4.13

Frank Lloyd Wright's 1943 Proposal for the Daphne Funeral Chapels in San Francisco, California (© 2009 Frank Lloyd Wright Foundation, Scottsdale AZ/Artists Rights Society (ARS), New York).

East and West Influences

Wright's observations of the environment were not exclusive to one specific region/location. For Wright, Nature became "an active figure in the representational process of architecture" (Levine 1996: 185). He believed that the spiritual lessons from regions across the world, East and West, enrich the built form (Wright 1910). He used the Hagia Sophia of the sixth century as an example of "The Byzantine sense of form [that] seems neither East nor West but belongs to both" (Wright and Brownell 1937/1993: 229). Wright used the Byzantine sense of form in his design of the Annunciation Greek Orthodox Church in Wisconsin. He related the domed religious monuments of late antiquity to modern times and called his design "the Romance of its Past Distinguished" where the new edifice became "a complete work of modern art and science belonging to today but dedicated to ancient tradition – contributing to Tradition instead of living upon it".[17] He based the plan of the church on the Greek square cross using the pure square and circle shapes as his inspiration (see plan of the church in Fig. 2.3.11). The church is a domical modern structure that abstracts in its geometry the traditional Byzantine domical churches (Fig. 2.3.15). Moreover, all of the details of the church are based on simple geometry and abstracted lines, which illustrate the square cross and Wright's interpretations of traditional Byzantine saint images (Figs 3.4.14 and 4.10.2).

Joseph Siry (1996) and Robert McCarter (2005a) show the influence of East and West on Wright's 1906 design of Unity Temple in Oak Park, Illinois. The Western inspiration may be found in the central plans of Santa Maria della Carceri in Prato, Italy, designed by Giuliano da Sangallo (1485), and in San Biagio, Montepulciano, Italy, designed by Antonio Sangallo (1520). The influence of the East is based on the plans of Tosho-gu and Taiyu-in-byo temples in Nikko, Japan.

3.4.14

Abstraction of Traditional Byzantine Saint Images in the Annunciation Greek Orthodox Church, Wisconsin.

The Japanese influence is also found in Wright's 1957 second design proposals for a Wedding Chapel in Berkeley, California. The proposed roof of the chapel would create "a contemporary pagoda-like feeling of lightness, airiness, and grace" (Boyd 1959: 173), (Fig. 1.7). Kevin Nute (2000: 147–148) notes that this Wedding Chapel and the bridge connecting the chapel to the hotel resemble a small *Ukimi-do* Buddhist chapel, which projects out into a lake at the *Mangetsu-ji* Temple (see Nute 2000: 148, figs 8.12 and 8.13). This Japanese chapel was designed to blend in with its surrounding tranquil nature. Moreover, it is plausible that Wright found inspiration for his own chapel in a Japanese wooden block print by Ado Hiroshige entitled "Descending Geese at Katata" (Nute 1996: 90) or "Geese Homing at Katata" (Nute 2000: 148), and in another print by Nishimura Shigenaga. Both prints feature this small Buddhist chapel and its bridge/passageway to the temple.

In summary, as is exemplified time after time, Wright's sacred architecture form manifests his belief in Nature as God. His work illustrates his design concept of harmony with Nature – all God's creations. He used horizontal lines to express the fundamental sacred elements of earth and air (horizon) in his houses of worship. These lines enhance the sacredness of these buildings.

Wright abstracted the geometry and order he found in Nature to create a composition of the universe as associated with spiritual meanings. He introduced this concept into the design of his houses of worship and created dynamic three-dimensional sacred spaces. He also believed that Nature's dimension of depth and the link to land portray American freedom: "Style is a free product: the result of the organic working in, and out of, a project entirely in character, altogether and in one state of feeling" (Wright quoted by Kaufman and Raeburn 1960: 96). The expression of the concept of American democracy and freedom in Wright's sacred architecture is the focus of the next chapter.

Chapter 5

Democracy and Freedom

America, more than any other nation, presents a new architectural proposition. Her ideal is democracy . . . This means that she [America] places a life premium upon individuality.

(Wright 1910/1992: 106)

Wright's religious philosophy tied Nature to freedom. This became a core concept in his search for a unique American architectural style, a style that would free the sacred built form from constraints of European traditions while expressing the American values of democracy and freedom. Wright cherished freedom: "As a young architect . . . I was the *free* son of a *free* people and I wanted to be *free*"[18]. He believed that his mission as an architect was to link this freedom to the American landscape in a democratic form as "Architectural features of any democratic ground plan for human freedom rise naturally by, and from, topography" (Wright 1958a/1995: 251). As such, he saw sacred architecture as an avenue where he could break out of old conventions: "Traditional church forms, like so many traditions now, must die in all minor forms in order that Tradition in great form may live! To understand this truth is to understand the changing growth that is already due to the idea of democracy" (Wright 1958a/1995: 322). When Wright completed Unity Temple, he said: "I knew I had the beginning of a great thing, a great truth in architecture. Now architecture could be free" (Wright quoted in Pfeiffer and Nordland 1988: 13; and in Hoffman 1995: 27).

Wright wanted all his designed forms to express the moment of creation, the feeling of change, and the wish for belonging, which he saw as embedded in the American mind (Scully 1996: 31). Thus, he was a great advocate of departing from traditional ecclesiastical architecture that had its roots in other countries: "Is this architecture? Is it thus tradition molded great style? In this polyglot tangle of borrowed forms, is there a great spirit that will bring order out of chaos? Vitality, unity, and greatness out of emptiness and discord?" (Wright 1910/1992: 106).

Wright's idea of departing from traditional church design was in part a reaction to the domineering Gothic Revival church design that came to

America from Europe during the nineteenth and early twentieth centuries. Gothic Revival became the dominant style for sacred buildings in Europe following Augustus Pugin, the Oxford movement, and the Ecclesiologists of the Cambridge movement (Turner 1979). Pugin's books *Contrasts* (1836) and *Glossary* (1844) transferred Gothic Christianity into architecture theory and practice. In his writing, Pugin determined that the Middle Ages style is the only truly Christian church form and sacred art, and therefore it is a moral obligation to build a church in this style.[19] The Oxford movement, which began in the 1930s, focused on the revival of traditional theology, while the Cambridge Ecclesiologists preached to restore the Church of England (Kieckhefer 2004: 216). Architect Ralf Adam Cram of Chicago, an American medievalist, followed the European theories and architecture of the Gothic Revival and considered the Gothic as "the fruit of a spiritual and aesthetic golden age" (Kieckhefer 2004: 224). Cram published several books in which he developed a theory of theological aesthetics that became a basis for church design (Cram 1924, 1925; see also Part 1, this volume). The influence of these theories and designs was so dominant that most congregations adopted the Gothic Revival image for their new churches. Despite some criticism on the use of this revived style, "Why have we gone back to the Middle Ages. . .? Why do we abuse the papists, and then imitate them?" (Kieckhefer 2004: 219), and the idea that churches should be built "out of that reality which we experience and verify every day" (Schwarz 1958: 11), most of the time, modern architects were required to make compromises. They were asked to provide an overarching Gothic-style image that would then be accompanied by small gestures in form toward the more modern styles (Kieckhefer 2004: 222).[20]

Frank Lloyd Wright sharply criticized the use of Classic and Gothic Revival styles in church building. In his point of view, this produced a "dead face", since "their spiritual center has shifted and nothing remains" (Wright 1931b/1992: 29[21]). His extreme criticism of the style did not stop with the architecture of the church. He believed that similar to freeing church design from stylistic constraints, the state of human spirituality should be freed from religious constraints. Wright felt that both physical and liturgical characteristics of the church needed to be changed (Wright 1932a/1977: 184; Wright and Brownell 1937/1993: 238). The change would reflect the growth of the Church in becoming more democratic in spirit, less of a sectarian institution and more liberal in thoughts, built for the people, or as he called it "The Church of Democracy" (Wright 1958a/1995: 322). Wright claimed that a style should articulate the meaningful forms of a culture and the technology that produces those forms (Alofsin 1993: 154).

Wright's reaction to the European traditional styles guided his continuous search for an American style that would express democracy and freedom, local environments, simplicity, and innovations in building technology (Pfeiffer 1990: 88). Wright believed that the architect "must be a great original interpreter of his time, his day, his age" (Wright 1939/1970: 262). In a letter to Spivey (September 20, 1938), president of Florida Southern College and Wright's client, he described his design of the campus's master plan and of Annie Pfeiffer Chapel as giving "a structural example of the freedom needed very much at this time in our national life".[22] In all, Wright preached for and practiced the creation of a new architectural grammar for his sacred architecture: a grammar that would manifest advanced democracy. This grammar was developed in the philosophical context of Wright's contemporaries. Thinkers such as William James, John Dewey, Henry George, Jane Addams, and others focused on the advance of social and economic freedom and democracy. In the 1930s, these ideas started to appear in art, literature, and social commentary: "American experience could indeed aid in the restoration of the nation's democratic traditions, spawn a new national strength and unity, and in turn recreate a culture that was truly American" (Owings Jr. 2003: 6).

Wright's thoughts on developing these ideas into a unique American architecture can also be studied in the context of Ralph Waldo Emerson's philosophy and Ernest Fenollosa's aesthetic theory. In his 1837 speech "The American Scholar", Emerson stated that artists should not import fashionable foreign styles; rather, they should develop their ideas based on their own culture and location. The same idea is found in Fenollosa's 1896 aesthetic theory. Interestingly, the notion of developing an original idea on the basis of one's own culture and location was also recognized in Europe. In 1902, Joseph A. Lux, a Viennese critic, called for creating an awareness of the timeless basic principles of "our own souls" and for the need to break away from stereotypes (Alofsin 1996: 215).

Wright's design for the Steel Cathedral (1926) in New York, which was intended to illustrate an article on the "Modern Cathedral" by William N. Guthrie[23], is an example of Wright's search for a unique form that would express freedom and unite all religions under the same roof. In this design, Wright used the basic geometry of a triangle as the cathedral's motif, creating open spaces that flow from one another, and freeing the sacred space from any structural elements. He used the triangle for the pyramidal roof (Fig. 2.3.1) and a series of hexagons in the plan. The design departed from the traditional box design and created a hexagon central sacred space free from structural elements. Six smaller spaces emerged from and into the central area. This design exhibited the aspiration for the "Modern Cathedral", which expresses American democracy and freedom.[24]

In his search for an original American style of sacred architecture, Wright introduced several prominent architectural ideas: the use of pure geometry as a basic motif for his design; free flow of continuous spaces; and the abstraction of forms to express faith symbols. The first concept may be traced to the geometry of ancient religious monuments, while the latter two illustrate Wright's innovative design forms.

The Use of Pure Geometry

Wright believed that three-dimensional volumes based on pure geometrical forms such as the square, triangle, and circle are noble forms, and as such can express the noble values of American democracy and freedom. In his eyes the forms' horizontal and vertical axes as related to the American landscape are associated with the soul of these values. In Part 2 of this volume, I introduce Wright's use of these basic forms as an expression of faith. In the context of this chapter, it may be said that Wright believed that abstracting these "noble" forms enabled him to free his sacred architecture from traditional European church design.[25] An example is his treatment of the roofs covering his central plans of the houses of God. Rather than using the historical precedent of a domed roof, Wright designed the roofs of his sacred "cube"-form churches using the triangle (for a pitched roof) and/or flat roofs. The square geometry dominates these types of roofs. One example is the double roof of Unity Temple in Oak Park, Illinois. The pitch of the outer roof is aligned with the center of the square plan, while the inner flat roof is pierced with square glass skylights. This project (Figs 3.5.1 and 3.5.2) and Wright's proposal for the Memorial for the Soil Chapel in Wisconsin (1936) (Fig. 1.2) illustrate Wright's use of the square as a basic form for his sacred architecture. In these designs the square becomes a symbol of integrity (Wright 1912/ 1992: 117), and of "harmony between body and soul, and the pursuit of a life that ethically and morally reinforces their union" (Joncas 1998a: 102).

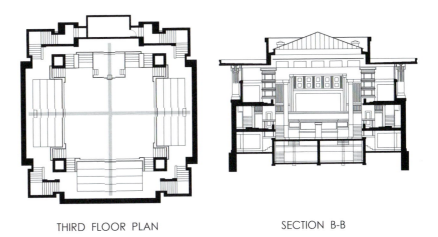

THIRD FLOOR PLAN   SECTION B-B

0   6' 12'   24'

3.5.1

The Plan and Section of Unity Temple, Illinois (note the temple's square cross plan) (redrawn under author's supervision).

Wright employed the triangle to create three-dimensional compositions of his houses of worship projects. Examples include the Unitarian Meeting House in Wisconsin (1947) (Fig. 3.5.3), the First Christian Church in Arizona (1950/1973) (Fig. 3.1), Beth Sholom Synagogue in Pennsylvania (1954) (Fig. 2.3.7), the Steel Cathedral in New York (1926) (Fig. 2.3.1), the Rhododendron Chapel for the Kaufmann Family in Pennsylvania (1952) (Fig. 3.4.11), and Trinity Chapel in Oklahoma (1958) (Fig. 2.1.4). The proposed Rhododendron Chapel shows a combination of the triangle and the square.

3.5.3
The Triangle as a Basic Motif of the
Unitarian Meeting House, Wisconsin.

Wright referred to the circle as a symbol of heaven and as the geometric form to be used for domical structures. Figures 2.3.13 and 2.3.15 show how Wright utilized the circle's geometry to serve as the basic motif for his design of the Annunciation Greek Orthodox Church in Wisconsin. The circle was utilized in all levels of the project (2.3.14). In the plan, it serves as a circumference to the square Greek cross (Fig. 2.3.11), while in the elevation and section it serves as the bowl that supports the dome (Fig. 3.5.4).

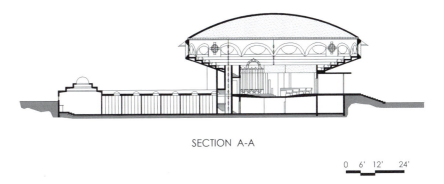

SECTION A-A

0 6' 12' 24'

3.5.4
A Section of The Annunciation Greek Orthodox Church, Wisconsin (redrawn under author's supervision).

Free Flow of Continuous Spaces

Wright demonstrated the idea of expressing freedom through design by breaking the conventional Western box of traditional constrained spaces and creating a composition of open spaces that freely flow from one to another – a "rhythmic geometry of movement" (Christ-Janer and Foley 1962: 196). Although the ideas of "breaking down the box" and "creating open spaces that flow from one to another" were also part of the European development of the International Style, Wright set himself apart from what he called "a-contextual style" (Wright 1932a; Levine 1996; Scully 1996). He claimed that most of these modernists did not interpret the structure as part of their own culture and geography (including local environmental conditions), nor did they express democratic art values.[26]

Wright developed his innovative compositions based on three major architectural design aspects and features. First, Wright changed the ratio of open space to solid structure. The religious building became a "creation of interior-space in light . . . Enclosing screens and protecting features of architectural character took the place of the solid wall" (Hoffman 1995: 22). Second, Wright moved the support's structural system inward and away from the salient corners. Wright explained this design concept of freeing the space when he described his design of Unity Temple in Illinois (Fig. 3.5.5): "I took those four corners and I pulled them away from the building. And there the thing began to appear . . . I followed that up with Unity Temple where there were no walls of any kind, only features" (Wright quoted in Hoffman 1995: 27). The same pattern appears in the interior of Annie Pfeiffer Chapel in Florida (Fig. 3.5.6). In his proposal for the design of the Steel Cathedral in New York and Beth Sholom Synagogue in Pennsylvania, Wright freed the interior from structural columns by designing a tripod structure holding the pyramidal roof (Fig. 3.5.7).

3.5.5 (top left)
A View Toward a Corner in Unity Temple, Illinois: the Column is Pulled Away from the Corner.

3.5.6 (left)
An Interior View of Annie Pfeiffer Chapel, Florida.

3.5.7 (top right)
An Interior View of the Tripod Structure Holding up the Pyramidal Roof of Beth Sholom Synagogue, Pennsylvania.

The third aspect of Wright's break from the traditional box was his introduction of the cantilevers as horizontal extensions of the roof's lines, or as extending horizontal balconies. The cantilever idea also appears as triangle overhangs that lift the roof toward the sky. Examples of these cantilevers include the horizontal overhangs of Unity Temple in Illinois (Fig. 3.5.2); the cantilever balconies of Annie Pfeiffer Chapel in Florida (Fig. 3.7.10); and the entrance to the Community Christian Church in Missouri (Figs 3.4.3 and 3.6.3). Examples of the triangular overhangs include the roof of the Unitarian Meeting House in Wisconsin (Fig. 3.5.3); and the roof of the Minor Chapel in Florida (Fig. 3.5.8). These measures enabled Wright to change the box's boundaries and open the space to the outside. This openness characterized Wright's departure from the conventional church design of his time.

3.5.8
The Overhang Roof of the Minor Chapel, Florida.

Abstract Forms of Faith Symbols

Wright's departure from the traditional church design of his time was also manifested in his attitude toward religious symbolism. He had criticized the use of symbols in conventional church design – pronouncing that their use made the church a cliché (Wright 1946a/1994: 298). In his view these symbols had lost their significance, replacing the church's original inspiration (Wright 1949/1994: 336). Still, Wright did not abandon the value of each faith's symbols. He abstracted their form and incorporated them into his design as an integral part of the project as a whole. Bruce Pfeiffer (1990: 87) writes that Wright strove to find these symbols and believed that by abstracting their design, the symbols would once again serve as religious inspiration. In this context, it is worth mentioning that Wright's 1926 all-faith project of the Steel Cathedral in New York served as the model for his 1954 design of the Jewish Beth Sholom Synagogue in Elkin Park, Pennsylvania. Although the two religious buildings required different attention to their symbols and rituals, the abstraction of the symbols and their relation to universal sacred meanings enabled Wright to reprocess these designs. Moreover, Wright's idea of designing a modern American house of worship governed the notion of "recycling" these designs. The Steel Cathedral was designed as a modern cathedral, while the design of the synagogue was geared "to build a [modern] American Synagogue for Jews to worship in" (Wright 1957: 210).

Examples of Wright's abstraction of faith symbols may be seen in his designs of the Icon Screens of the Annunciation Greek Orthodox church in Wisconsin (Fig. 3.5.9); the two Jewish candle holders (*menora*),[27] the fixture of the eternal light (*Ner Tamid*), and the wooden partition of the Torah Ark (*Aron Kodesh*) in the Sisterhood Chapel of Beth Sholom Synagogue in Pennsylvania (Fig. 2.3.10). These examples show Wright's use of basic geometry (a circle for the church and a triangle for the synagogue) as part of the holistic motifs of these projects.

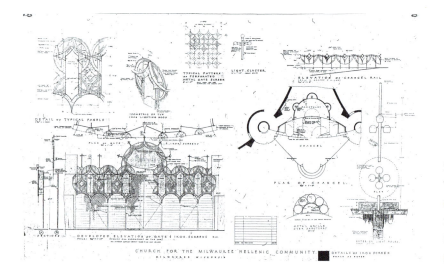

3.5.9
The Icon Screens of The Annunciation Greek Orthodox Church, Wisconsin (© 2009 Frank Lloyd Wright Foundation, Scottsdale, AZ/Artists Rights Society (ARS), New York).

Wright acknowledged that the principles of symbols and rituals evolve with people through history (Wright 1908/1992: 86). Accordingly, he called to adapt these faith principles rather than using explicit historic precedents (Wright 1957: 105). Indeed, Wright did not look at ancient religious monuments as precedents. Rather, he was inspired by their relation to Nature's order, principles, and geometry. The study of these geometric principles in monuments such as Mesopotamia's ziggurats, Egypt's pyramids and temples, Pre-Columbian pyramids and temples, and Japan's shrines reveals their relation to natural and cosmic systems as well as the principles' tectonic and symbolic spiritual meanings (Alofsin 1993: 215). Still, Wright considered his work as original design "not only in fact but in spiritual fiber" (Wright 1957: 205). He continued to declare that the Incas, the Mayans, and the Japanese "all were to me but splendid confirmation" (Wright 1957:205).

The American Institute of Architects, as well as several other scholars, all acknowledged and praised Wright's endless search for the unique American style. For example, Thomas Craven, an art critic, devoted a whole chapter to Frank Lloyd Wright's work in his book *Modern Art – The Men, The Movements, The Meaning* (1934/2007). The chapter is entitled "An American Architect" and refers to Wright's "lifelong battle for an American ideal" (Craven 1934/2007: 273–289). In this regard Peter Blake (1969: 11) called Wright "the last of the true Americans", believing that Wright was the last great representative of all the things this country once stood for.

In summary, Wright experimented with spatial compositions while seeking an American image for his sacred architecture.[28] Using line axes in his plans "like country cross roads in the boundless prairie" (Scully 1996: 18), he created three-dimensional forms both connected to Nature and growing out of the heart of America and its values of democracy and freedom. He freed his religious projects' styles from the constraints of his time's church design by using pure geometry and abstracting faith symbols; by introducing the cantilever; and by opening the spaces to create dynamic three-dimensional free-flowing sacred spaces, where "man was truly embodied in a world of his own making" (McCarter 2005c: 307).

Chapter 6

The Whole as the Equilibrium of its Parts

In organic building nothing is complete in itself but is only complete as the part is merged into the large expression of the whole.

(Wright 1953a: 66)

Frank Lloyd Wright's claim that a "part is to [a] part as [a] part is to [the] whole" played a major role in his departure from traditional religious buildings design. "[E]verything was integrated and related: form, structure, ornament" (Pfeiffer 1990: 88). The concept of the relationship between the whole and its parts served as the core of Wright's aesthetical values. He believed that the whole must consist of individual units, which are great and strong in their own sphere, but are united as a whole. Naturally, this idea was not developed in a vacuum of thought; rather, it may be viewed as part of the broader context of an era (the second half of the nineteenth and the beginning of the twentieth centuries) when major aesthetic theories were developed in Europe, Japan, and America. A key example is the foundation of the *Gestalt* theory in the 1910s in Germany and its influence on modern art and design. As described in Part 2 of the book, the formulation of this theory was based on the idea that a whole is not simply the sum of its parts, but an interdependent unique result of the whole's effects (Ash 1995: 88). Thus, the whole is generated by a dynamic interrelation of its parts. Max Wertheimer's 1923 paper entitled "Theory of Form" illustrates the *Gestalt* movement's ideas graphically and shows that the actual appearance of the parts is determined by wholes.

The resemblance between *Gestalt* theory and the Japanese aesthetic movement of the same period was proliferated by scholars such as Ernest Fenollosa, Arthur Wesley Dow, Kakuzo Okakura, and Denman Ross. In his 1891 manuscript *The Lessons of Japanese Art* and his two essays on "The Nature of Fine Art" (1896), Ernest Fenollosa argued that the particular is part of the whole and that both are universal at the same time. He continued to elaborate this concept in his 1896 manuscript *The Masters of the Ukiyo-e*, where he stated that wholeness is derived from the mutual interdependence of each particular, and that a synthetic whole holds a perfect equilibrium of its parts. Wright was a great advocate of this approach and expressed it in his process of design: "there was the general purpose of the whole to consider in each part: a matter of reasoned arrangement" (Wright 1932a: 180). Arthur Wesley Dow further developed the idea of an equilibrium composition as related to its parts. His graphic interpretations of Fenollosa's aesthetic theory focused on the whole as balanced by simple arrangements of lines: "There may be few lines, but each must have its part in the whole" (Dow 1899/1913: 38). Similarly, Wright related his plans, sections, and elevations to each other in creating a spatial holistic project.

Jonathan Lipman (2005: 264–285) illustrates the *parti* diagrams of Unity Temple in Illinois, the Annunciation Greek Orthodox Church in Wisconsin, and Beth Sholom Synagogue in Pennsylvania. These diagrams demonstrate a separation of the primary and secondary functions into two main volumes and show how the relation between these volumes creates the whole. In Unity Temple, Wright assembled the primary volume as the sanctuary based on a square plan (64'x64') while the secondary parts include the entry cloisters, the house, and galleries. These interdependent volumes create the balance of a dynamic sacred space (McCarter 2005c: 307). Lipman's diagrams also show that in section the volumes of the sanctuaries of the Annunciation Greek Orthodox Church and Beth Sholom Synagogue are separated from the main base but still work as a whole project (Lipman 2005: 281, 283). This analysis can also apply to Wright's proposal for Trinity Church in Oklahoma (Fig. 2.1.4). The latter example also reinforces Wright's idea of function and form as one. The separation of the main base from the sanctuary was designed to accommodate parking below the church. The separation of the sanctuary from its base creates the effect of "floating" in the air, thus adding an additional spiritual layer in these houses of worship. Air is one of the fundamental universal elements of sacredness, and upward movement is associated with the *axis mundi,* which links earth and heaven.[29]

In 1908, Wright expressed his holistic approach to design by writing the following about Unity Temple: "All the forms are complete in themselves and frequently do duty at the same time from within and without as decorative attributes of the whole" (Wright 1908: 160–161). Moreover, in his biography, Wright indicated that in order to achieve the holistic character of his design of Unity Temple, he dissected its design into pieces and then reunited them into one complete assembly (Wright 1932a/1992: 217). He started this process with a general idea of a noble room for worship that would then shape the whole edifice (Wright 1932a/1977: 177–184), and then proceeded to consider the whole as the equilibrium of its parts (Wright 1932a: 180).

The design of the whole as divided into its parts and then reunited into one complete holistic composition is exemplified in Wright's functional design of the assembly hall of the Unitarian Meeting House in Wisconsin

(Fig. 2.3.3). When the hall is used as a worship unit, the edifice's movable pews face toward the prow; when concerts and lectures are held in the hall, the pews are turned toward the hearth space; the pews are folded for dinner and social events; while during small gatherings, the hall is divided using a curtain with a design that coordinates with the motif of the whole space (Gaebler 1952: 89). Wright managed to provide all of these functions for the congregants while still designing a church that expressed an "overall sense of unity" (Wright 1953a/1970: 29). A structure where the three individual parts of conventional church design – the prayer hall, the sacred verticality, and the secular space – are gathered into one whole assembly (Patton 1947: 248, 268) (Fig. 3.6.1).

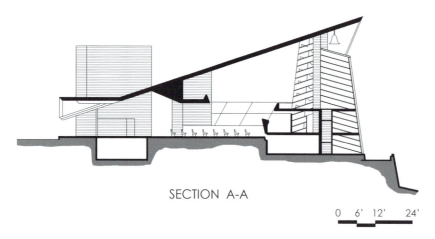

SECTION A-A

0   6' 12'   24'

3.6.1

A Section of the Unitarian Meeting House, Wisconsin (redrawn under author's supervision).

To achieve the equilibrium between the whole and its parts Wright created a sense of continuity among all of the individual units of each project: "Space. The continuity becoming: invisible fountain from which all rhythms flow and to which they must pass. Beyond time or infinity" (Wright 1953b: 6). This continuity became a major motif in Wright's design: "Let walls, ceilings, floors now become not only party to each other, but part of each other, reacting upon and within one another; continuity in all" (Wright 1955: 208–210). Wright extended this holistic concept by including the spatial continuity of the exterior of the building (Brooks 1979: 14; Scully 1996: 15). Examples of this are found in the Annie Pfeiffer Chapel in Florida where the peripheral balcony is a continuation of the central building (Figs 3.6.2 and 3.8.7), and the tower is part of this holistic design (Fig. 3.6.2). The balconies of the Community Church in Missouri create the continuous horizontal movement of the building (Figs 3.4.3 and 3.6.3).

Wright realized the idea of continuity using an underlying grid based on geometric modules/units. The grid system was configured into a balanced exterior and interior whole. It became the basis for open spaces flowing into one another, and served as the foundation for the shapes of interior features that define the vital whole (Wright 1908, 1912).

3.6.2 (right)
A Section of Annie Pfeiffer Chapel, Florida (redrawn under author's supervision).

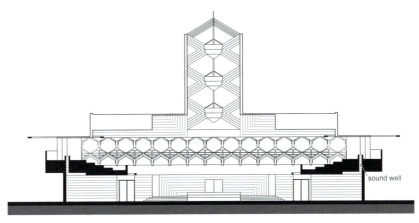

SECTION A-A

0 6' 12' 24'

3.6.3
Spatial Continuity of the Façade of The Community Church in Kansas City, Missouri.

Continuity and the Grid

An analysis of Frank Lloyd Wright's sacred architecture of all periods reveals that every one of his projects was planned on a grid using a pure geometrical module: "when you have the unit system established, every part of the building is sure to be in perfect accord with every other part"[30]. Wright's belief in the power of geometry and the aesthetic value of the whole motivated him to place every detail of the exterior and interior on the same grid and basic geometric module (De Long 1998: 17–18; McCarter 2005c: 303). Most of his religious projects were based on the square, the triangle, and their derivations (see more in subsequent text and in Chapter 5). Though, Wright used the circle in a few of his religious projects: for example, in his proposal for the Daphne Funeral Chapel, California (Fig. 3.4.13) and in the first alternative proposal for the Wedding Chapel in California (Fig. 3.6.4).[31]

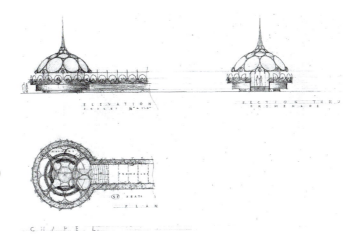

3.6.4
Frank Lloyd Wright's First Proposal for a Wedding Chapel of Hotel Claremont, Berkeley, California (1957) (© 2009 Frank Lloyd Wright Foundation, Scottsdale, AZ/Artists Rights Society (ARS), New York).

Wright used the circle combined with the square in one of his design alternatives for the Christian Science Church in California (Fig. 3.6.5), and in his project of the Annunciation Greek Orthodox Church in Wisconsin (Fig. 2.3.11).

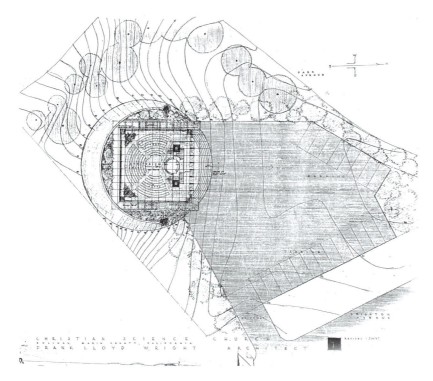

3.6.5

Frank Lloyd Wright's Proposed Site and Floor Plans for the Christian Science Church, California (1956) (© 2009 Frank Lloyd Wright Foundation, Scottsdale, AZ/Artists Rights Society (ARS), New York).

An analysis of Unity Temple's geometry shows that it is a complex inter-related design based on "many principles working all at the same time . . . held in balance by the ideal of an integrated order" (McCarter 2005c: 288). This practical application of a square grid was complemented by the idea that the grid and module system enhance the spiritual realm. The skylight in Unity Temple is formed on the building's square grid (Fig. 2.1.6). This design element creates the feel that the square is part of the whole sacred space.

Examples of Wright's use of the triangle grid system have been shown previously. In the context of this chapter it is important to illustrate the bell tower and spire of the First Christian Church in Arizona, which are based on the building's triangle grid system and express the church's religious associations (Fig. 3.1).

In his book *The Frank Lloyd Wright Companion* (1993), William Storrer elaborates on Frank Lloyd Wright's use of the grid and modules. Storrer describes these as the foundation for Wright's design of the whole building and its details. He presents Wright's plans and their specific grid systems, which are all based on a variety of pure geometric modules (e.g., squares, triangles, circles, overlapping modules, and modules rotated in various angles). The rotation of the modules is found in several of Wright's religious projects. For example, Annie Pfeiffer Chapel's grid in Florida is based on a six-foot square with 30 and 60 degrees reflex angles that create a hexagon. The Minor Chapel plan in Florida is also based on a six-foot square module that was set at 30 degrees from the Annie Pfeiffer Chapel (Fig. 3.6.6). Wright's grid of the Community Church (The Church for the Future) in Kansas City, Missouri is based on five-foot side equilateral parallelograms (also called "diamonds") of 60–120 degrees. Wright used the same type of grid in his design of the Unitarian Meeting House in Wisconsin, but with four-foot sides (Fig. 2.3.3).

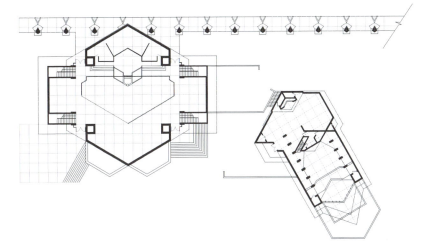

3.6.6

A Plan Showing The Minor Chapel, Florida set at 30 degrees from the Annie Pfeiffer Chapel, Florida (redrawn under author's supervision).

Most of Wright's sacred projects were based on a four-foot or six-foot grid. William Storrer (1993) explained Wright's use of these grids in terms of construction materials and building technology. He referred to the four-foot module as a standard design that is filled by three 16-inch blocks (Storrer 1993: 98). He went on to argue that the four-foot grid "rationalizes the maximum number of building elements into a single module". This flexibility is illustrated in Wright's proposal for the Johnson Desert Compound and Shrine. This project was based on the four-foot grid and included rectangular forms for the complex buildings and an octagonal form for the shrine. It should be noted that the number four is an even generative number (generating itself), which makes it inherent to and easily integrated into the geometry of a building and its details (Tabb 2007). Both the Unitarian Meeting House in Wisconsin and the Pilgrim Congregational Church in California were designed on a diamond grid with a four-foot unit side (Figs 2.3.3 and 3.6.7).

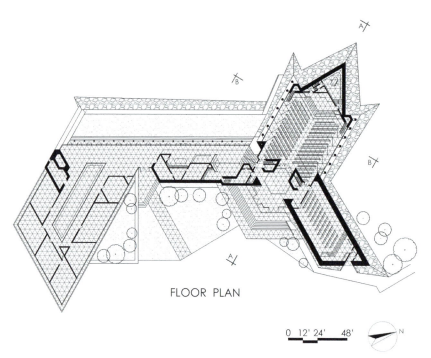

FLOOR PLAN

0 12' 24'   48'

3.6.7
The original Plan of The Pilgrim
Congregational Church, California
(1958) (redrawn under author's
supervision).

Wright exhibited the use of the six-foot grid in projects such as Unity
Temple[32] in Illinois and the Annie Pfeiffer and Minor Chapels in Florida.[33]
The grids of these three buildings are based on a square. While Unity
Temple reflects the square's pure geometry, the square in the Florida
Chapels is rotated to create a hexagon in the Annie Pfeiffer Chapel and the
30 degree orientation of the Minor Chapel. As described in Part 2 of this
volume, the utility of the six-foot module was influenced by the Japanese
building grid, which is based on the *tatami*, a padded floor mat measuring
six feet by three feet. This module is known as the basis for the traditional
grid of Japanese dwellings and shrines (Frampton and Kudo 1997: 3–6). It
is not surprising that Wright used this module in some of his religious
projects. He admired the Japanese house, finding spirituality in it since:
"Spiritual significance is alive and singing in everything concerning the
Japanese House . . . it is perfect unison with their Heaven" (Wright 1932a/
1977: 222). Wright used this notion as inspiration for his 1949 design
proposal for Father Harry John, Jr., a Catholic priest in Oconomowoc,
Wisconsin. In this design (the project was never built), Wright was asked
to include a house, a dormitory structure for eight homeless children, and
a small chapel as part of the house's mezzanine. Wright turned the small
and modest dwelling into a temple-like sacred space (Fig 3.6.8).

DETAIL VIEW FROM GARDEN
DWELLING FOR HARRY G. JOHN JR. OCONOMOWOC WISCONSIN
FRANK LLOYD WRIGHT ARCHITECT

3.6.8

Frank Lloyd Wright's Proposal for Father Harry John, Jr. House and Chapel, Wisconsin (© 2009 Frank Lloyd Wright Foundation, Scottsdale, AZ/Artists Rights Society (ARS), New York).

The notion of home as a sacred place can be understood by observing the relationship between people's heart and religion: "home is where the heart is, and where the heart is so there is religiousness in their broadest sense" (Osmen 1990: 7). In his sacred architecture, Wright carried this idea even further by emphasizing human scale rather than monumentality and calling for a praying space that is "A pleasant well proportioned room in human scale with a big fireplace and a plain table for flowers and the Book" (Wright 1946a/1994: 6). This belief was also expressed by Wright's uncle, Jenkin Lloyd Jones, a leader of the Unitarian church in Chicago, who referred to a church building as a dwelling in the country – a home for a large family, warm with human tenderness, filled with sunlight and air (Siry 1991a: 258; 1996: 14). In his 1958 book *The Church Incarnate: The Sacred Function of Christian Architecture*, Rudolf Schwarz, a German church builder, adopted this idea and claimed, "table, space and walls make up the simplest church" (Schwarz 1958: 35). An example of this principle is Unity Chapel in Spring Green, Wisconsin, which was designed by Joseph Silsbee in 1886 with Wright on the team (Fig. 3.6.9).

When collaborating on the proposals for the Unitarian Chapel in Sioux City, Iowa (1887) and the All Souls Church in Chicago (1897), Wright continued this design approach. The proposal for the chapel in Sioux City was not only influenced by the design of Unity Chapel, but by the Shingle style of the American vernacular domestic architecture at the turn of the century. The All Souls Church in Chicago was noted for having a fireplace that would provide "air of substantial comfort and warm the cockles of the heart of every one that will stop long enough to read the scriptural quotations cut into the wood of the mantels over the fireplaces" (Siry 1991a: 259, Note 17). Later, in his independent work, Wright introduced the fireplace – the hearth of a home, a comforting and warm feature – into some of his religious designs. His addition of the fireplace to houses of worship was meant to create human comfort as well as an association with the sacred symbol of fire. Examples of such fireplaces may be seen in his Pettit Memorial Chapel in Illinois (1906), the Unitarian Meeting House in Wisconsin (1947), and the Pilgrim Congregational Church in California (1958). In the Unitarian Meeting House in Wisconsin, Wright lowered the ceiling in the hearth's area in order to scale down the church to human size and retain heat from the fireplace. This also strengthened the effect of the rising ceiling in the edifice (Fig. 3.6.1). Wright emphasized the residential feel and human scale of the church by designing the prayer hall as a multi-function living room (Hamilton 1991: 19), and by designating the chimney as a focal point at the entrance of the building (Figs 2.3.3 and 3.6.10). The fireplaces in the Pettit Chapel in Illinois and Pilgrim Church in California are located in the prow area of the edifice (Figs 4.14.7 and 4.14.9). Again, in these examples, Wright continues to exhibit an integration of the physical (function and comfort) and metaphorical features (the spiritual elements such as light and sound). This brings us back to this book's conceptual model (Fig. 1.1), which illustrates this relationship.

All of these examples, which illustrate the human scale of Wright's religious projects, were designed on specific grid systems that help in integrating all parts of each structure into one whole assembly. The grids appear not only on the plan, but serve as a unified geometric module for the projects' sections, elevations, and details. Thus, they enable the continuity of spaces/volumes, "all in all and each in all sets forth" (Wright 1953a/1970: 29).

3.6.9 (left)
Unity Chapel in Spring Green, Wisconsin.

3.6.10 (right)
The Chimney as seen from the Entrance to The Unitarian Meeting House, Wisconsin.

Continuity and Details

Wright's use of different geometric units in his sacred architecture was previously discussed in the book in the context of ancient religious monuments, Nature's principles, and their symbolic and sacred meanings. In this section, I look at the influence of geometric units on details in Wright's sacred architecture. The premise for this examination is that Wright's use of the same unit throughout each project (including in the details) united all parts into a balanced whole, and enhanced continuity.

As mentioned before, Wright's use of the square as his basic geometric unit is demonstrated in his designs of Unity Temple in Oak Park, Illinois (1906) (Figs 3.5.1 and 3.5.2); and in his proposed projects for the Christian Catholic Church in Zion, Illinois (1911, 1915) (Figs 3.3 and 3.6.11), the Memorial to the Soil Chapel in Cooksville, Wisconsin (1936) (Fig. 1.2), the second alternative for the Christian Science Church in California (1956) (Fig. 3.4.12), and Taliesin Unity Chapel in Wisconsin (1958) (Fig. 1.8).

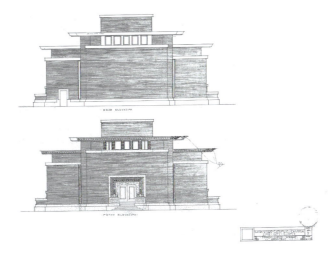

3.6.11

The Elevations of Frank Lloyd Wright's 1911 (ca) Proposal for the Christian Catholic Church in Zion City, Illinois (© 2009 Frank Lloyd Wright Foundation, Scottsdale AZ/Artists Rights Society (ARS), New York).

In studying the exterior and interior architectural features of these projects, one can note that Wright based the detail design on the square grid. For an example of this, we turn to Unity Temple in Illinois: the skylight ceiling is based on the square grid of the whole Temple (Fig. 2.1.6); the exterior columns that hold the roof of the Temple restate in miniature the pure geometrical square forms of the Temple; the same geometric pattern appears on the upper windows (Figs 3.5.2 and 3.6.12); the concrete planters at the entrance to the Temple are based on two squares (Figs 3.4.8 and 3.7.1); the vent holes in the hollow columns of Unity Temple exhibit this grid as well; and the form of the light fixtures and furniture repeat the pattern (Figs 3.6.13, 3.6.14, and 1.4). All of these details, based on the square grid, unite the individual parts of the sacred space into a continuous whole.

3.6.12
The Columns Holding up the Roof of
Unity Temple, Illinois.

3.6.13
Square and Round Light Fixtures in
Unity Temple, Illinois.

3.6.14
The Pulpit and Furniture of Unity
Temple, Illinois.

3.6.15

The Original Bell of the Unitarian Meeting House, Wisconsin.

As shown previously, Wright also used a triangle as his module in some of his religious projects. The triangle shaped the basic form of these projects' grid, their exterior and interior form, and their details. This triangular module also served as the basic form of the diamond shape grid of the plan, section, and main elevation of Wright's Unitarian Meeting House in Wisconsin and the Pilgrim Congregational Church in California. In the section of Wright's Unitarian Meeting House, the triangular room "rises from a low point at its rear to an apex high above the pulpit and choir loft" and creates an "acute point [that] projects north away from the body of the building" into nature (Hamilton 1990: 183) (Figs 3.5.3 and 3.6.1). Even the bell of this church was cased in a double triangle (diamond) module (Fig. 3.6.15).

Wright's design of the First Christian Church in Arizona was also based on a triangle in its module and volume. The worship center is a double triangle, which creates a diamond-shaped plan. The surrounding glass walls and the twenty-three exterior pillars of concrete that support the sanctuary are also based on the same triangular module (Fig. 2.3.5). The church's skyline, which comprises triangular colored glass, is located in a triangular indentation in the ceiling that embraces the worship area (Figs 3.1 and 3.6.16). As previously described, the triangle was the base for the church's spire and bell tower (Figs 3.1, 3.6.17, and 3.6.18). In all, the church as a whole as well as its individual features are all based on a triangular model that represents the Holy Trinity.

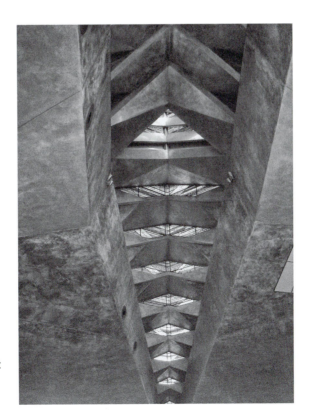

3.6.16

The Triangular Module of The Skylight of the First Christian Church in Phoenix, Arizona.

Wright also used the triangle as the fundamental form for the concrete base of the Beth Sholom Synagogue in Pennsylvania and its pyramidal roof (Fig. 1.3). Examples of other triangular architectural details of the synagogue are the entrance canopy (Fig. 2.3.8); the light fixtures (Figs 2.2.2 and 2.3.10); the stage – the *Bima* and *Torah Ark* (Fig. 3.6.19); the eternal light, the two candle lights (*menorah*), and the stage furniture in the Sisterhood Chapel of the synagogue (Fig 2.3.10); as well as the plaque of the building (Fig. 3.6.20).

3.6.17 (left)
The Spire of the First Christian Church in Phoenix, Arizona.

3.6.18 (right)
The Bell Tower of the First Christian Church in Phoenix, Arizona.

3.6.19
The Interior of Beth Sholom Synagogue, Pennsylvania: the Stage – *Bima* as the Focal Point.

3.6.20
The Plaque of Beth Sholom
Synagogue, Pennsylvania.

As illustrated before, the triangle also served as the basic unit in Wright's design of Pilgrim Congregational Church in California. This basic form appears in the church's plan (Fig. 3.6.7), section (Fig. 3.6.21), elevations (Fig. 3.4.1), structural and construction systems (Fig. 3.4.6), and in the floor pattern and details, such as the doors connecting the sanctuary to the secular part of the building (Fig. 3.6.22). Please note that the triangle pattern of the floor does not stop inside the chapel but continues outside as part of Wright's continuity effect for all details in the project.

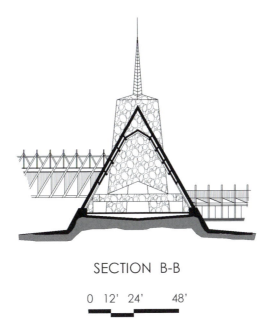

SECTION B-B

0   12' 24'   48'

3.6.21
A Section of the Pilgrim
Congregational Church, California
(redrawn under author's supervision).

3.6.22
A Detail of Triangular Windows in
the Pilgrim Congregational Church,
California.

Another interior feature that defines the vital whole in Wright's sacred spaces is the trim, which links all parts of the sacred space into one assembly. In the interior of Unity Temple in Illinois, where Wright designed features instead of partitions, wooden trim runs around the space and draws the space's interior elements together (Figs 3.5.5 and 3.6.23). Instead of using traditional trim design and running it on all four sides of each pier, Wright wrapped the trim around the two interior sides of each pier, allowing it to continue on to other parts of the interior including under the ceiling. The trim expresses the continuity between separate surfaces and areas, and creates "a single three dimensional form" (Brooks 1979:10). Thus, the trim, which is merely an ornament, is able to accent the importance of the central space.

Wright used the same motif in the Pettit Chapel in Illinois, where the trim unites the ceiling and the walls (Fig. 3.6.24). In this chapel, the outside cypress trim painted blue (wooden trim in the picture) and the indoor yellow pine trim represent the continuity between the interior and exterior of the building (Fig. 3.6.25).

3.6.23
The Ceiling's Trim in Unity Temple, Illinois.

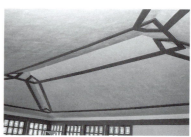

3.6.24 (above)
The Ceiling's Trim in the Pettit Chapel, Illinois.

3.6.25 (left)
The Exterior Trim in the Pettit Chapel, Illinois.

The links between the enclosed sanctuary, which in most of Wright's religious projects was designed as a space growing from within, and the exterior of the building and its surroundings are an additional example of Wright's holistic approach. These links are created through the bringing in of construction materials from the exterior façade to the interior sacred space. Examples of this are found in the Pilgrim Congregational Church in California (Fig. 3.6.26), the Unitarian Meeting House in Wisconsin (Fig. 3.6.27), and in the Annie Pfeiffer and Minor Chapels in Florida. In the latter, Wright used concrete blocks both as the exterior and interior material. In the case of the Minor Chapel in Florida, the amber and red colors of the chapel's stained glass match the colors used in its stage details and the pulpit.

3.6.26 (top)
The Continuation of the Construction
Materials from the Exterior Façade
to the Interior of the Pilgrim
Congregational Church, California.

3.6.27 (right)
The Continuation of the Construction
Materials from the Exterior Façade to
the Interior of the Unitarian Meeting
House, Wisconsin.

More is detailed on Wright's use of these geometric modules and their
combination in Chapter 7, which elaborates on the horizontal dimensions
of the journey from the profane to the sacred in Wright's sacred architecture. Chapter 8 further explores the vertical axis of Wright's sacred
architecture. These axes were also designed as part of the building's
module and as the continuation of one element into another to create a
holistic comprehensive project.

Chapter 7

Sacred Path/Plan

A good plan is the beginning and the end, because every good plan is organic. That means that its development in all directions is inherent-inevitable.

(Wright 1928a/1992: 249)

A number of civilizations in history drew their world map and built their cities in relation with horizontal and central dimensions (e.g., ancient China, ancient Greece, and medieval Europe). Other civilizations determined their horizontal setting in relation with the four cardinal sun/wind directions (e.g., ancient Egypt, the Pueblo world). Some, such as the Buddhist *mandalas*, created a circular or square central plan where Gods were superimposed on to the center of the plan where a process of transformation and purification occurred (Mann 1993: 98–100). The horizontal dimension and its centralized orientation were influenced by the perception of the cosmos and affected the form of sacred spaces/buildings.

The sacred plan, the core of religious building, creates an earthly meeting point between human and Divine. To reach this spiritual point, a path directs the worshiper from a secular space and into an esoteric plan "that is hidden . . . which needs to be rediscovered" (Mann 1993: 16). The path consists of a spatial sequence that encompasses a transitional zone between the outside world and the inside sacred space. This spatial sequence provides a symbolic narrative for the worshiper who travels along it, increasingly anticipating the arrival at the sacred place (Barrie 1996: 55, 58).

In this chapter I discuss the two main ideas behind Frank Lloyd Wright's design of the sacred path and sacred plan. The first illustrates how Wright designed the path to his sacred projects as a procession that separates the worshipers from the mundane and prepares them for their entrance into the sacred space. These progressions may be traced in ancient temples of the Egyptian and Greek, where the worshiper walked from an outer courtyard to a colonnaded space toward the holy of holies. There, as they progressed further into the temple, access became more restricted – fewer people were allowed close to the Gods. As such, it is fundamentally an undemocratic structure. Similar to these ancient religious monuments Wright designed the sacred paths for on-foot approach and maintained the move from secular to the sacred. However, his sacred paths were designed as a process rather than a dichotomy, taking away the elements of hierarchy and exclusion.[34]

The second idea of this chapter examines Wright's configurations of his various plans, their impact on the three-dimensional space, and their context in relation to historic precedents.

The Sacred Path

The sacred path's design elements consist of the path's specific approach to the building; its relationship to the entrance of the house of worship; the sequence of defined spaces within the path; the hierarchy of spaces; the focal point; the use of proportion and geometry; a consistent palette of materials; and the interplay of light and shadow. Thomas Barrie (1996: 47) claims that these design elements determine a path's dynamics and a person's experience of walking it. Furthermore, the path can provide the spiritual experiences associated with pilgrimage and procession, since it presents the elements of "preparation, separation and return" (Barrie 1996: 55). Often the path becomes "a spiritual quest as a test or affirmation of one's faith" (Barrie 1996: 28) that is defined by the focal point of its destination and is enhanced by light and shadow. In summary, all these features create a spiritual passage system. Already in ancient civilizations such as ancient Egypt the procession toward the holy of the holy space included a sequence of changing spaces and light (see Chapter 12, this volume). The procession to the holy top of the Ziggurat of ancient Mesopotamia was defined by a series of stairs and gates that restricted the movement of the worshiper. Each level changed its size and proportion toward the upper level of the monument.

The specific approach to a sacred building was important to Wright, and he claimed to design its path from the point of view of the attending worshiper (McCarter 2005a: 307). This point of view supported Wright's focus on the human scale and the individual's experience in his sacred architecture. The path becomes the passage from the secular to the sacred. Wright's approach to the design of the sacred path was based on creating a visual journey which maintains the idea that "All journeys have secret destinations of which the traveler is unaware" (Martin Buber). Indeed, Frank Lloyd Wright did not provide a straightforward entrance to his sacred spaces. Instead, he redirected the worshipers' movement to slow their pace and prepare them for a climax (Laseau and Tice 1992: 99). The indirect configuration creates an illusion of the path being longer in distance than its actual size (Barrie 1996: 111). Wright created a pilgrim's journey by designing a series of movements in the spiritual path that take the worshiper through a sequence of defined spaces determined by threshold gateways. His paths became an expression of movement and many decipher the underlying order of his design.

Often, the path and the plan were elevated and enclosed from the surroundings. This design obstructs the view of the sacred focal point at the start of the path. Wright's path along the building of Unity Temple in Illinois (1906) is a good example of this design approach (Fig. 3.7.1).

Walking along this path one climbs up a series of stairs moving toward the sacred. The exterior concrete walls of Unity Temple and the concrete railing walls, which serve as the boundaries of the path, are made of a pebbled aggregate which is pleasant to the touch, thus inviting rather than constraining the visitor or worshiper (Scully 1996: 200). In addition, these walls and their texture create an intricate play of light and shadow on the path, which adds to the mystery, enhancing the spiritual journey (Figs 3.7.2 and 3.7.3). Although the main volume of the Temple is clearly evident (Fig. 3.7.4), the entry sequence is obscured and the worshiper cannot see the entrance until turning into an open space leading to it (Fig 2.2.1).

3.7.1
The Entrance Path Along Unity Temple, Illinois.

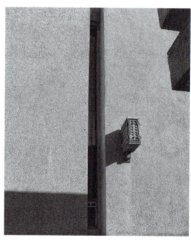

3.7.2 (above left)
Light and Shadow on the Path Entering Unity Temple, Illinois.

3.7.3 (above right)
Light and Shadow on the Path Entering Unity Temple, Illinois; Note the Light Fixture Design is Based on the Temple's motif.

3.7.4
The Volume of Unity Temple as seen above the Path of the Temple.

At the entrance to the Temple's edifice, a set of six stairs guides the worshiper upward toward the sanctuary. This interior path directs the worshiper to enter behind the pulpit. This design enables the worshipers to face the pastor as they exit from the sanctuary toward the foyer of the Temple. This arrangement seems to be more respectful than that of the worshipers turning their backs on the pastor as is common in traditional church design. In addition, people enter the Temple's sanctuary via two doors on the sides of the pulpit and leave through one central door. This exit procession was created by Wright to express his idea of unity. He believed that the members enter the space as individuals and leave as a united community.

An indoor procession was also created by Wright for the Beth Sholom Synagogue in Pennsylvania (1954), where he designed an entrance on the ground level, which is placed halfway between the two levels of the building (the main sanctuary and the sisterhood chapel). The position of the entrance creates a moment of pause, which prepares the worshiper to enter one of the sacred spaces. The passage includes a set of ramps that ascend to the temple above (Fig. 3.7.5), and steps that descend to the lower level chapel. Approaching the translucent temple up the ramp invokes the spiritual experience of reaching up to the divine light.

3.7.5
The Ramp Path Entering Beth Sholom Synagogue, Pennsylvania.

These types of processions create a dynamic spiritual experience based on a series of coordinated architectural events (Barrie 1996: 107). The journey separates the worshipers from the mundane (day-to-day life), and frees their state of mind from worldly thoughts. The path enhances the spiritual and physiological experience in reaching the holy of the holy (Geva and Mukherji 2007).

A more modest example of Wright's treatment of the sacred path as the indirect journey toward the sacred plan is his 1906 design of the Pettit Chapel in Belvedere, Illinois. The path (a covered porch) and the chapel's floor are raised. The procession starts with a climb toward the sacred built space. The centered stairs in the front elevation lead to a covered porch, which creates a drama of light and shadows (Fig. 3.7.6). This upward procession faces the wall of the chapel, while the entrance doors are located on each side of the chapel. The worshiper does not see the entrance while climbing the stairs (Fig 3.7.6). This indirect path creates an illusion of a longer passage and allows the transition between the mundane (outside) and the sacred (inside). The secondary path includes two sets of stairs, located on each side at the rear of the chapel (Fig 3.7.7). Again, these stairs bring the visitors upward, but do not direct them to the entrance doors. As mentioned before, the combination of the path and plan creates a crucifix (Fig 1.10).

3.7.6
The Main Stair Path Toward the Entrance to Pettit Temple, Illinois (1906).

3.7.7
The Secondary Stair Path Toward the Entrance to Pettit Temple, Illinois.

It should be noted that Wright's design of these routes to the main entrance was not unique to his religious buildings and also appears in his residential designs. Some may argue that this is a result of the sacred connotation which Wright assigned to the house (see Chapter 6). Others attribute this type of design to site's constraints; while scholars like Paul Kruty and Paul Sprague (2005: 24–32) believe that Wright's mysterious, subtle, and dramatic entry sequences are "the result of his practice of partially copying plans of earlier houses and incorporating them into the design of new ones". This explanation may also be generally applied to his sacred architecture, since Wright considered all of his projects sacred. Moreover, he demonstrated a fluid connection between his designs of secular and sacred projects and "recycled" some of his designs (see Part 5, Conclusion, this volume).

The proportion of the outdoor space in front of Unity Temple's entrance and its distance from the street (being elevated approximately 12 feet above grade) enhances the idea of a focal point (the entrance) at the end of the exterior procession. The overhang above the entrance and the inscription on it – "For The Worship of God and The Service of Man" (Fig. 2.2.1) – serve as the threshold between the outdoor path and the indoor procession toward the entrance of the temple. The outdoor plaza and the interior entrance foyer create a pause between the path and the plan, a small break before starting the interior procession toward the sanctuary. Since the foyer connects the temple with its house, it creates a physical division between the sacred and secular activities of Unity Temple's complex (Fig. 3.7.8).

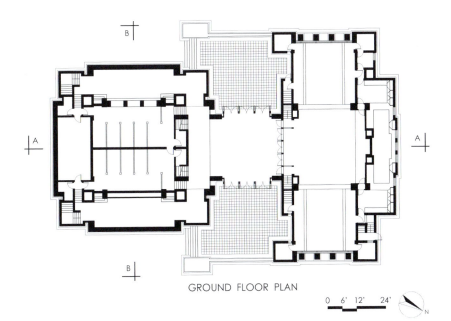

GROUND FLOOR PLAN

0 6' 12' 24'

3.7.8
Ground Floor Plan of Unity Temple, Illinois (redrawn under author's supervision).

Wright also designed a space for pausing in the Unitarian Meeting House (1947) (Fig. 2.3.3). The entrance to the building is elevated. Visitors walk to a small vestibule with double doors, then to a foyer, and only then to the sanctuary. This procession is accompanied by changes in proportion and ceiling heights culminating in the prayer hall's space (Figs 3.8.4 and 4.13.2). The changes in ceiling heights contribute to the interplay of light and shadow in the different parts of the interior path. When one enters the church's sanctuary directly, the procession moves through the assembly hall, which portrays more of a residential feel with its lower ceiling and fireplace (Fig. 2.3.3). To create a core area in the assembly hall that enhanced the worshiper's pause effect before entering the prayer hall, Wright designed a central hexagon indentation in the assembly's ceiling (see dotted lines in the plan drawing).[35]

The spiritual experience of the sacred path is also demonstrated in Wright's Annie Pfeiffer Chapel in Florida (1938). The path to the chapel is covered by one of the esplanades (covered walkways) that link the buildings of Southern Florida College's campus and creates a dramatic play of light and shadow (Fig. 3.7.9). Wright emphasized the transition from the secular esplanade to the sacred by ending the covered walkway at the bottom of the elevated entrance to the chapel. Again, he created a space for pause in the path by designing a set of monumental stairs that initiate an upward procession toward the entrance of the chapel (Fig. 3.7.10). The horizontal overhanging balconies create the dramatic play of light and shadow on the upward path.

3.7.9
The Path (One of the Esplanades) Leading to Annie Pfeiffer Chapel, Florida.

3.7.10
The Stairs and Entrance to Annie
Pfeiffer Chapel, Florida.

The idea of the elevated path also appears in Wright's proposed design of
the passageway to the Wedding Chapel of Hotel Claremont in Berkeley,
California (1957). This path was designed as an elevated bridge linking the
secular (the hotel) with the sacred (the chapel) (Fig. 3.7.11). Wright created
an elevated walkway that is separated from the secular and mundane, and
approached the sacred focal point of the chapel, which was enhanced by
a delicate and thin spire.

3.7.11
Frank Lloyd Wright's Second Proposal
for the Wedding Chapel of Hotel
Claremont, Berkeley, California. Note
The Passageway (Bridge) Leading to
Chapel (© 2009 Frank Lloyd Wright
Foundation, Scottsdale, AZ/Artists
Rights Society (ARS), New York).

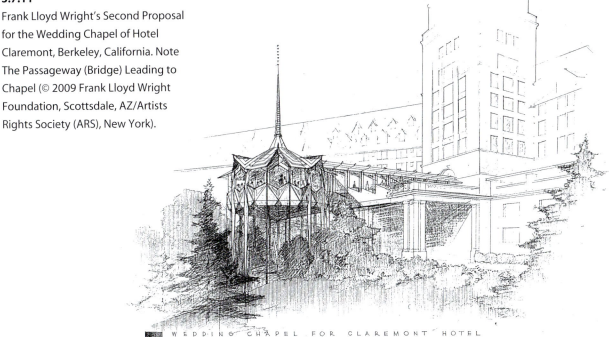

Wright's 1958 proposal for Trinity Chapel in Norman, Oklahoma is another example of an elevated procession. Wright had to include a parking area in the relatively small site. Therefore, he proposed a covered parking area underneath the chapel, and as such raised the chapel's floor. This elevated building not only accommodated the chapel's program requirements, but created an upward path to reach the sacred place. This path would enhance the spiritual experience of the worshiper's journey to the chapel. The proposed access to the chapel consisted of six ramps, two on each side of the triangular diamond building. The ramps generated a triangular entrance that enhanced the church symbol of the Christian Holy Trinity (Fig. 2.1.4).

Wright's design of the sacred path created the horizontal axis of the sacred place – an axis of movement and procession that is associated with a pilgrimage journey. All of these paths include a passage system that is directed toward a focal point – the entrance to the sacred building or space. The threshold areas create a pause – a transition of time, light, and space. The lit path culminates at the entrance that leads into the interior's darker set of spaces. These spaces then open up to the climax, which is the lit sacred space. Wright composed this progression from the outside light to the darker interior spaces and then to the inner light that represents the "holy" light by changing the proportions of the sacred space and its ceiling heights. The combination of light, shadow, proportions, and geometry creates a passage system that enhances the spiritual mood of the worshipers and their spatial experience while walking on the path and entering the sacred plan.

The Sacred Plan

Wright believed that the ground plan is the basic form of architecture and that a clear plan serves as the basis for the development of the three-dimensional volume of a building. Paul Laseau and James Tice (1992: 12) claim that Wright placed a higher value on the form of the plan, citing it as one of the fundamental aspects of his design. Henry-Russell Hitchcock and Philip Johnson (1932: 41) credit Wright for being the first architect to design free plans, which became the inspiration for the transformation of two-dimensional visions into three-dimensional spatial volumes. Indeed, Wright wrote: "There is more beauty in a fine ground plan than in almost any of its ultimate consequences. In itself it will have the rhythms, masses, and proportions of a good decoration . . . The plan? The prophetic soul of the building" (Wright 1928a/1992: 249).

What makes Frank Lloyd Wright's plans sacred is the fact that the plans' primary forms are based on pure and strong geometry. These forms are associated with universal attributes that can appeal to all faiths: "the cube or square, integrity; the circle or sphere, infinity; the straight line rectitude;

if long drawn out . . . repose; the triangle . . . aspiration, etc." (Wright quoted by Kaufman and Raeburn 1960: 77). These forms are derived from Nature – the creation of God, and from ancient sacred architecture. The plans were "transplanted as forms, they are tombs of a life that has been lived" (Wright 1986: 12).

Plans can be shaped as square/circle central forms, as a linear set of modules, as a combination of the two in straightforward configurations, or in more complex shapes (Schwarz 1958; Barrie 1996; Ching 1996). The most dominant plan configurations in religious structures are central and linear plans. Both types of plan emerged from religious symbols and rituals. Such is the case in Christianity where the linear plan represents the longitudinal cross of the Roman Catholic faith. A square/circle central plan is exemplified in the Eastern Orthodox Church and represents the square cross of that faith.

The linear plan consists of a series of spaces arranged along an axis that has a point of entrance facing an emphasized focal point (Ching 1996). The central plan is considered as a stable and concentrated composition that represents the universe, a symbol of completeness and eternity. Both linear and central compositions can be arranged to accentuate the orientation of the building, which is driven by faith. For example, and as described in Part 1 of this volume, mosques are oriented toward Mecca; synagogues toward Jerusalem; Shinto shrines are oriented north–south; and most Christian churches are laid out on an east–west orientation.

While Wright designed both linear and central plans of worship, most of his sacred plans were based on the central plan. It is plausible that this preference was driven by three major reasons: (a) Wright recognized the universal association of the central plan as the representation of the center of the cosmos/universe (see Part 1); (b) the central plan better fitted Wright's ideas of democracy and freedom in design, enabling the worshipers to see each other, to feel equal, and to become part of the community and the sacred space; (c) the use of the central plan was part of Wright's departure from the Gothic Revival church style that was based on the linear longitudinal plan.

As such, the square, triangle, and circle played a major role in Wright's design of the central plan of his religious projects.

The Square

The square is associated with the quaternity universal symbols: "four elements, four seasons, four stages of life, four points of the compass" (Alofsin 1993: 164). In addition, the square was used in ancient sacred structures as a symbol of earth (e.g., one of the universal fundamental sacred elements). Like Walt Whitman, Frank Lloyd Wright considered the square plan as a noble geometry associated with the Divine and the universal elements of earth and integrity. The Hindu faith considers the square as the mystical and absolute form, which does not permit any variation in the course of construction. Moreover, the location of the square within the ground plan of a Hindu temple corresponds with the importance attached to the deity (Geva and Mukherji 2007: 511). Unity Temple's square plan served as the base for the temple's "cube" volume (see note 14 in Part 1), which like the Hindu temples is an enclosed absolute form that defines an area of concentrated divine power. More so, its symmetry may symbolize the perfection of divinity (Siry 1996: 209). Wright's application of the stable image of a square plan is found in some of his built and unbuilt religious projects. Unity Temple's square plan, which is based on the square grid and modules, demonstrates Wright's consideration of this shape as an absolute form.

Wright also believed that the square expresses the nature of materials, and could be a result of the mechanized production of the Machine Age (Wright 1901/1992: 59–69; Alofsin 1993: 169). The concrete "cube" of Unity Temple and the concrete blocks of his Florida Chapels demonstrate the mutual relations between form, construction materials, and technology (see the Conceptual Model in Part 1 and Building Technology in Part 4, this volume). It should be noted that the square-based form and its construction materials catered to the low budget of Unity Temple's congregation. The size of the room itself "was determined by comfortable seats with leg-room for four hundred people" (Wright 1932a/1977: 179). The U-shape seating arrangement of the raised galleries around the auditorium in Unity Temple not only reinforces the square plan but serves as a practical solution which enables the members to see each other and face the pulpit.

As described in Part 2 of this volume (Faith), Unity Temple's prayer hall is part of a complex that also consists of the secular function of the house of worship (meeting space).[36] While the square plan of the prayer hall is a complete form that represents a central cruciform plan that is based on the Greek cross (Johonnot 1906: 7) (Fig. 3.5.1), the plan of the whole complex may be viewed as a linear plan based on the longitudinal cross (Fig. 2.3.2).

Interestingly, we can also trace the longitudinal cross when studying the circulation of the Unitarian Meeting House in Wisconsin. Again, the complex includes both sacred and secular functions, which create a cruciform plan (Fig. 2.3.3). Hence, the idea of portraying an abstracted cross plan that links the sacred and the secular is performed both with a square (Unity Temple) and a triangular (Unitarian Meeting House) plan. The only house of worship that portrays an explicit cruciform plan is the T-plan of Wright's Pettit Chapel in Illinois (Fig. 1.10).

An additional example of Wright's use of the square in his sacred architecture is the central plan of his design proposal for the Memorial to The Soil Chapel, Cooksville, Wisconsin (1936). This square plan was smaller in dimension than Unity Temple, and consisted only of a chapel prayer hall (Fig. 1.2). This proposed project illustrates "Wright's predilection for strong geometric precision in organizing masses of concrete and architectural details" (Pfeiffer 1990: 93).

The dominance of the square in Wright's plans evolved to other configurations, such as the multiple squares system, derivations of the square, and combination of the square with other geometric forms (e.g., the circle) (Alofsin 1993: 298). All plans were created as simple forms, which were meant to be translated into three-dimensional volumes (see example below).[37]

The multiple squares geometry, or as Anthony Alofsin (1993: 179) called it, the multiple frame, was used by Wright to accentuate some of the entrances to his proposed churches. Wright used this form in the two alternative designs of the entrance for the unbuilt project of the Christian Catholic Church in Zion City, Illinois. Multi-squares defined the entrance of the 1915 proposed second alternative design (Fig. 3.6.11). The other design alternative (1911) was conceived of a series of receding arched planes (part of a circle) that were used as a multiple frame at the entrance (Fig. 3.3).[38]. In these proposals Wright used the square as a basic shape for the plan and utilized the multiple squares configuration as part of the elevations. The use of the multi-frame entrances can be traced back to the ancient Mesopotamia ziggurat of Ur. It also appears in eighteenth century Japanese prints, and early twentieth century Viennese Secessionists art.

The plan of Annie Pfeiffer Chapel in Florida illustrates Wright's use of square derivations. The plan combines an intersecting rectangle (36'x 84') and a hexagon (102' diameter). The geometry of this plan is based on a six-foot square grid. This grid allowed Wright to abstract the formal traditional centralized and longitudinal sacred plans (Doremus 1985: 150) (Fig. 1.12). He accentuated this abstraction with a skylight along the intersection of the two plans. The skylight ends with a bell tower above the pulpit located in the front.

The Community Christian Church (or the Church of the Future) built in Missouri (1940) is an additional example of a linear plan imposed on a central plan. Wright placed the altar at the front and highlighted it with a perforated dome above it (Fig. 4.12.11). Rudolf Schwarz (1958) wrote that one could consider the integration of the two types of plans enhanced by vertical light as the ultimate church plan.

Combination of the Square and Circle

The combination of the square and circle geometrical plans is observed in ancient patterns of art and architecture all over the world. The common thread is not just the use of these geometries together, but mainly their association with spiritual meanings. The circle motif, its derivations (e.g., overlapping circles), and the combination with other pure geometries (e.g., the square, triangle) symbolize the universe and its celestial realm, the sun god, god's eye, heaven, and more. In Part 1, I discuss the Pantheon's floor and dome in Rome as a historic example of the combination of the circle and the square as associated with spiritual and civic symbols. The circle implied heaven while the square represented the earth. Together they manifested the combination of the power of the Roman Empire and the power of its gods.

In his plan of the Greek Orthodox Church in Wisconsin (1956), Frank Lloyd Wright utilized the combination of the square with the circle to enhance the spiritual experience of the visitor as well as to abstract historic precedents. The configuration of this central plan is based on the Eastern Orthodox Church's square cross which is framed by a circle symbolizing God (as in Byzantine architecture) (Fig. 2.3.11). This combination appeared not only in the plan, but in the church's sections and elevations. It created a design where "the very structure of the building signifies the building's meaning" (Lipman 2005: 282). As described previously, Wright used a domical and arched structural system, and circular ornaments in the interior as part of this holistic use of geometry and religious symbolism (Fig. 2.3.15).

One of Wright's unbuilt proposals for the Christian Science Church in Bolinas, California (1956) also shows his use of the combination of the square and circle. He designed a square platform bounded by a circular retaining wall and arranged the seating space in a circular configuration (Fig. 3.6.5). The arch as a derivation of a circle appears in combination with the square in the proposed elevations of the design (Fig. 3.4.12). The combination became a geometric motif that contributed to the continuity of the plan from outside to inside, and the transformation from the horizontal level of a two-dimensional design (the plan) to the vertical dimension of the building.

The Triangle

The triangle, a symbol of aspiration and fertility, may be traced to openings and art in sacred temples of ancient and medieval religious monuments (Berlage 1912; Alofsin 1993: 190–193). Wright utilized the triangle as a basic form for some of his religious projects' plans. He associated the triangle plan with spiritual symbols such as the holy trinity and unity. One such example is his design of the Southwest Christian Seminary in Phoenix,

Arizona (1950) that was later used to construct the First Christian Church on the same site (1971–1973) (Figs 2.3.4 and 3.1). Additional examples are his design of the Unitarian Meeting House in Wisconsin, and his proposed design of Trinity Chapel in Oklahoma.

Wright also used the triangle as the basis for the plan of Beth Sholom Synagogue in Pennsylvania. The base of the building has six sides, suggesting the shape of the Jewish Star of David; while the tripod structural system can be associated with the three Jewish fathers (Abraham, Isaac, and Jacob). The triangular configuration of the synagogue's plan allows the floor of the sanctuary to slope inward gently as if to suggest that the congregation is resting in the hands of God.[39] Moreover, the 1020 seats are organized around the *bima* (stage) in a manner that allows the worshipers to see each other from all directions, thus creating the feeling that they are joined together in the holy act of worship (Fig. 3.6.19). Again, with this design, Wright used a geometric module for all facets of the building (plan, elevations, sections, and details).

The use of the fundamental triangle as the basic module for the design of Beth Sholom Synagogue received a special meaning when Wright linked it to traditional Native American art. He believed that using these symbols of many meanings was a way to also tie his work to American roots (Alfosin 1993: 231). In the case of Beth Sholom Synagogue, the Native American meaning of the symbolic triangle was meant to link the Jewish community to America.[40] Specifically, the influence of Native American teepee design can be seen in the general shape of the synagogue's roof as well as in details in the building[41] (see Figs 2.2.2, 2.3.9 and 2.3.10).

In Wright's sacred buildings the triangle became a basic system for various triangulations such as the Pythagorean hexagram where two equilateral triangles overlap in opposite orientations around a center; or polygons used for the unit of composition. As mentioned before, examples include Trinity Church in Oklahoma and the Unitarian Meeting House in Wisconsin. Richard Joncas (1998a: 103) states that in Wright's proposal of the Steel Cathedral's structural system, he used the triangle as part of a comprehensive triangulation form. This was Wright's first "uncompromising use of the triangle in architectural design". The proposed design for the Steel Cathedral in New York became one of the more interesting examples of the use of a triangle and its derivation in combination with a circle and its derivation. Otto Antonia Graf (2005: 149–169) provides graphic analyses of these geometric derivations and demonstrates the complexity of the combination system found in the cathedral's plan. These analyses illustrate the influence of ancient religious monuments on the proportion and geometries of this proposed project. Indeed, Wright felt that their design was original, not imitating any previous forms, and thus expressed the "true" form. In other words, he proposed that these geometric forms were used in design during the origin of culture itself (Alofsin 1993: 158).

Anthony Alofsin (1993: 193–201) also shows the resemblance between Unity Temple's plan (1906) and the secular plan of Olbrich's European Secession Building in Vienna, Austria (1898). The latter was based on the Viennese Secession movement.[42]

Historic Precedence

Numerous scholars (Tselos 1953, 1969; Siry 1991a, 1996; Alofsin 1993; Scully 1996; McCarter 1997, 2005a; Nute 2000) examine Wrights' design forms and details along archeological and historic evidences while also linking them to the context of his era's aesthetic values and theories (e.g. Fenollosa, Dow, the Viennese Secessionists). I agree with the major conclusions of these studies, especially with Alofsin (1993) and Nute (2000), who claim that Wright's greatness was his ability to abstract the preceding forms and create his unique style. Nevertheless, Wright claimed that the similarities with historic forms only served in confirming his design ideas: "To cut ambiguity short: there never was exterior influence upon my work, either foreign or native" (Wright 1957: 205). Still, Wright did admire historical precedents for their philosophy, aesthetic values, and spirit. For example, he expressed his admiration for early Italian Renaissance architecture and referred to it as the Gothic spirit, believing that this spirit would fix the new forms: "I suggest that a revival, not of the Gothic style, but the Gothic Spirit, is needed in the Art and Architecture of the modern life of the world" (Wright 1910/1992: 101, 106).

Wright also admired the archeology associated with lost cultures and their spiritual expressions (Tselos 1969: 68). An example of his appreciation is his commentary on archeological excavations conducted in Pre-Columbian sites. He found them to be "long slumbering remains of lost cultures . . . mighty, primitive abstractions of man's nature". He then related the findings to the sacred: "These were human creations, cosmic as sun, moon, and stars!" (Wright 1957: 111). Worldwide archeological evidence of the origins of these pure geometrical forms served to enhance their important tectonic and symbolic meanings (Alofsin 1993). Most of their symbolism related directly to sacred spaces and represented the fundamental sacred universal elements (see Part 1, this volume). Wright transformed and abstracted these ancient primary forms in his sacred plans. He compacted nature's shapes using "human geometry and numerical control" (Scully 1996: 12) to achieve an abstraction of the ancient forms and their geometries.

Studied extensively, Unity Temple has become "the" example in illustrating Wright's design's resemblance to ancient sacred monuments. In the context of archeology, the temple's plan, which is organized in three parts (Fig. 2.3.2), is similar to the plans of the temples in Arroyo group, Milta (Tselos 1969: 67, fig. 18). Tselos claims that this resemblance may be accounted for by mere coincidence or that it may be considered as a confirmation of Pre-Columbian influence on Wright's design style. Others, as described before, show that Unity Temple's plan resembles the *gongen-style* plans of seventeenth century Japanese temples (the Shinto Shrine Tosho-gu in Nikki from 1634; and the Buddhist Temple Taiyu-in-byo in Nikki from 1653). In addition to the temple plans, the entrance elevation can also be traced to the Japanese temples (Nute 1996: 96, fig. 10). Wright compared his design of the base of Unity Temple to the stylobate of Ancient Greek Temples, such as the Parthenon in Greece (Wright 1908: 159). He followed the same ratio of length to width (9:4). Moreover, the six exterior columns supporting the roof on each side of the square temple (Fig. 3.5.2) resemble the ancient Greek order of hexta-style temples. Joseph Siry (1996: 195–226) summarizes the different religious historic precedents that influenced the architectural interpretations of Unity Temple (including the Unitarian liberal perspectives of the time). He concluded that Unity Temple may be read both as an ancient temple and as a religious structure built for a modern liberal religion. The first read evokes multiple cultural memories while the second illustrates the usage of the most innovative materials and techniques of the time.

Additional examples of Wright's sacred architecture plans' resemblance to historic precedents are the Annunciation Greek Orthodox Church in Wauwatosa, Wisconsin and the Annie Pfeiffer Chapel in Lakeland, Florida. The first is an example of Wright's abstraction of the Byzantine central plan of domical religious buildings. In this case, Wright utilized both Eastern and Western Byzantine influences (Pfeiffer 1990: 101). Furthermore, similar to the "dramatic feats of structural engineering" of the Byzantine era (Joncas 1998a: 104), Wright introduced innovations in building technology such as a shallow concrete dome and the use of aluminum in construction (see Part 4 on Building Technology, this volume). The second example, the chapel in Florida, illustrates the influence of Pre-Columbian sacred monument details (Scully 1996: 29). His 1938 master plan for Florida Southern College has been compared to the plan of the villa at Tivoli from the second century AD, designed by the Roman emperor Hadrian (Scully 1996: figs 104 and 105). These examples show that both Eastern and Western influences, the "classic" and the "primitive" (exotic), can be seen as the framework of Wright's sacred architecture plans.

In summary, it may be argued that Wright's design of sacred projects emphasized the importance of the plan and its path. His plan and path created a separation from the mundane. Wright created a path that enhances movement, spatial sequence, time, and generates a visual anticipation in the person entering the building. Once passing the threshold area of the entrance, the worshiper begins a spiritual journey to the sacred space of the edifice, based mostly on a central plan. The specific interpretations of the various typologies of paths and plans determined the worshiper's spiritual experience of Wright's sacred architecture.

This sacred procession through the path and plan may be viewed as a "horizontal" journey, which prepares the worshipers to be engaged with the vertical path that connects them with the Divine. This vertical axis connects earth and heaven and thus creates the *axis mundi* – the axis of the world – in the holy space: "In the beginning God created the heaven and the earth" (Genesis, ch. 1:1). In the next chapter I elaborate on this sacred verticality.

Chapter 8
Sacred Verticality

[C]ertain geometric forms have come to symbolize for us . . . for instance: the spire, inspiration.

(Wright 1912/1992: 117)

Throughout history and across the world we see mountains as focal points of religious life. A few examples of this are the Mount of Olives in Jerusalem, Israel, Mount Fuji in Japan, Mount Kaliash in Tibet, the Black Hills and Taos Mountain in the US, and Uluru Mountain (Fig. 3.8.1) and Kata Tjuta in Australia. Mountains symbolize the link between heaven and earth as the spot where the sacred manifest itself (Cohn 1981: 63–79). The belief that great gods dwell in mountains is even demonstrated in the Old Testament with regard to the sanctity of Mount Sinai where the Ten Commandments were given to Moses: "Now Mount Sinai was altogether in smoke, because the LORD descended upon it in fire; and the smoke thereof ascended as the smoke of a furnace, and the whole mount quaked greatly" (Exodus 19, 18); "And the LORD came down upon mount Sinai, to the top of the mount; and the LORD called Moses to the top of the mount; and Moses went up" (Exodus 19, 20).

3.8.1
Uluru Mountain (Ayers Rock) in Australia.

Many stories and myths were created around these mountains. Examples of these are the belief that the echoes surrounding mountains are the voices of spirits (Hale 2007: 52), or that the heavily wooded mountains in Japan are the home of the gods (Frampton and Kudo 1997: 3). In addition to the sacred mountains of Nature, humans erected their own "mountains". Sometimes on top of a sacred mountain such as the Chapel of the Holy Trinity atop of Mount Sinai, Egypt (Fig. 3.8.2); or the shrines, chapels, and other secrets in the mountains of Italy, and sometimes imitating the mountains themselves (e.g., the ziggurats of ancient Mesopotamia, the Egyptian and Pre-Columbian pyramids; Borobudur Temple in Java). Some artists illustrate a comparison between Gaudi's La Sagrada Famillia Cathedral in Barcelona, Spain, and the rocks of Muela del Diablo in Bolivia. Both, as do so many other religious buildings, manifest the religious connotation of mountains.

3.8.2
The Chapel of the Holy Trinity atop of Mount Sinai, Egypt.

Early on in the Old Testament man-made pillars are mentioned as sacred: "So Jacob rose early in the morning, and took the stone that he had put under his head and set it up as a pillar and poured oil on its top" (Genesis 28: 18). The definition of such a pillar can be as simple as "a vertical element, such as a column, obelisk, or tower, [establishing] a point [on] the ground plane [which] makes it visible in space" (Ching 1996: 120). This establishment of a point on the ground is usually associated with the center of a sacred plan, above which rises the vertical element. This center and pillar/tower combination represents both sacred symbols and a place of orientation. For example, the center of a Hindu Temple's plan represents the holy sanctuary, above which rises a tower representing holy Mount Meru; in Christianity, a steeple rises above the church's central intersection of the crucifix plan. The pillars have the symbolic meaning of sacredness as they represent gods in Nature. Frank Lloyd Wright created a sacred volume by adding a third dimension to a simple two-dimensional plan. In his view, this third dimension – the vertical axis – was Nature, or as he referred to it, "Nature worship" (Wright 1949/1994: 361). The vertical axis triggers the worshiper's imagination, providing a spiritual experience and a greater understanding of form (Wright 1953a: 349).

Just as a sacred plan creates the image of the universe, the sacred vertical elements are considered to be the Cosmic Pillars. Examples of this are found in the Canaanite stone in Hazor in northern Israel which has carved hands raised to the sun, and the twin pillars of the Temple at Ur (ancient Mesopotamia) which were raised before the moon god. In the UK, Stonehenge is composed of vertical pillars that create a circle revering the celestial gods (see, e.g., Fig. 1.9). Stonehenge serves as an excellent example of the interwoven relation between sacred vertical elements, the central sacred plan, the sacred path, and holy light.

The vertical axis that creates the *axis mundi* connecting earth and heaven is embraced in religion not only as mountains and pillars, but as trees. These represent both cultural and mystical motifs. The "world tree" or "tree of life" links heaven with earth as well as underground where the roots find their center. In both cases the tree is rooted down into earth, while its branches reach up into the light. In Japan, most of the ancient structural systems of the pagodas were based on one central cypress pillar. Thus the pagoda could be perceived as a man-made tree that links heaven and earth.

Others used the human body as the place where the "synthesis of earth and heaven occurs" (Mann 1993: 34, fig. 45). Examples are the figure of the 'human module' or the "proportions of the human" by Leonardo da Vinci (1452–1519), where a standing man is framed by a circle (heaven) and a square (earth); and the vertical indicators drawn on a Samadhi – a seated human figure – which create the axis of Enlightment: Patanjali (Osmen 1999: 189). The Hindu Mandala is another example, where a human figure is imposed on to the square/circle grid of the Hindu temple.

A sacred building's *axis mundi* can be developed in three positions: (a) the location of the building where the height of the sacred site creates the region's *axis mundi*; (b) the vertical elements of the building, which establish the *axis mundi* inside the sacred space. Some such elements, as domes, skylights, or peaks of a sloped roof, may be seen, and may also serve as the community's vertical axis; and (c) the vertical elements attached to the building (e.g., steeples, spires, bell towers) or are freestanding near the building creating the *axis mundi* as a beacon for the sacred place. Beams of light can also create an *axis mundi* as a beacon for the sacred place (see Part 4 of this volume for examples of Wright's use of light in this manner). In all developments, the verticality of the sacred building is visible from both outside and the interior.

The Height of the Sacred Site (Location of the Building)

Across all religions the location of a house of worship is a manifestation of its importance and power. The sacred building is distinct not only for serving as the center of community life or for being oriented toward a specific location defined by faith requirements; it is distinct in its vertical dimension. The site selected for these structures usually has the highest elevation in the area. The location generates a bridge from the profane (the earthly world) to the sacred, and places the worshiper as part of the *axis mundi* and in touch with the eternal (Geva and Mukherji 2007).

Wright's 1936 proposal for the Memorial to the Soil Chapel in Cooksville, Wisconsin, is an example of a vertical location of a house of worship. The chapel grows upward out of an earth berm (Fig. 1.2). Thus, the vertical location of the chapel is accentuated by the union of site and building as one sacred place, in harmony with nature – the ultimate sacred place in Wright's view.

Another example of verticality is the location of Annie Pfeiffer Chapel on the campus of Florida Southern College. It is located on the highest site of the relatively flat campus and radiates the spiritual message of the Methodist Liberal Arts College. This location, as well as the chapel's form, expresses the Methodist College's modernity and religious ideas (Siry 2004: 525). The chapel's bell tower is attached to the building and is called a "lantern" (Pfeiffer 1990: 94). In addition, the bell tower was designed to house eighteen bronze bell-shaped gongs. Indeed the resonance of these bells was so strong that the neighboring community requested they not be played. Still, the effect of a vertical marker as the light of the campus and the sound of the bells that impacted on the whole area strengthen the spiritual focal point of the campus.

The Vertical Elements of the Building

The vertical configuration of a building comprises three vertical elements which create the *axis mundi* of a sacred space: (a) the building itself as a whole vertical element; (b) the roof (e.g., domes, extensions of the roofs, or parapets) which may be seen from both the outside and the inside of a sacred space; and (c) interior vertical elements such as changing floor levels, changes in ceiling heights, skylights, ornaments, and furniture.

The Building Itself as a Whole Vertical Element

One of the most impressive examples of Wright's usage of vertical elements (spaces) as a symbol of monumentality is his 1926 proposed design for the Steel Cathedral in New York. The building would have soared at more than 1500 feet high and, if built, would have been one of the tallest buildings in the world at that time (Fig. 2.3.1). Its elevation shows an enormous steel and glass pyramid placed on a massive star-shaped concrete platform. Wright designed a tripod of steel open girders to support this platform. The pyramid's steel beams enclosed heptagonal and octagonal chapels for various faiths, all under the same roof. Within the perimeter walls of the cathedral, Wright designed a spiral roadway leading to a garden at the top, or – as it can be interpreted – a sacred path upward toward the "Garden of Eden" (Joncas 1998a: 103; Pfeiffer 1990: 92). The tripod structural system was another expression of Wright's triangulation design. It demonstrates the cathedral's building technology accommodating form.[43]

Like the Steel Cathedral's plan, Wright's 1954 design of Beth Sholom Synagogue in Elkins Park, Philadelphia was based on a triangulated tent structure of steel, glass, and fiberglass (Figs 1.3 and 2.3.8). This structure is supported by a steel tripod frame and is seated on a concrete podium. The translucent pyramid structure rises to 100 feet and is meant to express spiritual enlightenment (Fig. 3.5.7). This pyramidal synagogue creates an *axis mundi*, which serves as the vertical axis for the whole community. This vertical axis is accentuated at night when the building becomes a beacon of light (Fig. 1.14) (for details see Chapter 12 on Light in Part 4, Building Technology).

The shape of the synagogue resembles not only a sacred mountain, but the "cone of Astarte in her horned enclosure at Babylon" (Scully 1996: 111, fig. 126). This comparison further emphasizes Wright's admiration of ancient civilizations. His design is a combination of ancient religious symbols, the local historic Native American teepee architecture and its sacred symbols and the religious symbols of the Jewish faith.

Another example of Wright's design of a vertical configuration is his 1958 proposal for the Trinity Chapel in Norman, Oklahoma. The entire building is based on a vertical axis as a soaring spire that widens at its base in interlocking triangles. The proposed vertical proportion of the diamond shape of the colored glass window in the spire also accentuates the verticality of the chapel (Fig. 2.1.4).

A more modest example of the verticality of a building itself is Wright's proposal for the Memorial to the Soil Chapel in Wisconsin. As mentioned before, a central vertical mass grows out of an earth berm and rises up to create an area where the worshiper can perceive the center of the space as the chapel's *axis mundi*. Even Wright's drawings for this proposal reinforce the vertical aspect of the project (Fig. 1.2).

The Roofs

Frank Lloyd Wright manipulated interior/exterior features to create a vertical axis for his sacred buildings that point to the sky. Behind the pulpit and organ of his Unitarian Meeting House in Wisconsin, the glass walls reveal the peak of the church's roof which points to the sky (Fig. 3.5.3). This effect is visible both from outside and inside. Another example of a pointed roof that is visible from the interior is the roof of the Minor Chapel in Florida. The shape of an extended pointed roof enhances the vertical effect of the building (Figs 3.5.8 and 3.8.3). Wright also changed the ceiling heights inside the building and extended these changes to the outside of the building. For example, in his Unitarian Meeting House in Wisconsin, the ceiling height in the entrance and hearth areas is lower than in the sanctuary, and the ceiling of the sanctuary rises toward the peak of the roof's large eave (Figs 3.8.4, 4.13.1, and 4.13.2).

The four cantilevers that extend the roof of Unity Temple are horizontal and do not point to the sky. Rather, they emphasize the form of the square and stabilize the "cube". Wright designed the vertical axis of Unity Temple using an interior skylight, which was formed by a double roof. This roof includes a pitched glass roof and a flat concrete slab with square glass openings. The filtered light that pours through the skylight and the light of the upper windows create the Temple's *axis mundi* (Fig. 1.4).[44] A high concrete parapet screens the double roof from the street and maintains the shape of the "cube" (Fig. 3.5.2).

The dome of Wright's Annunciation Greek Orthodox Church in Wisconsin is visible as a vertical element from the outside, but also generates a vertical illusion inside the building (Fig. 3.2). The sacred verticality of the

3.8.3 (left)
The Roof of the Minor Chapel in Florida, as seen from inside the Chapel.

3.8.4 (right)
The Change in Ceiling Heights from the Entrance and Hearth Areas to the Pulpit Area of the Unitarian Meeting House, Wisconsin.

dome is increased by its blue color, which refers to the sky. The gilded color in the inside of the dome makes it look lighter and higher. Moreover, it highlights the relationship to Byzantine religious monuments, and adds to the sacredness of the space.

Interior Vertical Elements

Wright's changes in floor levels and ceiling heights created a hierarchy of volumes, which was complemented by special light treatments and vertical ornaments. Some of the exterior and interior processions described previously demonstrate the vertical aspect of the pilgrimage paths that moved upward toward a sacred place. One specific example is Unity Temple's interior procession from the foyer to the sanctuary. A set of stairs brings the worshiper to the sacred space. The movement upward under a lower ceiling changes dramatically when the worshiper enters the more open, tall, and lit holy space. This vertical change helps to connect the worshipers to the sacred space's *axis mundi* and brings them closer to the divine. The changes in ceiling heights and light in the prayer hall of the temple are a result of Wright's design of the galleries. The low ceilings in the galleries enhance the vertical dimension of the main floor and its focal point – the pulpit (Figs 1.4 and 3.5.1).

In order to draw attention toward the skylight, Wright changed the ceiling heights in the Annie Pfeiffer Chapel in Florida. This change enhances the vertical movement of the space and creates the drama of verticality, light, and shadow (Fig. 1.5) (see also Chapter 12 on Light in Part 4, Building Technology).

Wright changed the ceiling height in the area of the *bima* (stage) of the Sisterhood Chapel of Beth Sholom Synagogue, Pennsylvania. This change created a hierarchy of volumes and a greater sense of holiness (Fig. 2.3.10). This hierarchy was not created as a gradual change, but rather as a dramatic variation that provides a focal point while increasing the verticality of the place and its sacredness (Fig. 4.12.14). It should be noted that in this example the special treatment of light is based only on artificial light.

Another interesting example is the First Christian Church in Phoenix, Arizona. Here, the dramatic change from a low ceiling entrance made of concrete and rockwork to a taller and smoother concrete ceiling in the main space draws the worshiper into the sacred prayer hall. The vertical effect of the sanctuary is further enhanced by a colored glass skylight, which extends from one side of the sanctuary to the other (Figs 2.3.6 and 3.6.16), and by a lantern that rises to become a stained glass spire (Fig. 3.8.5).

Other interior features that enhance the *axis mundi* are vertical ornaments and furniture. Examples of such ornaments are the hanging vertical electrical fixtures in Unity Temple, Illinois (Fig. 3.5.5); and the vertical electrical fixture in the Annunciation Greek Orthodox Church[45] (Fig. 3.8.6).

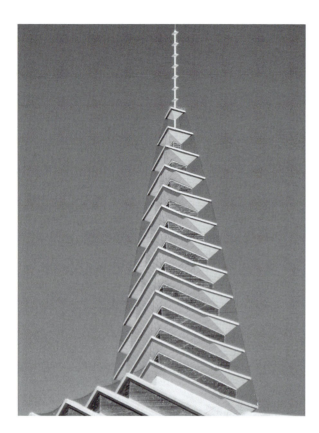

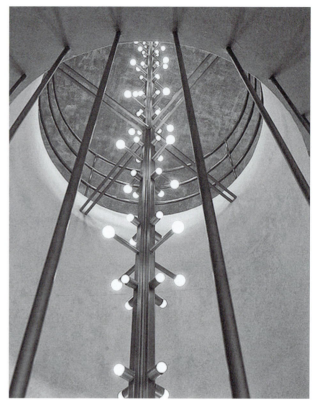

With their tall backs, the square-based chairs of Unity Temple and the triangle-based chairs in Beth Sholom Synagogue are part of the whole vertical dimensions of these religious buildings. In all these projects the various vertical elements add to the creation of the interior *axis mundi* and enrich the relation between verticality and light/shadow.

3.8.5 (left)
The Stained Glass Spire of the First Christian Church in Phoenix, Arizona.

3.8.6 (right)
The Vertical Electrical Fixture in the Annunciation Greek Orthodox Church, Wisconsin.

The Vertical Elements Attached and Adjacent to the Sacred Building

Despite Wright's belief that there is no need for a spire or bell tower in the modern church – "why the steeple of the little white church? Why point to heaven?" (Wright 1932a/1992: 212), and his opinion that the steeple is "A perversion of sentiment-sentimentality" (Wright 1932a/1992: 212) – he did design several of them. Some of his religious projects have a type of spire, and one project, Trinity Chapel in Oklahoma, was designed as a spire building. Wright's towers catered to the functional requirements of the faith (e.g., bell tower, religious icon) while instantiating the symbol of heaven (e.g., Annie Pfeiffer Chapel in Florida, First Christian Church in Arizona). As with his departure from traditional church design (see Chapter 5, this volume), the design of these towers was also a departure from conventional tower designs of the time. For example, Wright introduced a concrete and steel tower in the Annie Pfeiffer Chapel in Florida (Figs 3.6.2 and 3.8.7). The tower is composed of two central concrete panels decorated with rectangular patterns and supported by triangular steel beams (Fig. 3.4.7).[46] The bell tower, visible from every place on campus, creates the traditional *axis mundi* not only for the chapel but for the entire surrounding area (Figs 3.4.7, 3.8.7, and 4.14.3): "The tower of the chapel is the one strongly vertical element dominating the site" (Pfeiffer 1990: 94). As described earlier, it used to operate as a bell tower with such an effective resonant space that the sound of its carillon disturbed the chapel's neighbors and eventually led to its removal (Storrer 1993: 260).

3.8.7
Annie Pfeiffer Chapel, Lakeland, Florida.

The major link between Annie Pfeiffer Chapel's interior with the exterior is the vertical view of the sky through the skylight (Figs 3.4.5 and 3.8.8). Wright designed this vertical axis window "to bring God's outdoors into man's indoor" (Rogers 2001: 8). The soaring sky-lit form and the tower above it cast dramatic shadows across the stage and pulpit and directs the attention toward the sky. It should be noted that this connection to the sky is one of the fundamental vertical spiritual elements, which enhances the connection to the divine since it symbolizes eternal transcendence and heaven.

A modest spire was proposed by Wright to rise above a small chapel which was part of a dwelling design for Father John, a Catholic priest in Oconomowoc (Fig. 3.6.8). "It [the spire] denotes the ecclesiastical nature of the project and gives a certain striking drama to what is a rather simple residential building" (Pfeiffer 1990: 96). Here again we witness Wright's ideology that a house can be a temple and vice versa (see Chapter 6, this volume).

The spire of Wright's 1950 design of the Southwest Christian Seminary in Arizona, which was built in 1973 as the First Christian Church, is attached to the church and rises to seventy-seven feet (Figs 3.6.17 and 3.8.9). The bell tower is a freestanding tower and is 120 feet tall (Fig. 3.6.18). Both the spire and the tower have four triangular sides. The spire's sides are equal to one another, while each of the bell tower's sides is unique. The height of the cross on top of the bell tower is twenty-two feet, which extends the verticality of the tower (Fig. 3.8.9). Both towers may be viewed as an abstraction of the triangle and triangulation, which are associated with the Christian tradition of the Holy Trinity (Fig. 3.1).

This section addressed Frank Lloyd Wright's incorporation of the vertical axis in his sacred architecture design as part of his holistic approach. His abstraction of traditional vertical elements such as domes, spires, and bell towers strengthens the religious connotation of the sacred *axis mundi* and the spiritual experience of the worshiper.

3.8.9
The Two Vertical Elements and the Cross on Top of the Bell Tower of the First Christian Church, Arizona.

Summary of Part 3 (Form)

In conclusion of Part 3, we can identify major innovative aspects in Frank Lloyd Wright's sacred architecture design. He considered form and function as one, truth and beauty as one, and man and God as one. These ideas were part of his holistic approach to design, where the whole was a balance of its parts. In addition, these ideas helped Wright to link his sacred architecture to faith, form, and building technology. This link illustrates his attitude to Nature, and highlights his democratic design for religious houses that featured human scale, perception, and movement.

Wright manipulated various design tactics to create sacred spaces free of traditional constraints. His sacred sites were governed by geometric modules as found in Nature – God's creation. The three-dimensional forms of these projects were enhanced by the horizontal axis of the path, the plan of the *imago mundi*, and by the sacred verticality (the *axis mundi*), which brings worshipers closer to the divine. Wright's sensitivities to universal faith aspects and to faith specifics were translated to sacred form such as using the crucifix shape for a plan but creating a three-dimensional volume that resembles more an ancient religious monument; or abstracting traditional faith symbols to link them to the local culture and religion of native American symbols (see the description on Beth Sholom Synagogue). The use of pure geometric forms enhanced the relation of faith and form in his sacred architecture, since it represented fundamental elements of faith on the one hand, while, on the other, the combination of these forms catered to the specific faith needs. In summary, the relation of faith and form as shown in the book's model can be applied to Wright's sacred forms.

Wright achieved these forms by experimenting with building technology, including the reuse of old materials in new, modern ways. In Part 4, I introduce Wright's innovative use of materials, his manipulation of structural systems, and his method of creating the sacred ambience while catering to each faith's special needs (e.g., light, acoustics, and climate comfort). Part 4 illustrates Frank Lloyd Wright's sacred architecture through building technology.

Notes

1 Frank Lloyd Wright's quote is cited from a short description of the Wedding Chapel that appeared in *Architectural Forum* (October 1957: 7) under News, 'Wedding Chapel by Frank Lloyd Wright With Fountain Below'.
2 Frank Lloyd Wright's Office used Wright's original proposal (design, drawings, and details) for the 1950s Southwest Christian Seminary in Phoenix, Arizona to build the First Christian Church on the same site in 1973.
3 The proposition that "Form Follows Function" originated in the nineteenth century, and was developed out of an assumption that a linear link exists between Nature/environment, function, and form (see a quote by Architect Leopold Eidlitz (1828–1908) in Nute 2000: 182, note 2).
4 It should be noted that the concept of truth and beauty as one was part of the transcendental philosophy (1830s–1850s), which was based on the premise that truth is innate in all of creation and that knowledge of it is intuitive rather than rational.
5 From 'Buildings for Democracy: The Mildred and Stanley Rosenblaum House and Marin County Civic Center', *Frank Lloyd Wright Quarterly*, (2004) 15(2): 4–21, p.7.
6 Ernest Fenollosa was one of the first scholars to actively relate the ideas of European philosophers such as Hegel and Kant, and American studies of Emerson, to the study of Far Eastern art. Thus, he integrated Western and Eastern philosophies and aesthetic values.
7 This statement is a later repetition of Wright's 1910 introduction to the book *Ausgefuhrte Bauten und Entwurfe von Frank Lloyd Wright*.
8 See Part 1, n. 7.
9 Wright's diagonal plan of the Florida Southern College campus was once again a direct response to the local environment of the site (the lake, the existing orchards, and the local breezes). In this case the site is characterized by lush vegetation and a hot and humid climate that is very different than a desert context.

10 This statement was written on Frank Lloyd Wright's drawing of the Memorial to the Soil Chapel.

11 See Part 1, n. 7.

12 See Part 1 for more details on the sacredness of the universal elements of sky and air.

13 From 'Buildings for Democracy: The Mildred and Stanley Rosenblaum House and Marin County Civic Center', *Frank Lloyd Wright Quarterly*, (2004) 15(2): 4–21, p.15.

14 A "News Report" in *Progressive Architecture* (November 1960: 70) quoting Taliesin Associated Architects, responsible for overseeing this project.

15 Over the years, most of the orange orchard surrounding the Annie Pfeiffer Chapel in Lakeland, Florida, was cut down. Although there are indications that vegetation was hanging from the tower (see a photo by Ezra Stroller in Christ-Janer and Foley 1962: 196), historic photographs of the chapel from the 1940s (MacDonald et al. 2007: 19), as well as current photographs by the author show the tower as almost bare with no vegetation as proposed by Wright (see Chapter 14 on Thermal Comfort).

16 During my visit at the Pettit Chapel in Illinois, there was no vegetation in the flower boxes.

17 The quotes were taken from unpublished manuscripts located in the Frank Lloyd Wright Archives and Wright's personal letter written on September 9, 1958.

18 Wright quoted in 'Buildings for Democracy: The Mildred and Stanley Rosenblaum House and Marin County Civic Center', *Frank Lloyd Wright Quarterly*, (2004) 15(2): 4–21, p.5.

19 Nikolaus Pevsner (1968) interprets this moral duty as moral honesty. It is interesting that the concept of honesty in architecture was manifested by modernists as purity of materials, colors, etc., and served as the basis for truth and beauty.

20 Kieckhefer (2004: 212) describes Marion Mahony Griffin's design of the All Soul's Unitarian Church in Evanston, Illinois (1902–1903) as a compromise that transformed a proposal of a modern church with gestures toward the Gothic style into a Gothic Revival church with gestures toward the Prairie School style.

21 This article is part of six lectures presented by Wright at Princeton University in May 1930.

22 Wright believed that his Florida Southern College campus master plan manifested the current times and freedom.

23 William Guthrie's article on the 'Modern Cathedral' was written for the *New York Times*.

24 See ibid for Guthrie's critics where he condemned the Gothic Revival style of American churches/cathedrals and welcomed the Modern Cathedral.

25 It should be noted that the development of Japanese aesthetics at the turn of the twentieth century called for geometric abstraction in art and design.

26 Oscar Niemeyer, the famous Brazilian modern architect, reacted to the International Style in the same manner as Frank Lloyd Wright. When Walter Gropius, the major advocate of the International Style, criticized Niemeyer's house (1953) in saying that it was not multipliable, Niemeyer's answer was: "how can you repeat a house that has a definite environment, level curves where to settle, a light, a landscape. How can you build it over again?"

27   Originally, Wright designed the two candle holders (*menora*) as seen in Fig. 2.3.10 for the major sanctuary of the Beth Sholom Synagogue in Pennsylvania.

28   See Part 2, Faith for a discussion on Wright turning to ancient civilizations that did not exhibit any form of democracy and freedom.

29   It is interesting to note that the relationship between plan and elevations as part of a holistic approach may actually be found in the Gothic Cathedral of Chartres, France (Tabb 2007: 90, fig. 70).

30   Wright quoted in 'Eye Music' *Frank Lloyd Wright Quarterly* (1998) 9 (2): 4–9, p. 8.

31   Wright's first alternative proposal for the Wedding Chapel in California was influenced by his design of the Annunciation Greek Orthodox Church in Wisconsin (see Part 5, this volume).

32   To be more accurate, Wright utilized a unit of six feet and ten inches in laying the plan and elevation of Unity Temple (Siry 1996: 120–126).

33   The use of the six-foot module as an aesthetic value that displays the relationship of the whole to its parts was also demonstrated in Wright's master plans for the Broadacre City and Florida Southern Methodist College. In the latter case, Joseph Siry (2004: 507) quoted Wright as saying: "they [the buildings] will make much of association with the ground and through-going harmony, each to each and each to all".

34   Thanks to Belinda Bragg for her insightful addition to this paragraph.

35   This central piece in the ceiling is based on the whole church complex's triangular grid.

36   This brings us back to the meaning and the use of the term "temple" in reference to a sacred complex (see Part 2 on Faith).

37   It is interesting to note that various ancient and medieval civilizations also utilized derivations of the square (e.g., the rotated square, the square within a square, the multiple squares) in their sacred architecture (Cirlot 1971; Alofsin 1993).

38   Later, Wright adapted the form of multiple arches in his secular design of the entrance to the built Morrison Gift Shop in San Francisco, California (1948) (see Part 5, Conclusion).

39   An article entitled 'Frank Lloyd Wright: A Selection of Current Work' appeared in *Architectural Record* (May 1958) and included a description of two of Wright's churches and one synagogue.

40   Based on the author's conversation with the synagogue's manager (*Gabai* in Hebrew).

41   The Native American teepees also became the basis for Wright's secular proposals for Lake Tahoe's Summer Colony (1923) and the Nakoma Country Club in Madison, Wisconsin (1923–1924). In addition to the triangular form, the latter included a fireplace in the middle of the space as inspired by the smoke hole in the center of a teepee (see Riley 1994: 198–199, plates 172, 174, 175).

42   The Austrian movement was called the *Vereinigung Bildender Künstler Österreichs*, and was established in 1897 by a group of Austrian artists and architects.

43   This brings us back to the book's conceptual model, which illustrates the relationship between form and building technology (Fig. 1.1).

44   See more in Chapter 12 on Light in Part 4.

45   Joncas (1998a: 105) claims that these fixtures resemble Sullivan's devices as

designed for the Chicago Auditorium. Indeed, in many of his writings, Wright called Sullivan his beloved master and admitted to Sullivan's influence on his work.

46 Today's tower (as seen in the images) was rebuilt after a hurricane damaged the original tower on October 19, 1944. The new tower is shorter than the original and consists of substantially more reinforcing steel (MacDonald et al. 2007: 29–31).

Part 4
BUILDING TECHNOLOGY

4
BUILDING TECHNOLOGY

Architecture is the triumph of human imagination over materials, methods and men, to put man into possession of his own earth.

(Wright quoted in Pfeiffer and Nordland 1988: 48)

The interchangeable connections between Faith, Form, and Building Technology as described in the book's conceptual model (Fig. 1.1) show a mutual relationship between building technology and the sacred form. This mutual relationship is best expressed in Wright's Unity Temple where "The building is a harmonious unit; the style fitting the material and the material the form" (Johonnot 1906: 15–16). The book's conceptual model also implies a mutual relationship between building technology and the sacred ambience. While the ambience factors of light, acoustics, and climate comfort are influenced directly by each faith's programmatic and spiritual needs, which inspire the form, they also influence and are directly affected by building systems. These reciprocal influences are accentuated by the impact of a building's setting, i.e., environmental conditions and time.

In part 4, I show the relationships between building technology, form, and sacred ambience as described in Figure 4.1, and explore Wright's experimentation with new innovations in building technology in his sacred architecture.

4.1

A Diagram Illustrating the Relationship of Building Technology and the Sacred Form and its Ambience.

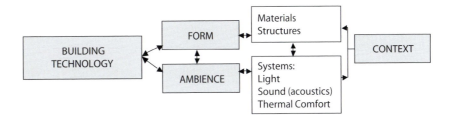

Figure 4.1 illustrates two aspects of building technology and their relationship to sacred form and ambience. First, it shows the relationship

between building materials, structural systems, and form; second, building systems (light, acoustics, thermal comfort) help achieve the ambience. A mutual relationship also exists between materials and building systems. Both are affected by the building's setting (e.g., environment and time). Environmental conditions impact on the use of local materials, the quality of light, the surrounding sounds, the climate variables, and much more. Time expresses the temporal conditions of the environment and is a major factor in the development of building technology (for example, when Wright first used electricity in Unity Temple in 1906, he had to work with 6-watt bulbs). It should be emphasized that these aspects of building technology became constituent parts of Wright's sacred buildings (Kaufman and Raeburn 1960: 47).

> I know well that my buildings see clearly not only the color. Drift and inclination of my own day but feed its spirit. All of them seek to provide forms adequate to integrate and harmonize our new materials, tools and shapes with the democratic life-idea, of my own day and time.
>
> (Wright quoted in Tselos 1969: 72)[1]

Materials, Structures, and Form

This section describes two aspects of the relationship between Wright's use of materials and structural systems and his sacred form. First, I look at how form influenced his selection of materials and structures. Second, I examine how materials and structures determine Wright's sacred form.

The first set of relationships is found in Wright's 1926 proposal for the Steel Cathedral in New York. The proposed form for this cathedral was a spider's web (Fig. 2.3.1), which was "a good inspiration for steel construction" (Wright quoted in Pfeiffer and Nordland 1988: 80). Similarly, in Beth Sholom Synagogue in Pennsylvania, corrugated glass and plastic sheets comprise the pyramidal roof shape that defines the aesthetics of the building (Fig. 1.3). Wright believed that each architectural form determined the use of a specific material and its characteristics (Wright 1957: 229).

The second set of relationships between building technology and form illustrates how building technology defines the form. Often, Wright's design principles were "profoundly affected by materials and construction methods" (McCarter 2005a: 12). He claimed that "Each material may become a happy determinant of style" (Wright 1957: 229), and that buildings' forms can be driven out of building technology. For example, when talking about Unity Temple in Illinois, Wright asked, "What shape? Well, the answer lay in the material . . . That [concrete] would make their temple [Unity Temple] a cube – a noble form in masonry" (Wright 1960: 76).

Wright's selection of construction materials, their dimensions, and their appropriate structural systems also influenced the development of the grid/module system for his projects.[2] This determination became the grammar of the form: "The grammar of such style as is seen here [in Unity Temple] is simply and logically determined by the concrete mass and flat layer formation of the slab and box construction of the square room, proportioned according to concrete-nature or the nature of the concrete" (Wright 1932a/1977: 218). Moreover, the building system "appears to be the major property by which Wright defined the nature of a material" (Patterson 1994: 4). This in turn impacted on the structural system that he used and enhanced his holistic approach to design and construction. Frequently, building technology was stretched to become the aesthetic of his religious buildings: "The reinforced concrete slab [in Unity Temple] as a new architectural expression is here used for its own sake as 'Architecture'" (Wright 1925/1992: 212).

In other projects, such as the two chapels in Florida (Annie Pfeiffer Chapel and the Minor Chapel), Wright used concrete blocks as the "architecture" of the buildings. In Annie Pfeiffer Chapel the pour-on-site concrete of the upper level and the tower complement the image of the chapel (for construction pictures see MacDonald et al. 2007: 13, 15). The use of concrete blocks in the Minor Chapel (Danforth Chapel) was complemented by stained glass, which shaped and styled the building's form (Pfammatter 2008: 174) (Fig. 2.1.1).

A mixture of stone and concrete shapes the images of the Pilgrim Congregational Church in California (Fig. 2.1.3) and of the First Christian Church in Arizona (Figs 4.2 and Fig. 4.3).

4.2 (left)
A Mixture of Stone and Concrete Interior Walls of The First Christian Church in Arizona.

4.3 (right)
A Mixture of Stone and Concrete Exterior Walls of The First Christian Church in Arizona.

Stone and copper define the entrance elevation of the Unitarian Meeting House in Wisconsin (Fig. 3.6.10). On his drawings of this building Wright specified the masonry details to be a nine-inch-thick stone with a slope of four to twelve vertical units and two-foot back course steps measuring two inches on the front wall.

In his 1994 book *Frank Lloyd Wright and the Meaning of Materials*, Terry Patterson analyzes Wright's use of materials along the aspects of form, workability, strength, and durability. These analyses allude to Wright's development of new technology while using traditional materials (i.e., stone and wood). His use of traditional materials created new tectonics, while his experimentation with modern materials (i.e., concrete, steel, and glass) generated new possibilities. In addition, Patterson evaluates Wright's own writing about materials and their actual application. I agree with Patterson's conclusion that Wright's use of materials reflected the spirit of the material more than the actual strength of it. Patterson observes that although Wright claimed to respect the strength of materials, he did not always seem "to view it as necessary to accomplish the task he assigned to" (Patterson 1994: 6). In this respect, one important example of Wright's sacred architecture comes to mind: the strength and durability of the porous and highly permeable concrete blocks used in constructing Annie Pfeiffer Chapel and the Minor Chapel in Florida Southern College, Lakeland, Florida. In 1993 the *RIBA Journal* (August: 40–41) published a case study under their "Refurbishment" column. The article describes Wright's concrete blocks as suffering from the "omission of coarse aggregate, incomplete compacting and insufficient curing". This investigation of the blocks confirms Patterson's conclusion that Wright's "material's decisions were not consistent with any discernible paradigm except, ultimately, the production of beauty" (Patterson 1994: 8, 237).

These observations are not surprising in the context of Wright's religious architecture. As detailed before, Wright believed that truth and beauty are one and viewed them as an organic divinity – a divinity in architecture (Wright 1954: Credo; Wright 1953b/1995:62). As such, Wright attempted to express truth embedded in beauty in his sacred architecture: "To me, a church building should express a reverence for the beautiful. Beauty is truth, and truth beauty." Wright thought that "Beauty then, fundamentally, is the Order of the Natural, whether of mind or body, because we are Nature ourselves in this sense" (Wright 1929/1992: 329). Beauty was so important to Wright that when he referred to ancient architecture, he emphasized the making of beauty with a capital B: "So the Persian of old made the God of Beauty and passionately dreamed his life away godward" (Wright and Brownell 1937/1993: 230).

Wright's selection of materials in his design of the Wedding Chapel for the Claremont Hotel in Berkeley, California was driven by this search for beauty. Wright proposed using seamless-role terne roofing: "Because of its inherent adaptability in both form and color, terne permits the visible roof area to become a significant part of structural design" (Boyd 1959: 172).

In his sacred architecture Wright introduced another consideration in his selection of materials. It was important for him to show a harmony between his selection of materials and the design of structural systems. This harmony relates to his view of beauty and truth in the sense that it reveals the aesthetics of the building (see, e.g., the tripod structural system and the translucent materials of the pyramidal roof of Beth Sholom Synagogue in Pennsylvania – Figs 1.3 and 3.5.7; or the concrete bent columns exposed outside and partially inside in the Pilgrim Congregational Church in California – Fig. 3.4.2). Sometimes he focused on the material and hid the structural system. See, for example, the Unitarian Meeting House in Wisconsin, where the enormous wooden roof (Fig. 4.4) is entirely hidden above the ceiling (Fig. 4.13.1), or the Minor Chapel in Florida, which is framed in Florida tidewater red cypress woodwork and is also not visible. In a way, these examples contradict his idea of beauty and truth as one. Still, and as Patterson (1994) observes, beauty became the dominant factor in some of Wright's projects, even on the account of revealing the true material.

4.4

The Unitarian Meeting House, Wisconsin: The Wooden Roof Under Construction (picture taken of a picture at the church).

Furthermore, Wright believed that new materials and structural systems of his day freed the design and provided new options for open plans, shapes, and details. Wright expressed these ideas in his development of the cantilever structural system, which boasts a significant projection of a structure beyond any base or point of direct support and materials (see, e.g., Unity Temple's concrete cantilevers – Figs 3.5.2 and 3.7.4).

During his time as a designer, Wright was exposed to tremendous and rapid developments in technology in general as well as specifically in construction technology (Frampton 1994: 58–79).[3] He believed that similar to other civilizations in history, we in modern times should build and experiment with the new technologies and materials of our era. Indeed, just to name a few of his achievements, in 1906 he was one of the first American architects to build a monolithic concrete pour-on-site building (Unity Temple in Illinois; Fig. 4.5); he manipulated new structural systems to open and free spaces from interior support beams and corner columns (examples include the Annie Pfeiffer Chapel in Florida – Fig. 3.5.6; and Beth Sholom Synagogue – Fig. 3.6.19).

4.5
Unity Temple Under Construction: Monolithic Concrete Pour-on-site (picture taken of a banner in front of the church).

In addition to his use of new materials, Wright did not dismiss the use of traditional construction materials (e.g., stone, wood, copper); rather, he believed that they should be explored and used in unconventional forms that determined the basic rhythm of the design (Frampton 1994: 58). Wright alleged that traditional materials and systems could be used in a modern way through the use of the machine:

> The machine, by its wonderful cutting, shaping, and smoothing and repetitive capacity, has made it possible to so use it [wood] without waste . . . Our modern materials are these old materials in more plastic guise, rendered so by the Machine, itself creating the very quality needed in material to satisfy its own are equation.
>
> (Wright 1960: 66)

In Wright's opinion, materials such as machine-made glass distinguished between ancient and modern designs. Wright felt that machine-made glass was underutilized, despite the fact that it does not disintegrate. He felt that it should be regarded "as crystal – thin sheets of air in air to keep air out or keep it in", or as "catching reflections and giving back limpid light" (Wright 1928c/1992: 291). He believed that wood could benefit from the use of the machine as well: like "[t]he walls [that] take on character of the surface left by the mason's use of his tools", so the machine allows "wood to be wood at its best" (Wright 1928c/1992: 272 and 282). The timber structural system of the Unitarian Meeting House in Wisconsin (Fig. 4.4) although not seen to be admired is an example of the potential of wood that was used to create "an astonishing structure. Exterior appearance of a center ridge is illusory; actually two ridges converge at the prow . . . Each Pair of [wood] trusses acts like a center-hinge arch" (Gaebler 1952: 87) (for details of the roof trusses see Patterson 1994: 19, fig. 2-11).

Wright preached the use of the machine in construction and aimed to discover some of the potential of machine-made materials and systems. He believed that "each structure is an ordered fabric; rhythm and consistent scale of parts and economy of construction are greatly facilitated by this simple expedient: a mechanical one" (Wright 1925/1992: 213). Although he admired the machine, he warned that the machine is a tool and not a "Creator". Therefore, the role of the architect's imagination is to create the artistic values of the material, its details, and décor. The machine is only a tool that helps achieve the architect's design (Wright 1960: 225). In his design of Unity Temple in Illinois, Wright recognized this tool and used it to reveal the nature of concrete. The concrete was freshly exposed at the exterior and then washed out and brushed to show the rough-textured pea gravel aggregate (Bell 1974: 161; Pfeiffer 1990: 88).[4] Wright's experiment with this material resulted in using four different kinds of concrete: conventional concrete for the structural system; cinder concrete for the floor and the cantilevered roof; lightweight cinder concrete for the roof topping; and Portland cement for the exterior walls (Knecht 2001). Siry (1996: 145) claims that the kinds of concrete and its finishes were a function of "Wright's late changes in the surface's aggregate (granite to gravel) and in method of finishing (floating to acid wash)".

The application of machines, the use of reinforced concrete, and of outward opening casement windows instead of the neo-colonial sash all enhanced Wright's "ingenuity as a space-planner" while economizing on the construction (Frampton 1994: 62). Budget constraints pushed Wright to find new solutions in construction/finish materials. Examples include the concrete for Unity Temple in Illinois (concrete was cheaper than stone construction); the change of Wright's initial design of colored glass to clear glass in the prow of the Unitarian Meeting House in Wisconsin,[5] and the change from the copper roof of the First Christian Church in Arizona to foam and colored green to resemble oxidized copper.[6] It should be noted that when budgets improved, some congregations tried to complete Wright's original selection of materials. Such is the case with the Minor Chapel in Florida where the original intended copper roof was installed in the 1990s.

Wright's use of materials and systems was enriched when he combined the tectonic and sacred symbolism in his religious work, and created the preferred sacred ambience.

Building Technology and the Sacred Ambience

The second aspect of Figure 4.1 illustrates the relationship between building systems and the sacred ambience. Wright's use of building technology in his sacred architecture answered not only the monumental/religious and integrity aspects of the design but created the sacred ambience of light, sound, and thermal comfort (Geva 1999, 2000, 2002a, Geva and Mukherji 2009). The investigation of these factors in Wright's sacred architecture shows his attentiveness to local conditions and his incorporation of various techniques to manipulate these conditions to achieve a sacred ambience. In addition, it illustrates Wright's innovations in building systems. For example, he was one of the first architects in Chicago to introduce electrical lights in his buildings (in Unity Temple) and to design light fixtures for this technology; he was one of the first architects in the United States to utilize the radiant floor heating system in his designs. The latter can be found in his designs of Unity Temple in Illinois, the Unitarian Meeting House in Wisconsin; Annie Pfeiffer Chapel in Florida, and the Pilgrim Congregational Church in California the (see Chapter 14 on Thermal Comfort).

Light and acoustics are special components of sacred ambience and building technology in religious projects, since they reinforce the spiritual experience of a sacred space. They are considered an integral part of the *axis mundi* (Plummer 1987; Cirillo and Martellota 2006; Andrews 2007). Sara Osmen (1990: 31, 35) argues that light is the most central element of a sacred space and acoustics represent life, since "life itself is music". In his designs, Wright provided a link between the worshiper and the divine through the design of the "holy" light and "divine" sound (voice and music): "Light! – living in mathematics of form to match with the mathematics of sound" (Wright 1928c/1992: 270). The relationship between both light and sound with mathematics is also linked to Wright's inclusion of light fixtures and sound screens as part of the geometric modules and grid systems of his sacred buildings.

Wright's sacred architecture's environmentally conscious design is especially unique, since Western religions do not necessarily consider thermal comfort as a factor in the design of their houses of worship (Geva 1995, 2009b; Geva and Morris 2010). In his 1882 sermon on the "Ideal Church", Jenkin Lloyd Jones, Wright's uncle, claimed that Gothic cathedrals were never thermally comfortable and proceeded to request: "O architect, build it low with humility, and make it warm with human tenderness . . . Flood it with sunlight and fill it with pure air" (Jones 1882: 204 quoted by Siry 1991b: 258). Wright also believed that "a chapel building is a thing of the spirit and for the spirit, [it] can best serve its purpose when the body is comfortable, which never was in Gothic architecture" (Wright quoted by Siry 2004: 509). It is interesting to note that unlike Western religions, Eastern religions such as Hinduism and Buddhism promote the provision of all-round comfort in their temples. These buildings are built with heavy stone (mainly granite in Hindu temples) and small openings, which provide coolness and shadow as a refuge from the outside heat and glare. By the time the pilgrims reach the holiest innermost chamber their physical stature and state of mind are comfortable and relaxed enough, no longer plagued by exterior's harsh conditions (Geva and Mukherji 2007). Similarly, Muslim devotees find refuge from the environment's extreme conditions in the sacred space of their mosques (Serageldin and Steele 1996). It is not surprising that Wright turned to Eastern religious concepts. This was part of his departure from traditional European church design: his way to accommodate environmental conditions and cater to human needs.

As shown in the previous parts, Wright believed that freedom and democracy are also fundamental to human needs. Therefore, he searched for a unique American style in his sacred architecture that would express these values. In his search he turned to the American landscape (nature), which in his point of view linked between humans and the Divine. Chapters 9 and 10 describe Wright's use of materials and structural systems along his design concepts of nature, and freedom and democracy. Chapter 11 illustrates his holistic approach in the use of materials and structures as part of his design of sacred buildings. Chapters 12, 13, and 14 focus on Wright's use of building systems to create a sacred ambience as required by the faith. In the latter chapters I introduce some empirical analyses, which further explain Wright's design. The computerized light and energy simulations assess and evaluate Wright's treatment of light and climate in his sacred architecture.

Chapter 9

Nature

Every new material means a new form, a new use if used according to its nature.

(Wright 1928c/1992: 270, 294)

In this chapter I describe the relationships between building technology and Nature in Frank Lloyd Wright's sacred architecture along two levels. First, I examine Wright's use of materials and structural systems in relation to Nature. In a sense, this reflects his organic architecture concept and his holistic approach to design. The second level addresses Wright's attitude about and understanding of the nature of materials and the appropriate structural systems they require.

Relationship between Materials and Structural Systems with Nature

A summary of Wright's articles that were published in the April to August and October 1928 issues of *Architectural Record*[7] reveals his poetic descriptions of and attitude toward materials as related to Nature: "These materials are human-riches. They are Nature – gifts to the sensibilities that are. Again. Gifts of Nature" (Wright 1928c/1992: 270). As such, Wright described stone as part of nature's strata – a rock formation, which gleams in its mineral color(s) and is shaped by winds and tide. Timber in Wright's eyes has a universal beauty and symbolizes the essence of a forest. Brick is part of the fabulous heat of the kiln that highlights a rainbow. Concrete is the "secret stamina of the physical body of our new world", which can be molded in the form of wood. In a poetic way, Wright believed that the shape of concrete could be determined by snow or sand. Steel has a sense of terror and romance (like "pages in the Arabian Nights"), and evokes "aesthetic gloom" (Wright 1927a/1992: 224). And glass is a crystal – a thing that has the effect of a jewel, or a mirror that may be "seen in Nature in the surfaces of lakes, in the hollows of the mountains, and in pools deep in shadow from trees; in winding ribbons of the rivers that catch and give back the flying birds, clouds, and blue sky" (Wright 1928c/1992: 295). These descriptions of brick, concrete, steel, and glass illustrate Wright's under-standing of man-made materials as concepts of Nature.

In another set of articles that appeared in the January, September, and December 1939 issues of *Southern*,[8] Wright stated that using natural materials "gives indigenous character to buildings". This statement strengthened his previous writings about the importance of the rela-tionship between materials and Nature in the context of historic religious monuments (Wright 1928c/1992: 273–274). He observed stone-made historic religious monuments and pointed out how the Mayans, Egyptians, and Chinese all understood the nature of stone as a construction material. Wright felt that these civilizations used stone to mimic the natural surface of the surrounding landscapes' stone. He criticized the Greeks, Romans, and the Goths for their lack of feeling for and understanding of the nature of this material. He did, however, acknowledge that the Goths made the most of stone when building their cathedrals, giving the stone a spiritual meaning: "It was as though stone blossomed into a thing of the human-spirit." Still, he believed that stone as a material was not the inspiration for Gothic design and that it was not expressed as part of Nature. The Goths used stone "scientifically", and thus, in Wright's point of view, the stone was used as "a negative material".

Wright continued to experiment with the use of materials as part of Nature and realized that "Nature furnished the materials for architectural motifs out of which the architectural forms as we know them today have been developed" (Wright 1908/1992: 86). He concluded that a different choice of materials would imply different forms (Scully 1996: 13; McCarter 2005a: 325). Examples of his selection of man-made materials demonstrate the relationship between the material and the form of his sacred architecture. The grammar of the square/cube design of Unity Temple in Illinois is determined by concrete masses proportioned according to concrete nature (Kaufman and Raeburn 1960: 76; Alofsin 1993: 115); his use of a combination of glass and plastic sheets in the roof of Beth Sholom Synagogue in Pennsylvania defines the pyramidal shape of the building (Fig. 1.3.); the grammar of the circular design of the Annunciation Greek Orthodox Church in Wisconsin is established by the concrete dome and bowl-shaped support of the dome (Fig. 3.2).

Frank Lloyd Wright also experimented with traditional materials such as stone and wood, using them in contemporary ways. He showcased the relationship of these materials with Nature. For example: "The stone may show a natural face in the wall, or a face characteristic of the tool used to shape it – or be flatly smoothed" (Wright 1928c/1992: 271–272). The materials' substance, which comprises texture, color, and layers of paint, "embodies the memory of their making and contributes to our subtle experience of them" (Tabb 2007: 95). One example of Wright using tradi-tional materials in contemporary ways is his application of terne roofing.

Terne is a 200 year old material which is durable, economic, and has design potential in its color and form. Wright suggested using it in his design proposal for the Wedding Chapel in Berkeley, California to enhance the form of the chapel (Boyd 1959: 175). In Unity Chapel in Wisconsin, Unity Temple and Pettit Chapel in Illinois, Wright used the traditional method of ceiling rib-banding to enhance the charm of wood (Figs 3.5.5 and 3.6.24). Another example of the relationship between materials and nature is the original design of the copper roof of the Unitarian Meeting House in Wisconsin. The roof, left to weather and become an oxidized green, was laid on wooden trusses like tree branches spreading below it: "Bring out the nature of the materials, let their nature intimately into your scheme" (Wright 1908/1992: 87). Wright also saw Nature's inherent structure as part of his pattern of design (Wright 1954). He interpreted the third dimension of space, which is depth, as actually representing Nature. He saw in it "a new structural integrity" (Wright 1953a: 224). Moreover, he developed the structural systems as part of the primary geometry that enhanced the spiritual experience. For example, each unit of the choir screen in the Annie Pfeiffer Chapel in Florida rises at a 30 degree angle from a narrow base, which acts like a parapet beam carrying the entire load of the screen "much like branches cantilevered from the trunk of an orange tree" (Siry 2004: 517). The chapel was built near a citrus orchard and thus the screen's decorative pattern represents the relationships between the structural system and the chapel's surrounding nature. Moreover, the 30 degree angle of the screen is a continuation of the same angle of the outside campus's diagonal plan.

The most obvious relationship between building materials and Nature is Wright's use of local materials in construction. For example, 1,000 tons of local stone were transported from a quarry near Sauk City, Wisconsin for use in the construction of the Unitarian Meeting House. Ninety-one tons of rocks and boulders were quarried and transported from the area of Shasta Lake and from the Iron Mountain mine in California, and then mixed with cement (concrete) for the building of Pilgrim Congregational Church in California. In that church, Wright also used local cedar veneer (milled in Anderson). This is also the case in Minor Chapel in Florida, which is framed by Florida tidewater red cypress woodwork. Wright used the same wood for the original seats and pulpit of Annie Pfeiffer Chapel (also in Florida). The use of local cypress and local materials, such as sand and coquina stone in the mix of the concrete blocks of the chapels, tied the material to the indigenous character of the "Florida feel". Furthermore, the use of the coquina stone added a symbolic meaning to these blocks. Since coquina stone contains evidence of oceanic life's long history, it conveys the message that "natural evolution [was] championed by modernist theology" (Siry 2004: 515).

The Nature of Materials

Frank Lloyd Wright asserted: "Every true aesthetic is an implication of nature, so it was inevitable that this aesthetic ideal should be found to enter into the actual building of the building itself as a principle of construction" (Wright 1932a/1977: 171). In his view, every material and its handling "had new possibilities of use peculiar to the nature of each" (Wright 1954: 23).

Wright claimed that he started studying the nature of materials because he could not find any work addressing this subject's interpretation (Wright 1932a/1977: 172). Therefore, he felt that his technique of understanding the nature of materials was based on his instincts rather than on prior knowledge (Wright 1949/1994: 361). He believed that architecture could overcome and subdue violent forces of nature such as changes in climate, earthquakes, fires, and floods through the understanding of the nature of materials and systems (Levine 1996: xviii).

In his sacred architecture Wright explored each material in its unique nature as a means to enhance the spirituality of the project: "Each material has its own message and, to the creative artists, its own song" (Wright 1928c/1992: 270). For example, he considered stone as a precious solid and a durable material and wrote: "Stone has every texture, every color, and as in marble – also exquisite line combined with both." He linked stone to earth since a particle of stone reveals the grammar of earth (Wright 1928c/1992: 275). As previously discussed, earth is one of the fundamental universal elements that define sacredness. Wright's use of stone growing out of the earth enriched sacredness of his houses of worship. An example of this is the use of stone in the base and walls of the Unitarian Meeting House in Wisconsin. The local stone highlights the material's relation with earth. The use of stone in Pilgrim Congregational Church in California presents the same relationship. In addition to the local stone that connects the building to its physical location, members of the congregation included special stones, which they brought from their homelands (i.e., Tahiti, Hawaii), in the construction of the church's walls. These stones represent the members' roots, which for some are associated with sacredness.

Wright felt that wood was "universally beautiful to Man. And yet, among higher civilizations, the Japanese understood it best" (Wright 1928c/1992: 277). His work with wood was a natural continuation of his admiration of Japanese construction "where wood always came up and came out as nobly beautiful". He believed that wood is the most humanly intimate of all building materials (Wright 1928c/1992: 277). Moreover, Wright deemed the nature of wood to be a religious sentiment that expresses simplicity.[9] He used wood in all his sacred projects in roof trusses, shingles, frames, ceilings, trims, and furniture (see, e.g., the Pettit Chapel in Illinois, Figs 3.7.7 and 4.9.1; and the wooden ceiling of the Pilgrim Congregational Church in California, Fig. 4.9.2).

4.9.1
The Wooden Details in the Interior of
The Pettit Chapel, Illinois.

4.9.2
The Wooden Ceiling of the Pilgrim
Congregational Church, California.

Still, it seems that Wright was fonder of wood veneers, which create the appearance of wood while dispensing with nearly all of its properties. When discussing honesty and truth as part of Wright's general design principles, Patterson (1994: 240) explains that Wright's use of wood veneer, as well as his technique of hiding expressionless wood construction, "does not necessarily mean that the nature of material [was] violated" (Patterson 1994: 240). For Wright, wood in construction and ornamentation meant using a light and continuously flowing design (Wright 1931a). Moreover, he believed that wood veneer expresses the utility of machinery while highlighting the beautiful aspects of wood (Wright 1928c/1992: 280).

The interesting question is why Wright exposed concrete or steel structural systems but hid wood construction. One plausible explanation may be the fact that at the time of design, concrete and steel were innovative materials, expressing modern technology. It may be assumed that Wright wanted to showcase his use of up-to-date materials and construction systems.

Wright understood concrete's plasticity and its ability to incorporate the forms of wood or metal molds (Wright 1927a/1992: 242). In 1908 he wrote that the formwork itself modifies the shape that the concrete naturally takes "if indeed it does not wholly determine it" (Wright 1908/1975: 59). Thus, Wright used concrete as a construction material with decoration possibilities in several of his designs. Examples include the ornamental impressions cast in Unity Temple's columns (Fig. 3.6.12); the perforated concrete choir screen in Annie Pfeiffer Chapel (Fig. 4.13.3), the decorative patterns of the chapel's tower (Figs. 3.7.9 and 3.8.7), and the patterns of the chapel's concrete blocks (Fig. 4.9.3).

The Nature of Material as its Own Decoration

Ornamentation also contributes to the form's natural pattern and reveals the building's character (Wright 1932a, 1953a). Frank Lloyd Wright claimed that "The very nature of the material itself becomes its own decoration" (Wright 1928c/1992: 273). Thus, the ornaments manifest the structure's constitution. The blocks of the two Florida chapels show Wright's use of the concrete's texture as the building's ornamentation. In addition to the concrete patterns he included painted glass inserts in the blocks, which add to the decorative patterns and enhance the effect of light inside the chapel (Fig. 4.9.3). Annie Pfeiffer Chapel includes about 6,000 individual concrete blocks with forty-eight different designs (Siry 2004: 515). The blocks' designs are created from the concrete's blend of cement, coquina (crushed oyster shells)[10], and local sand. The nine-inch by thirty-six-inch blocks were cast in wooden molds. These block walls were built using a technique similar to Wright's *textile-block* construction system (*c.* 1923): two columns of blocks (width) with two-inch air spaces between the columns (Fig. 4.9.4). The air spaces provide insulation and soundproofing. The blocks were laid dry with their edges grooved to hold the steel reinforcement rods and grouting. There are no mortar joints on the face of the blocks.

To achieve the elegant image of a wall, Wright "smoothed" the concrete and applied plaster or stucco. These finishing treatments can be observed in the Pettit Chapel in Illinois, the Annie Pfeiffer Chapel in Florida, the Greek Orthodox Church in Wisconsin, Beth Sholom Synagogue in Pennsylvania, and in some of his unbuilt proposal designs such as Trinity Chapel in Oklahoma. In the case of Annie Pfeiffer Chapel, the smooth finish (stucco) was applied on the second floor contrasting the ornamented concrete blocks of the first floor. Stucco was also applied to the two concrete sections of the tower: the concrete blocks of the plain broad central surfaces, and the concrete of the patterned surfaces of the tower's flanking elements (Fig. 3.8.7). In the case of the synagogue, the smooth finish was applied to the base of the building to contrast the translucent light of the pyramidal structure (Fig. 1.3).

4.9.3
The Concrete Blocks of Annie Pfeiffer Chapel, Florida.

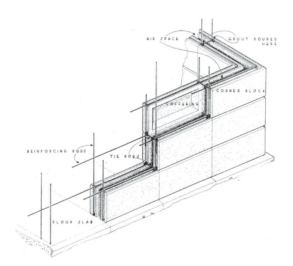

4.9.4
Wright's *Textile-block* Construction System (c. 1923) (© 2009 Frank Lloyd Wright Foundation, Scottsdale AZ/Artists Rights Society (ARS), New York).

Wright utilized the plasticity of concrete for more than just decoration. For example, the dome of the Annunciation Greek Orthodox Church in Wisconsin and its bowl-shaped volume reflects the plasticity of concrete. Moreover, the details of this church's semicircular openings with their beveled edges "further supplement the plastic image of the church" (Patterson 1994: 193).

Another factor of Wright's focus on the nature of materials in his design of houses of worship was his particular use and design of joints. These structural musts serve as additional examples of the ornamentation potential of various materials. The joints also reflect environmental constraints. For example, Wright used wooden joints interlocked with a beaded insertion so that environmental shrinkage is allowed and the joint ornaments express Nature (Wright 1928c/1992: 280). Another example is the expansion joints between different sections of concrete walls, which include slit windows between central walls and corner stair blocks (Fig. 4.9.5). These joints insured the thermal independence of each poured section while ornamenting the building's form.

4.9.5

The Slit Windows Between Central Walls and Corner Stair Blocks of Unity Temple, Illinois.

Glass was another material used either with ornamentations or made transparent to connect the worshiper and the building with Nature. Wright created several design patterns of prism glass during his collaboration with the Luxfer Prism Company in Chicago (1894). These patent designs not only showcased a variety of ways to utilize prism glass technology as part of a composition, but contributed to the improvement of daylight conditions in buildings. Although Wright introduced this material into some of his secular projects (Pfammatter 2008),[11] it is interesting to note that he did not use this technology in his sacred architecture, working instead with clear, stained, or painted glass. In addition, he introduced geometrical patterns and abstracted vegetation images into the glass to add to the ornamentation of the sacred space (see details later). His use of clear glass was often a result of budget constraints and a tight schedule, or the recognition of the need for better illumination. The latter condition is demonstrated in Wright's early design alternative for the prow of the

Unitarian Meeting House in Wisconsin (1947). He specified narrow vertical bands of glass alternating with concrete, and cast concrete blocks containing colored glass inserts as "a non-supporting screen mosaic of light and pattern" (Hamilton 1991), a technique he had previously used in his design of Annie Pfeiffer Chapel in Florida (1938). To add natural daylight, Wright replaced this design idea with clear glass panels that transformed the hall into an almost transparent space. Mary Hamilton (1991: 22) mentions that perhaps Wright also "intended to admit a view of Lake Mendota into the auditorium". Indeed, this window's view exemplifies Wright's idea of bringing Nature/God into the building and linking the worshiper with the Divine (which, in his view, was Nature).

In addition to understanding each material, Wright also utilized a combination of materials (like stone and wood) that would "naturally [meet] in nature" (Wright 1932a/1977: 195). For example, in the Pilgrim Congregational Church in California, a combination of stone and concrete rises from the ground and prepares the way for the wood (Fig. 2.1.3). Wright utilized a different combination of natural and man-made materials (stone and glass) in his second alternative for the Christian Science Church project in Bolinas, California. In this proposal, the stone sets the way for the glass (Fig. 3.4.12). This combination also illustrates Wright's conception of man-made materials as being part of Nature. Another example of this combination is his use of four slim, sharp, and precise steel pipes as columns that support the overhang above the entrance of Beth Sholom Synagogue in Pennsylvania. These pipes are visible in the upper part of the entrance, while at the bottom they blend into the mullions of the glass. This combination creates the illusion that the steel grows out of the glass and its mullions (Fig. 2.3.8).

Frank Lloyd Wright believed that understanding the nature of materials and structural systems, as well as relating them to Nature, would create new options in design and construction. His belief freed his design of sacred architecture from any traditional constraints. He was able to design a free and open plan with spaces flowing from one into the other. The next chapter on building technology and its relationship with democracy and freedom examines this notion, and demonstrates how Wright's use of materials and systems expressed his search for an American style of sacred architecture.

Chapter 10

Democracy and Freedom

The cantilever is . . . [a] new structural resource . . . It can do remarkable things to liberate space.

(Wright 1932a/1943: 341)

Wright was fascinated by the potential of construction materials and structural systems, exploring it endlessly throughout his entire career (Storrer 1993: 61). He believed that by using old materials in new ways and applying new materials and systems creatively, architecture could express the "body of our new democratic world" and "the culture of modern life" (Wright 1957: 23). These materials and systems helped his design explore modernity in all faiths and allowed him to depart from traditional church design. To achieve these developments in building technology, Wright explored the potential of the machine and its use in construction. As mentioned before, in his view, the machine was a tool used to advance his aspirations for a unique American style for his sacred architecture: "The machine is a tool to a greater freedom: new power to manipulate new materials by new strategy" (Wright 1957: 155). Kenneth Frampton (2005: 170–189) claims that this attitude was part of Wright's approach to construction as a production process. Joseph Siry (2008: 78) demonstrates Wright's serious relationship with engineering as part of his production approach, and claims that Wright responded to engineering and construction "while choosing among his era's contested theories and methods".

Indeed, Wright utilized modern building technology to develop the open space plan, which is free of structural components, and to introduce the cantilever. Although the free open plan was demonstrated in some of his secular projects (see, e.g., the Larkin Office building, and the Guggenheim Museum) and in most of his residential projects (see, e.g., the schematic plan of a Usonian house in Brooks (1979: 12, fig. 10c)), all of his religious projects (built and unbuilt) exhibit a free and open interior space. This space creates an egalitarian atmosphere for all worshipers and expresses Wright's interpretation of democracy. The cantilever helped free Wright's religious projects from traditional constraints and elevated "the spirit of the material [concrete] in the building image" by its dynamic nature that magnifies concrete's characteristics (Patterson 1994: 201).

Free and Open Space

Wright's combination of modern materials and systems to free his sacred architecture from any interior structural support is best exemplified in his proposal for the Steel Cathedral in New York (Fig. 2.3.1) and in his built Beth Sholom Synagogue in Pennsylvania (Fig 1.3). Both projects were designed as tripod airy structures of steel and glass (in the synagogue he also used plastic and aluminum) supported by a concrete base. Both designs also demonstrate Wright's use of his time's modern materials in his abstraction of an ancient monument's form (e.g., pyramids).

As mentioned before, the design of Beth Sholom Synagogue was inspired by the proposal for the Steel Cathedral in New York. The synagogue is smaller in size, but is still a very impressive building. The 160-ton steel tripod frame system of the synagogue, which is supported by a concrete base, completely frees the 1,030-seat sanctuary from internal supports. This freedom and the treatment of light in the sanctuary allowed Wright to create a greater spiritual and communal experience. Glass and plastic were utilized to construct a translucent pyramidal roof. The translucent corrugated wire glass is bound by aluminum strips to cream-white corrugated one-and-a-half-inch plastic sheets with five inches of air space between the two layers (Fig. 4.10.1). This double layer of translucent panels controls daylight as well as heat gain and loss (Aitken 1998: 15).

The domical structure of the Annunciation Greek Orthodox Church in Wisconsin is another example of Wright's use of modern materials and structural systems creating a free and open interior sacred space. The church's lightweight shallow concrete domical structure expands to 106 feet in diameter. Wright introduced curved transverse reinforced concrete ribs and upper arched openings to raise the dome and give an impression of its being lighter and almost floating above the prayer hall (Figs 2.3.15, 3.5.4, and 4.10.2; see also Chapter 12 on Light). The dome is supported by a concrete bowl and as such frees the interior space (Fig. 3.2).

Wright deemed concrete to be the "Physical body of modern civilized world" (Wright quoted in Pfeiffer and Nordland 1988: 77), but he also experimented with new processes and materials of his time such as steel and aluminum. In Beth Sholom Synagogue in Pennsylvania, Wright used steel to reinforce the concrete base. Steel is the main structural material of the building's tripod legs and the material of the secondary structural elements between the tripod and the base. Wright used aluminum as the legs' cladding. He applied aluminum gold-anodized cladding with the

4.10.1

Zoom on The Translucent Wire Glass of the Roof as Bound by Aluminum Strips in Beth Sholom Synagogue, Pennsylvania.

same patterns of the horizontal cladding outside the synagogue on to the ceiling niche of the Sisterhood Chapel (Figs 2.3.10 and 4.12.14). In the Annunciation Greek Orthodox Church in Wisconsin, Wright also used gold-anodized aluminum brackets that radiate from the face of the building. These appear precise and sharp, reflecting the spirit of the material and creating an illusion of a crowned dome (Fig. 4.10.2).

4.10.2
Upper Arched Openings of the Annunciation Greek Orthodox Church, Wisconsin. Note the Gold-Anodized Aluminum Brackets that Crown the Dome.

Wright used glass to create a sense of continuous flow spaces – both in interior spaces and in the transition from a building's interior to the exterior. His work with glass supports the idea that "continuity [becomes an] invisible fountain from which all rhythms flow and to which they must pass. Beyond time or infinity" (Wright 1953b: 6). This in turn created free and open space. As mentioned before, he studied and experimented with glass and used it extensively as "an intrinsic component of his architecture" (Lind 1995: 10). His work with glass is characterized by simplicity, delicacy, and an interlocked pattern, which is part of his holistic design approach. This approach is seen in his design of the Minor Chapel in Florida. His attention to the glass's detail as an integrated part of the building is displayed through the alignment of the tip of the stained glass with the tip of the roof's overhang copper trim (Fig. 3.5.8).

Another structural measure that frees a space is demonstrated in Wright's Pilgrim Congregational Church in California, and in the First Christian Church in Arizona. In both churches the interior side columns extend the boundary of the sanctuary to the outside of the building and free up the interior space. The continuity of the structural system strengthens Wright's holistic approach to design, creating a mysterious image of a concrete grove (Figs 4.10.3 and 4.10.4).

4.10.3
The Columns Extend the Boundary of the Sanctuary to the Outside of the Pilgrim Congregational Church, California.

4.10.4
The Columns Extend the Boundary of the Sanctuary to the Outside of the First Christian Church, Arizona (note the play of light and shadows on the ground).

The open space and support-free corners of Unity Temple in Illinois and Annie Pfeiffer Chapel in Florida are a result of a design based on four major columns (see plans in Figs 3.5.1 and 1.12 respectively; and Figs 3.5.5 and 3.5.6 for the support-free corners images). As mentioned in Chapter 5, Wright moved the support's structural system internally, away from the prominent corners, and described it as if the corners were pulled away from the building. Similar to Unity Temple, Wright utilized only four columns in the Annie Pfeiffer Chapel to free up the corners. These supported the superstructure and the cantilever balconies.

In Annie Pfeiffer Chapel and the Minor Chapel in Florida, the concrete blocks' structural system and construction method freed Wright's design and allowed for a greater manipulation of the interior space (Christ-Janer and Foley 1962: 195). The blocks were stack-bounded and horizontally and vertically reinforced using grooves and hollow cores with three-eighths-inch steel rods (Fig. 4.9.4). These grooves run along the center of each direction and hold the steel reinforcement and mortar (MacDonald et al. 2007: 12). "This achieved strength, modular coordination and visual clarity without the use of piers or obstructive structural elements."[12] Once more, Wright utilized construction materials and structural systems to determine the form while beautifying the building.

In summary, in his sacred architecture, Wright turned to advanced technology using modern materials (e.g., concrete, steel, and glass) and, for his time, sophisticated structural systems, which were not commonly used. He also repurposed traditional materials such as stone by using innovative structural system methods. For example, the tower of the First Christian Church in Arizona, capped with a twenty-two-foot tall cross, has no internal support structure. Rank Grossman, a steel detailer, followed Wright's specifications as noted on the original drawings of 1950, and created an alloy skeleton that supports the tower's 304 tons of concrete, stone, and steel.

These different methods of freeing the sacred space from structural elements created equal views for the worshipers and a communal feeling that enhances democracy. To extend the expressions of freedom and continuity from within the building to its outside, Wright introduced the cantilever, which became his "preferred system" (Siry 2008: 78).

The Cantilever

Wright believed that his design of the cantilever system was almost the ultimate expression of freedom. In his view, the cantilever expressed modernity and technological advances. As described in Chapter 5, Wright introduced the cantilever as horizontal planes extending the horizontal lines of a flat roof. The extension of the horizontal lines creates an illusion of a larger building. See, for example, Unity Temple in Illinois (Fig. 3.5.2); the 1911 proposal for the Christian Catholic Church in Zion, Illinois (Fig. 3.6.11); and the Community Christian Church in Missouri (Figs 3.4.3 and 3.6.3). The horizontal cantilever was also used to extend the appearance of horizontal balconies (see Annie Pfeiffer Chapel in Florida, Fig. 3.8.7).

Wright also employed the cantilever idea for triangle overhangs that enhance the verticality of the roof. This is seen in the Unitarian Meeting House in Wisconsin (Fig. 1.11), and in the Minor Chapel in Florida (Fig. 3.5.8). This type of overhang is based on the extension of a roof's eaves. As mentioned before, Wright's cantilevers and overhangs exhibit a significant projection of the structure. In the context of sacred architecture Wright's cantilever system represents the sacred symbols of earth and sky. Donald Hoffman (1995: 15) states that "nothing but the cantilever could so daringly assert the horizontal or so grandly culminate a series of planes parallel to the earth". The huge triangle overhangs are associated with the vertical aspects of the sacred building as it metaphorically soars toward the heavens (the sky).

The cantilever system not only expressed Wright's departure from tradition but had a pragmatic purpose: structural support and protection of the upper openings and walls from rain and sun. Wright used the cantilever to support not just itself, but other heavy parts of the building. One such example is the cantilever use in Annie Pfeiffer Chapel in Florida. The cantilevers partially support the weight of the central lantern.[13] Joseph Siry (2004: 523) explains that Wright adapted this exceptional structural system from the cantilevered footing technique, which originated in the construction of public/commercial buildings in Chicago at the end of the nineteenth century. Still, in his sacred architecture Wright made the cantilever a precedent example "to crown a spiritual space". An example of this "crowning" is the introduction of the horizontal cantilever system in Unity Temple, Illinois. This system was an addition to his innovative use of concrete as the construction material and construction method. The cantilevers on each side of the temple create the shape of a square cross while enhancing the cubic form of the Temple, reinforcing the connection of the building to the stable earth and the horizon, and showcasing concrete construction (Figs 3.5.1, 3.5.2, and 3.7.4).

Wright's proposal for the Community Christian Church (the Church of the Future) in Kansas City, Missouri is another example of his use of horizontal cantilevers and modern/new materials (Fig. 3.4.3). The cantilever design emphasized the horizontal lines of the church while providing shade for the horizontal openings. The style of his proposed structural system was unique for its time (1940). Wright proposed a system that is "a light *tenuous* steel frame, flexible in shape – a *hex* – *resting for the sake of flexibility on rock ballast foundations*" (Wright 1943a/1994: 187). In his design of the church, heavy paper, strung with steel wires (Steeltex) and securely connected to the skeleton, covered each side of the light steel frame. He then specified that a cement gun be used to apply thin but sufficient shells over the insulating paper with a two-and-a-quarter-inch space. These shells would be secured to the paper using the wires much like plaster is secured to a lathed wall. Wright also included the use of the Guntie process in the proposed building structure.

Although Wright had used this system before, he could not convince the leadership of the church to adopt it for their building: "The cost figures came in finally, but only after no one in K.C. had confidence enough in the church and its architect, or faith in the novel technique, to bid" (Wright 1943a/1994: 187). His client, the building committee, along with the commissioner and the contractor of the church were conservative traditionalists who did not appreciate Wright's new developments. They questioned his revolutionary construction methods as well as the novel radiant heating floor system that Wright proposed to install instead of conventional visible radiators. In the end they did not accept Wright's innovative proposal.[14] This rejection, trust issues, and the client's modifications of Wright's original design and construction specifications resulted in Wright distancing himself from the built project.

It should be noted that the lack of support from the Kansas City Church's leaders was a rare case. The rest of Wright's sacred projects had the full support of the people involved in design and construction. The congregations and their build teams supported Wright's search for a sacred architecture style that would express American's core values of democracy and freedom through the introduction of a unique form, modern materials, innovative systems, and construction methods. These design challenges combined with budget constraints engaged most of the congregations in the process of design and construction.

In his *Autobiography*, Wright acknowledged the involvement of Charles E. Roberts,[15] a dominant figure on the building committee of Unity Temple in Illinois. Roberts was delighted with the design of the Temple and suggested that Wright build a model for the rest of the committee. With this presentation, Wright and Roberts won the votes of the majority of the committee members.

Skilled members of both the Unitarian Meeting House in Wisconsin and the Pilgrim Congregational Church in California performed professional construction tasks. Other congregations also involved members, including women and children, in the construction of their houses of worship. In the case of the Unitarian Meeting House in Wisconsin, Harold Groves, a distinguished professor of economics at the University of Wisconsin, and his wife, Helen Groves, overcame their initial objection to the selection of Wright as the architect of the building, and worked closely with him[16] (Hamilton 1991: 6). In Pilgrim Congregational Church, California, David Packard, a member of the congregation, served as the first moderator of the construction and as the building's re-bar installer. Members who worked with him on this project called him "a true David when the church confronted a real Goliath".[17] Other members of the congregation, including women and children, performed many tasks on the construction site such as hauling the stone, cleaning the forms for reuse, and more.[18]

Another example of community involvement in the construction process is the work of Dr. Spivey, the president and campus religious leader of Florida Southern College. Together with Robert D. Wehr, a faculty and construction superintendent, and William Weley, Wright's on-site supervisor, the three facilitated Wright's unconventional design of the Annie Pfeiffer Chapel and were committed to its implementation and construction (1938–1941). They involved students of the college in the construction process. The construction work became part of the daily "pleasant" routine of the students (MacDonald et al. 2007: 14). Dr. Spivey also worked directly with Wright and his on-site supervisor Nils Schweizer to conceive and construct the Minor Chapel in 1954.

These examples of community engagement in the design and construction of houses of worship epitomize the American value of democracy – these projects were designed for the people and built by the people.

Chapter 11

The Whole as the Equilibrium of its Parts

Form and function thus become one in design and execution if the nature of materials and method and purpose are all in unison.

(Frank Lloyd Wright 1932a)

The integration of form, function, materials, systems, and construction methods was part of Wright's holistic approach to design and construction. It was a continuous feature of his projects: "the form itself in orderly relationship with purpose of function: the parts themselves in order with the form: the materials and methods of work in order with both: a kind of natural integrity" (Wright 1955: 58). This approach was already in place in 1912 when Wright stated that "in design, that element which we call its structure is primarily the pure form, an organization in a very definite manner of parts or elements into a large unity – a vital whole" (Wright 1912/1992: 116–117). He believed that materials and systems determine the organization of the parts into a whole balanced project. One example of this is the concrete shell dome of the Greek Orthodox Church in Wisconsin. The dome is carried by thousands of ball-bearings that are set in steel rails and are supported by reinforced concrete cylindrical trussing in the form of arches. Four concrete piers support these trusses and create the shape of the Greek cross in the building's plan (Fig. 2.3.11). All of these parts, materials, and structural systems work in harmony to create and define the whole domical church. The entire building represents a spiritual continuation of domical Byzantine church architecture. This continuation of history into modern times was possible owing to Wright's interpretations of the historic style and his innovative use of materials and systems. Referring to the Byzantine religious monument of Hagia Sophia, Wright wrote, "The effect of the whole was robust nature. It was worship by way of heavy material, masterful construction and much color" (Wright and Brownell 1937/1993: 229).

Wright's holistic approach to defining the sacred form (see Chapter 6) is accompanied by his unique use of materials and structural systems as part of the design aspects of the grid, continuity, and detailing. In this chapter, I explore Wright's use of building technology as part of his production/construction approach.

In his 2005 article 'The Text-tile Tectonic: The Origin and Evolution of Wright's Woven Architecture', Kenneth Frampton demonstrates that Wright's holistic approach to design was aimed with the goal of producing a building (2005: 170–189). This production took into consideration the economic/tectonic advantages of construction materials, tools, structural systems, and methods (Siry 1996: 142). Wright believed that "the process of construction [is] a conscious aesthetic feature of the whole. [The] 'style' is due to the way it was 'made'" (Wright 1925/1992: 212). In Wright's view, the nature of each material and the process of working with it actually craft the building (Wright 1928b/1992: 268). He believed that his use of advanced building technology combined with his holistic approach to design and construction was "superior in harmony and beauty to any architecture" (Wright 1954: 19). The sense of this harmony in his sacred architecture was often associated with a spiritual dimension: "Spirituality was expressed in bold and simple forms and flat colors, whether in wood-block prints or the materials of the building" (Alofsin 1996: 9).

Part of a building production's considerations was Wright's development of geometrical modules and grid systems. The grid allowed all the pieces of a project to be part of its designed grammar, relating to one another and to the whole (Siry 1996: 121). The use of the grid system helped simplify the fabrication of the building's parts and its construction process, creating a greater focus on the production of the building as a whole: "Now why not let walls, ceilings, floors become seen as component parts of each other" (Wright 1932a/1943: 146), and "openings should occur as integral features of the structure and form" (Wright 1908/1992: 87). Indeed Wright's design and construction includes repetitive orderly components such as columns and windows. Some examples of this repetition as presented in column form are found in Unity Temple in Illinois (Fig. 3.6.12) and in his design alternative of the Christian Science Reading Room in Illinois (Fig. 4.11.1). Examples of repetitive windows can be seen in Unity Temple (Fig. 1.4) and in the Pettit Mortuary Chapel (Pettit Chapel) in Illinois (Fig. 4.9.1).

The repetitive decorative glass of these openings also became part of the grid that unites the building's parts into one whole project. The glass pattern of Unity Temple's entrance doors and its slit windows express the building's square module (Figs 2.2.1 and 4.11.2).

Another example is the repetitive arched windows of the Annunciation Greek Orthodox Church in Wisconsin. The glass patterns express Wright's abstraction of the faith's images. Wright used arched lines as part of the circular module of the whole church.

4.11.1

Frank Lloyd Wright's Design Alternative of The Christian Science Reading Room, Illinois (© 2009 Frank Lloyd Wright Foundation, Scottsdale AZ/Artists Rights Society (ARS), New York).

4.11.2

The Glass Pattern of the Slit Windows of Unity Temple, Illinois.

Wright also referred to the nature of metal bars in windows as repetitive "grilles" with inserted glass (Patterson 1994: 218). It is interesting to note that in Annie Pfeiffer Chapel in Florida, he used the concrete blocks as the repetitive "grilles" that hold the inserted glass (Fig. 4.9.3).

Another part of Wright's holistic approach to design as related to materials and structures is his belief that their relationship defines the aesthetic of the building: "The structure depended upon its shape, graceful simplicity, and lightness of treatment for aesthetic effect" (Wright 1943a/1994: 187). As Patterson (1994) concluded, aesthetic of the building was one of the most important aspects in Wright's selection of material and in his pursuit of harmonious relation with the building's structural system. In essence, this view emphasizes that the continuity of materials, from inside to outside, reveals their nature and thus their beauty and truth (see Chapter 6). It also implies the continuity of structural components, from inside to outside (see Chapter 10). The concrete floor, with its triangle pattern, does not stop inside the Pilgrim Congregational Church in California, but continues outside. Figures 4.11.3 and 4.11.4 illustrate the structural columns of the church that extend from the outside into the building to create the whole as the equilibrium of its mutual parts.

Wright's proposal for the Kaufman Chapel in Pennsylvania presents a continuous line of materials, creating a balance of parts. The suggested stone for the base of the building continues and appears at the top of the building as a backing for the glass triangles (diamonds) of the proposed pyramidal roof (Fig. 3.4.11).

As described in Chapter 10, the idea of continuity uniting the building's parts into one holistic project was also expressed by Wright's use of glass. Wright was fascinated by glass design and saw glass as a means to bring Nature and light into a space: "Glass and light – two forms of the same thing!" (Wright 1928a/1992: 196).

Other construction and finish details were also part of Wright's holistic approach to design and construction. His drainage solution for the humongous copper roof of the Unitarian Meeting House in Wisconsin illustrates his ability to include every detail as part of the whole. In order

4.11.3 (left)
The Structural Columns of The Pilgrim Congregational Church, California Extend from the Outside into the Building (looking outside the church).

4.11.4 (right)
The Structural Columns of The Pilgrim Congregational Church, California Extend from the Outside into the Building (looking inside the church).

to enhance the visual effect of the roof, he designed horizontal seams, which ran parallel to the roof's lower edges (Figs 4.11.5 and 4.11.6). This design caused water to collect in the angle between the seams and the roof deck. Wright solved this problem by positioning "battens beneath the seams to raise them above the roof, allowing rainwater to flow harmless over them"[19] (Hamilton 1990: 185). This solution maintained the roof's aesthetic while contributing to the "architecture" of the church.

4.11.5
The Horizontal Seams of the Roof of the Unitarian Meeting House, Wisconsin, ran Parallel to the Roof's Lower Edges.

4.11.6
A Zoom on the Horizontal Seams of the Roof of the Unitarian Meeting House, Wisconsin.

Wright's holistic approach was expressed both in the form, function, and building technology of his projects: "The complete assembly, indoor and out, can be regarded as a single environmental device, controlling heat, light, view, ventilation, and . . . shade as well. Not only are the parts unified as a structure, they work together as well" (Banham 1966/1981: 157). These building technology measures helped Wright in shaping the form of his religious projects and catered to some of their various faith requirements. The next three chapters discuss Wright's sacred design and innovative techniques in creating the sacred ambience.

Chapter 12

Light

The best way to light a house is God's way – the natural way . . . The sun is the great luminary of all life.

(Wright 1954: 154)

Light and darkness create dramatic visual and spiritual experiences in a sacred setting. These experiences contribute to the connection between worshipers and a higher order of things – the immutable truth. They are the link to the celestial body as well as to spiritual and mystical transcendence (Fig. 4.12.1).

4.12.1
The Sky's Mystical Transcendence.

As described in Part 1, we can read about the relationship between light and darkness and the cosmic forces in Genesis 1:35: "Then God said let there be light and there was light – God saw how good the light was . . . evening came and morning followed – the first day." This relationship may be traced back to early human worship of light deities such as the sun, the moon, and the stars. In Part 1, I discussed the relationship between light/darkness and the cosmos as part of a universal set of beliefs. In this chapter, I investigate the influence of light on sacred architecture and its ambience.

For most faiths, light represents the Divine and is also associated with life. Therefore, it is often perceived as a prime symbol of the sacred, drawing attention to religious ambience (Yi-Fu 1978). Divine light and its association with heaven is a spiritual element, which in religious buildings enhances the *axis mundi*, where heaven and earth melt into one (Schwarz 1958: 180–181). I mentioned earlier that heavenly light is associated with cleanliness, purity, knowledge, and cosmic powers, while glimmering lights are associated with hope and inspiration (Plummer 1987). The various interpretations of these associations and their rooted meanings produce different treatments of light and darkness in sacred settings. Darkness is perceived as an expression of death and the underworld. It represents a void and the unknown, and thus provokes many interpretations. Still, darkness is necessary to complete the experience of light (Mukherji 2001). Even crypts and underground elements of religious buildings, which are associated with darkness, when lit with artificial lighting such as candles enhance the mysterious spiritual experience. Thus, shadows enhance the beauty that light creates (Tanizaki 1977).

Like Western religions, Hinduism associates light and darkness with the presence of the Divine. The Vastupurushamandala, which is the diagram of a Hindu temple's physical and spiritual plan, shows the Vastu, the residence of the deities along the solar and lunar cycles. According to the Rigveda, ancient Hindu scriptures, the God Surya

> is the sun of the heaven and his name is derived from the word svar [light] . . . Surya is the golden ornament of the sky, a flying falcon, and the very countenance and eye of the gods. Traversing heaven and earth in a single day, Surya observes the whole world from on high.

Despite the importance given to sun in these Hindu scriptures, natural light is very sparsely used in Hindu temples (Geva and Mukherji 2007). According to the Hindu faith, when worshipers are in the presence of the Divine, there should be nothing to distract their senses, including vision. Only then can God reveal himself gradually to the devotee (Deva 1995). As such, the innermost sanctum of the temple is shrouded in total darkness and the progression into the temple is a ritual movement through darkening spaces leading into the darkest and most sacred chamber (Michell 1987). The temple's holy of holy, the garbhagriha (the womb chamber), the place for the main deity, the seat of Brahman,[20] is dark, representing the black square in the center of the Vastupurushamandala (Volwahsen 1969). It is the dark location in the central shrine where worshipers are in the presence of the Divine, and where their souls are completely absorbed and transcendent beyond the unknown.

While Hinduism cherishes holy darkness, numerous studies demonstrate that in other faiths light provides premonitions and points of departure for spiritual and mystical transcendence. As previously described, light creates a bridge from earthly profanity to the sacred, bringing the devotee in touch with the eternal (Eliade 1958/1996; Arnold 1975; Hayes 1983; Gelfenbien 1987; Plummer 1987; Millet 1996; Geva and Garst 2005; Geva and Mukherji 2007). This eternal is symbolized by light streaming from the direction associated with heaven and God's presence (Schwarz 1958: 76–78) (Fig. 4.12.2).

4.12.2

Light Streaming From the Direction Associated with Heaven and God's Presence.

Wright believed that "Sunlight is to nature as interior light is to man's spirit" (Wright 1953a: 253). Indeed, the Scriptures tell us that the spiritual experience is not influenced solely by the exterior elements of light, but rather is based on the belief that the "Lord is the Light": "And there shall be no night there; and they need no candle, neither light of the sun; for the Lord God giveth them light: and they shall reign for ever and ever" (Revelation 22: 5); "The sun shall be no more thy light by day; neither for brightness shall the moon give light unto thee: but the LORD shall be unto thee an everlasting light, and thy God thy glory" (Isaiah 60: 19). The belief that the Lord is the light attributes to light the power "to calm, relax, revere, and inspire" (Clarahan 2004: 42–44). Light offers "a hopeful sanctuary in a shadowy void, a safe-haven in the ontological night, a friendly harbour in the cosmic sea" (Plummer 1987).

As such, the design of sacred buildings should attempt to enrich this inner spiritual experience by providing natural light. This light is perceived to connect the worshiper to the Divine, while the design of artificial light can highlight the rituals and symbols associated with the connection between light, the Divine, and the worshiper (Geva and Garst 2005). Dynamic lighting design is based on natural light, reflecting temporal changes and their dramatic effects, as sunlight moves throughout a space at different times of the day and throughout the seasons. Artificial light, a static technique, provides an additional dramatic effect. Still, both types of light may be considered as the "True Light itself" (John the Scot quoted in Plummer 1987).

Wright related the "true light" to nature and religion and saw the sacred building as "a creation of interior space in light" (Wright 1931b/1992: 89). "Light began to become the beautifier of the building – the blessing of the occupants" (Wright 1931b/1992: 89).[21] He linked light to freedom and democracy, and to the expression of a non-sectarian and more spiritual form. This belief guided him to design light to wash the entire sanctuary as opposed to the traditional European church design where light appears from one source, usually from behind the altar. This one source of light symbolized the Divine and enhanced the concept of one God.

Frank Lloyd Wright left no record of his daylight design process, except for an early sketch (on a tablecloth) of his lighting ideas for the Beth Sholom Synagogue in Pennsylvania (Aitken 1998: 4). It seems that his lighting design was based on intuition combined with the availability of electricity and its technology. Still, it is intriguing to discover that Wright's lighting approaches and techniques accommodate contemporary guidelines and standards for lighting design in houses of worship.

The modern standards, established by the Illumination Engineering Society (IES), require that light reveals the sacred space while highlighting the building's architectural and artistic value. More specifically, the four main criteria of these standards as interpreted by Clarahan (2004), who called them the four "layers of light", consist of: (1) task lighting (function) for the pragmatic and mundane needs of a specific faith (e.g., reading the sacred texts, performing rituals to be observed by those present, and safety issues of the worshipers); (2) accent lighting (spiritual) that draws the worshipers' eyes to brighter areas while highlighting specific features such as religious items of importance; (3) architectural lighting (function and spiritual) that adds to the drama of the service by illuminating the sanctuary and its symbols; and (4) celebration light (spiritual) that represents the Divine.

Examining Wright's lighting approaches and design techniques along the four IES standards demonstrates that his lighting design focused on natural light with which he attempted to combine the spiritual meaning of light with task lighting as called for by each faith's programmatic requirements. Although he was fascinated with the potential of artificial light and its fixtures, he treated this feature as a complementary and secondary source to natural lighting. This approach is one of the general sustainable approaches of today's lighting design guidelines. More particularly, Frank Lloyd Wright's treatment of light accommodated the spiritual aspects of lighting design that evokes sanctity in his sacred architecture. In his treatment of the "holy" light he used a combination of light sources and techniques departing from traditional European church design of one focal point of light. He wanted to bring God into the sacred building by streaming the heavenly light from all around the sanctuary. Though it is interesting to note that in some of the projects Wright's lighting design approach also followed traditional lighting solutions, which highlight focal points of the sacred place. This effect was achieved by illuminating the pulpit, as in Unity Temple in Illinois, the Unitarian Meeting House in Wisconsin, and the Minor Chapel in Florida. Alternatively, Wright created a mysterious effect of light and shadow in the area of the altar/pulpit in the Pilgrim Congregational Church in California (Fig. 2.1.3).

Wright's Spiritual and Architectural Lighting Design

The spiritual lighting journey of Frank Lloyd Wright's sacred architecture starts with his design of the sacred path. This path is enriched by a repeated interplay of light and darkness (Scully 1996).[22] For example, Wright applied covered walkways for their shading effect and directing people to the building (see Chapter 7). The shade creates a gradual adjustment of a worshiper's eyes to the dimmer light of the interior of a sacred place (Aitken 1998: 11). The journey from the exterior bright light toward the sacred dimness of the building contributes to calm the worshipers' state of mind. This path serves as a transition between the mundane and the spiritual realm (Geva and Mukherji 2007: 511). The paths of Unity Temple, Illinois (Figs 3.7.2 and 3.7.3), Annie Pfeiffer Chapel, Florida (Figs 3.7.9 and 3.7.10), and the First Christian Church in Arizona (Fig. 2.3.5) demonstrate this approach. It is interesting to note that the treatment of light in the procession from the outside toward the holy sanctum in Hindu temples also ensures that by the time the pilgrims reach the innermost chamber (garbhagriha) their eyes have become accustomed to the darkness (Geva and Mukherji 2007: 511). This notion is also found in ancient Egyptian temples where the worshiper's procession from the secular light to the holy darkness moves through a sequence of increasingly smaller and darker spaces (Barrie 1996: 88). This relationship between light and shadow became part of Wright's sacred path design as well as his lighting technique within a sacred place (Fig. 4.12.3).

4.12.3
The Play of Light and Shadow at the Entrance to the Pilgrim Congregational Church, California.

Inside the sacred place, Wright's spiritual lighting design utilized one of two strategies. In the first, Wright used the building itself as a mountain of light. This design technique relies on translucent building materials to control direct sunlight and glare. In the second strategy, Wright utilized multiple sources of light and a combination of several lighting design methods and techniques. This approach enabled Wright to achieve a balanced, uniform, and contrast-free soft light in the sacred space. The interplay of light and shadow evokes the mysterious associations attributed to light and darkness. Wright's use of indirect lighting in his sacred buildings' darker spaces suggests "a sense of inwardness, an invitation to meditation" (Kieckhefer 2004: 123). This sensation corresponds to Wright's ideas of catering to the individual in faith and design, while creating a community experience.

Mountain of Light

Frank Lloyd Wright's 1926 "tripod of light" design proposal for the Steel Cathedral in New York displays his attention to both task and spiritual utilities of light. In order to cater to all religions in this all-faith cathedral, Wright proposed to equally illuminate all of the chapels under the cathedral's pyramidal roof (Fig. 2.3.1). This practice would accommodate the task lighting of the central area of the cathedral and all the chapels surrounding it. Sunlight would pour into the central cathedral's space and embrace the "Hall of the Elements" (Pfeiffer 1990: 92). To enhance the spiritual and architectural aspects of light, Wright proposed to include a fountain shooting water upward in that center. The water would glow with the sun's spectrum of colors, enhancing the spiritual effect of sacred verticality. In addition, the natural light reflected in water would create a sense of purity and sanctity in the cathedral's central space (Joncas 1998a: 104).

Wright repeated this type of light treatment in his design of Beth Sholom Synagogue in Pennsylvania (1954). The synagogue was built as a "mountain of light" (Davis 1974), using a double-shell pyramidal roof made of corrugated glass and fiberglass, with a five-inch air space between the two layers (Fig 1.3). This double layer translucent "tripod of light" controls daylight and lets in the light's varying colors and tones during different hours of the day and during different seasons. In the morning, the temple's light is celebrated with silver tones; while in the afternoon it changes to gold tones. These tones enrich the spiritual atmosphere of the synagogue and the meaning of light.

The synagogue's image as a mountain of light symbolizes Mt. Sinai, "where God first revealed the Torah, the guide and Law of life" (Davis 1974: 35). This symbolism connects the congregation to its sacred roots and heritage. Moreover, the illumination from above creates a holy atmosphere, reminding the worshipers of Genesis's "*Yehi or*" – "Let there be light" (Figs 3.5.7 and 3.6.19). The soft and diffused light creates a feeling of reverence – "Wherefore glorify ye the Lord in the fires" (Isaiah 24: 15).

This natural light solution also achieves the congregation's required task lighting. It accommodates the faith's requirement for an equal distribution of light so that the whole congregation can read the sacred text. This lighting also fulfills the need for the congregation's members to connect to the Divine through the sky (Gothold 1977: 46; Shainberger 1977: 82). In an early tablecloth sketch for the Synagogue's lighting design, Wright suggested this passage of light through a translucent envelope. This way, the glass surfaces bring light into the sanctuary during the day (Fig. 1.13) and deliver it out to the heavens at night (Fig. 1.14) (Aitken 1998: 4).

An additional example of a more modest "mountain of light" is Wright's 1952 proposal for the Rhododendron Chapel in Pennsylvania – a small chapel for the Kaufman family (Fig. 3.4.11). The roof design was composed of diamond-shaped glass and copper crystalline panels. Wright attempted again to bring diffused soft natural light into the sacred space during the day and deliver the artificial light out at night.

Multiple Sources of Light and a Combination of Lighting Design Techniques

The second strategy in Wright's spiritual lighting design was his use of multiple light sources as part of his holistic approach to design. His innovative lighting design was based on his ability to balance the light emanating from these sources and a combination of lighting design methods and techniques. He created this balance by capturing the quality light of the specific context of the building; by filtering natural light through openings and skylights; by reflecting light to generate a subdued soft and "glowing" light. These measures enrich the divine light ambience and its focal points. Wright reflected light off walls, ceilings, and cantilevers to create an interplay of light and shadows. He created these effects using the shape, texture, and color of his architectural features: "Sun-acceptance in building means . . . wall-surfaces that eagerly take the light and play with it, break it up and render it harmless or drink it in until sunlight blends the building into place with the creation around it" (Wright quoted in Aitken 1998: 9).

Context

As described in this book's conceptual model (Fig. 1.1) and in Figure 4.1 in this part of the book, the relationship between the sacred ambience, building technology, and the building's context implies that the lighting design guidelines are affected by light quality of a specific location and the time of day and season. For example, the solar angles are different in Florida and Wisconsin. The sun in Florida is more vertical (89 degrees altitude in the summer; 38 degrees in the winter) than in Wisconsin, where the angles in the winter are almost horizontal (17 degrees altitude angle in the winter; 64 degrees in the summer). In terms of lighting design, these data show that vertical sun angles cast light on horizontal surfaces while horizontal sun angles work better with vertical surfaces, especially in the winter.

Wright understood the impact of the building's context on lighting design. As such, his composition for Annie Pfeiffer Chapel in Florida and the Unitarian Meeting House in Wisconsin addresses the sun angles of their respectful locations. The chapel in Florida is based on horizontal lines and includes upper horizontal windows on both sides of the chapel, while the prow of the Unitarian Meeting House in Wisconsin is vertical, capturing the light and reflecting it on to the high ceiling.[23]

The type of glass used in a sacred building's openings is also influenced by the building's context. Wright carefully selected his projects' glass and translucent exterior building materials (Aitken 1998). This selection reflected the light quality he intended to provide for the building's sacred ambience (see section on Glass later in this chapter).

Windows

Wright recognized the importance of a bright overhang and ceiling in reflecting daylight into the inner sacred space. He utilized the daylight penetration to a distance ratio rule of thumb: 2–2.5 times the height of the window (Aitken 1998: 9). As such, in his sacred buildings, he placed most of the windows at the top of the walls.[24] This placement is close to bright ceilings or skylights as well as to exterior cantilevers or eaves. Therefore, the upper windows transmit the reflected daylight deep into the inner space of the building (for examples see Unity Temple in Illinois, Ann Pfeiffer Chapel and the Minor Chapel in Florida, Annunciation Greek Orthodox Church in Wisconsin, and Community Christian Church in Missouri).

Wright's windows were usually protected either by a roof overhang, a projected cantilever, or a deep balcony (see Unity Temple, Illinois; Unitarian Meeting House, Wisconsin, and Ann Pfeiffer Chapel and the Minor Chapel in Florida). These structural features provide shade; glare protection; as well as reflect light. They create a "glow". In some of his designs, Wright enhanced this effect by using a brightly painted floor, which reflected light upward (e.g., Unitarian Meeting House, Wisconsin; Minor Chapel, Florida, and the Pilgrim Congregational Church, California). He also utilized interior features such as trim and furniture to reflect and bounce light toward the core of the sacred space. These techniques create a dramatic play between light and shadow, which elevates the worshiper's spirit toward God: "They shine through the darkness, a light for the upright; they are glorious, merciful and just" (Psalm 112: 4). This dramatic play is featured in all of Wright's houses of worship. For example, in the Unitarian Meeting House in Wisconsin, "The interior space expands from the darker interior of the building toward the light that bursts through full-height windows at both sides of the pulpit" (Hamilton 1990: 183), highlighting the altar/pulpit area as the focal point of the church (Figs. 3.8.4 and 4.13.1).

Another well-known example is Unity Temple in Illinois. There, huge concrete cantilevers on all four sides of the temple protect the upper windows. They shade the windows, control glare, and act as light shelves. They reflect the light through the windows up toward the skylight ceiling and then back down to the main floor of the temple. The light from the windows and skylight balance one another (Figs 1.4 and 3.4.4). The windows, which are located on all four sides of the temple, enable different light penetrations at each hour of the day. The exterior columns supporting the temple's roof create interesting shadows on the windows (Fig. 4.12.4).

4.12.4

The Shadows of the Exterior Columns on the Upper Windows of Unity Temple, Illinois.

Wright's lighting design techniques using window design can be observed in a host of his religious projects. In the following sections I analyze some of these examples.

The repetitive upper square windows of the Pettit Memorial Chapel in Illinois face north, east, and south (Figs 3.6.25 and 4.9.1). These windows are made of thick, opaque glass decorated with a gilded square frame (Fig. 2.1.5). Their design controls direct sunlight penetration and glare creating a soft light in the chapel. In addition, the obscured view to the outside adds to the spiritual relationship between the interior space and its exterior surroundings. The huge overhang eaves that extend the rooflines both protect and shade the strip of the upper windows while serving as an external shelf that reflects light back on to the bright ceiling of the chapel (Fig. 4.12.5). The reflected light is diffused through the opaque glass, enhancing the feeling of holy mystery in the edifice (Fig. 4.9.1). The shading effect reduces sunlight penetration and helps control glare.

4.12.5
The Huge Overhang Eaves of the Pettit Memorial Chapel, Illinois.

In the Unitarian Meeting House in Wisconsin and the Minor Chapel in Florida, we find an enormous overhang that extends the rooflines and protects the windows and walls beneath it. In both houses of worship a glass wall is designed at the edge of the prow, behind the pulpit area. In both buildings, Wright used additional side windows as sources of light and various bright surfaces to reflect this light. These measures balance the light penetrating from the glass wall and soften the light ambience of these sacred buildings.

In the Unitarian Meeting House, morning light penetrates the space from the east on one side of the clear glass wall, while late afternoon light arrives from the west. This creates different qualities of light throughout various parts of the day. The temporal light entering the sacred space links the

4.12.6

The Glass Wall of the Sanctuary of the
Unitarian Meeting House, Wisconsin.

worshiper to the sky as well as to changes in time. Wright blocked the
potential glare of this glass wall by enclosing the glass in two-inch by
twelve-inch louvers and angling it at a 25 percent slant (Fig. 4.12.6), and by
shading the glass with the roof's huge overhang. This overhang also serves
as a light shelf and helps to control the glare.

Wright balanced the light entering through this glass wall using a combination of techniques. First, he designed bright painted walls and a rail
on the church's mezzanine to face the glass wall (Fig. 4.12.7). Light
bounces from the walls and the rail's surface into the edifice. A reflective
floor and pieces of furniture also enhance the quality of light in the edifice.
The second technique was Wright's use of wide glass entrance doors as
an additional light source. The doors are protected by the low roof's huge
eaves (Fig 3.6.10). Thus, light bounces back to the space from the roof's
bright surface.

4.12.7

The Unitarian Meeting House,
Wisconsin: the Church's Mezzanine
and Entrance.

In the Minor Chapel in Florida, light quality is particularly enchanting during sunset, when light filters in through a stained glass wall located in the prow of the chapel (Fig. 2.1.1). The wall's stained glass enhances the light's expression of spirituality while minimizing glare. The light also reflects into the space off the bright surface of the roof's huge overhang. This design allows light entering through the stained glass wall to reach deeper into the inner space. In addition, the light bounces off the bright upper gallery's rail (a plastered wall), the whitewashed interior columns, the benches, and the bright red painted floor (Fig. 4.12.8). To balance this effect, Wright also utilized light streaming through the sides' upper windows (Fig. 4.12.9).

4.12.8
The Minor Chapel, Florida: the Bright Upper Gallery's Rail (a Plastered Wall), The White-Washed Interior Columns, and the Brightly Painted Floor.

4.12.9
The Sides' Upper Windows of the Minor Chapel, Florida.

Although Wright's proposal for the Rhododendron Chapel in Pennsylvania was crafted as a "mountain of light" design, he also included diamond-shaped side windows, which allowed light into the interior's ground level pierced stone walls (Fig. 3.4.11). The overhanging roof was designed to shade these windows and serve as a light shelf. The crystal-shaped windows, which would capture a spectrum of sunlight colors, were meant to diffuse "soft" light into the space. The concept of diamond-shaped windows was reused on a larger scale in Wright's design of the Trinity Chapel in Norman, Oklahoma. In that proposal, Wright set the large windows on each side of the building (Fig. 2.1.4). Natural light would pour through these large windows and be filtered through the proposed stained glass.

Wright used a different approach to window design in the Pilgrim Congregational Church in California and in the First Christian Church in Arizona. In his design of the First Christian Church in Arizona, the envelope of the building is a clear glass wall with operable openings. The Pilgrim Congregational Church in California uses a clear glass wall on only one side of the building's envelope (west side), and an east wall clerestory, which was later replaced with stained glass windows and roofed over. In both churches, light penetrates from the sides of the edifice and washes over the prayer hall. The structural elements cast shadows around the glass wall and enhance the spirituality inspired by this light.

Skylights

In addition to Wright's technique of using high placed windows that are protected by overhangs (eaves, cantilevers), he also designed skylights. Two examples are Unity Temple in Illinois and Annie Pfeiffer Chapel in Florida. The light entering through the buildings' skylights balances the light entering from the high-placed windows. The skylights create an atrium that allows daylight to penetrate deep into the core of the sacred space. The skylight of Wright's Larkin Building in Buffalo, New York (1902) is cited for "its pioneering contribution to the rediscovery of glass-topped, enclosed atrium[s and] for bringing useable daylight deep into the interior of the building" (Aitken 1998: 13). This solution influenced Wright's design of the skylight in Unity Temple in Illinois (1906). In the temple, Wright designed a double roof comprising an exterior clear glass pitched roof and an interior amber-tinted flat skylight ceiling (Fig. 2.1.6). This double roof, which covers the entire prayer hall, filters the light into the space. The painted glass contributes to the diffusion process and controls the glare. Moreover, the amber color of the glass creates a warm and inviting light. It introduces a soft distribution of light throughout the interior and creates a natural glow, which enhances the concept of "holy" light in the Temple. This effect highlights the Unitarian belief in unity through simplicity and solidarity. The use of equally distributed light also reinforces Wright's democratic and Unitarian ideals that congregation members should be able to see one another and unite in their faith.

Unlike the brightly lit edifice, the design of the galleries around it created dark spaces beneath the mezzanine floor. Wright's attempt to provide light in these areas from slit windows on the sides of the galleries (Figs 1.4, 4.9.5, and 4.11.2) did not create functional light (e.g., reading, seeing, safety). Therefore these areas had to be illuminated with electrical lights (Figs 1.4 and 4.12.21). Still, the electric light technology of the Temple's time of design did not provide enough watts for functional lighting.

Wright created a dramatic game of light and shadow with the skylight's clear glass in Annie Pfeiffer Chapel in Florida. Moving slowly, sunlight streams through the bell tower above the skylight and highlights the chapel's rostrum (Siry 2004: 518) (Figs 1.5 and 3.4.5). Although this effect enriched the ambience in the church, it also interrupted services as the congregation moved into shade and cooler areas of the hall (MacDonald et al. 2007: 28).[25] The four small skylights flanking the central one (two are located above the west balcony, and the other two above the choir loft) were covered from beneath (Fig. 1.5). Figure 1.5 illustrates the use of electrical lighting in place of natural light in these covered skylight areas to supplement the overall light quality of the chapel. In addition, Wright designed concrete planters to be used for hanging plants inside the Annie Pfeiffer Chapel tower. These plants would filter some of the Floridian sun-glare (see Chapter 14 on Thermal Comfort). The proposed vegetation was supposed to symbolize the Floridian outdoor garden while partially shading some of the skylight.[26]

In this chapel, the skylight serves as the focal light, illuminating the center of the church and its main stage. The area under the gallery at the back of the church is more dimmed. This area is surrounded by the chapel's perforated exterior walls, which are pierced with small colored glass squares (Figs 1.5 and 4.12.10). The effect of these glass pieces contributes to the holy atmosphere in the church and suggests a Gothic spirit of stained glass (see following section on Glass).

The special treatment of a skylight as a focal point can be seen in the First Christian Church in Phoenix, Arizona (Figs 2.3.6 and 3.6.16). Although Wright provided upper side windows and an envelope of glass, the strength of the skylight as a focal point is its shape of triangular glass panels placed in triangular niches in the ceiling and the glass colors.

Wright designed a different skylight in the Community Christian Church in Missouri. This skylight is located above the altar area (apse) and filters in light that partially illuminates the altar (Fig. 4.12.11). The light penetrates the church's perforated pitched roof over that area (4.12.12). The light pattern creates a dramatic effect of light and shadow that accentuates the focal point of the cross on the wall, and enhances the spiritual ambience of the church. Although this lighting follows the traditional design of highlighting the church's apse, Wright still managed to bring light from all sides above the altar and not just the traditional light behind it.

4.12.10

The Perforated Exterior Walls, Pierced with Small Colored Glass Squares in the Background of Annie Pfeiffer Chapel, Florida.

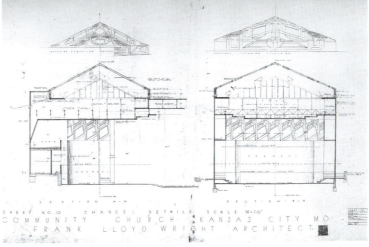

4.12.11 (left)

The Skylight Above the Altar of the Community Christian Church, Missouri.

4.12.12 (right)

The Skylight Drawings of the Community Christian Church, Missouri (© 2009 Frank Lloyd Wright Foundation, Scottsdale AZ/Artists Rights Society (ARS), New York).

Glass

The use of glass as a building material in Wright's sacred architecture is discussed in previous chapters of this book. In this section I examine glass as a lighting design technique in Wright's houses of worship. Wright's intricate use of clear glass in skylights and openings brought light into his buildings, symbolizing the presence of the Divine (e.g., Annie Pfeiffer Chapel, Florida; Unitarian Meeting House, Wisconsin; Pilgrim Congregational Church, California; First Christian Church, Arizona). The glass's translucence serves as a link between the earthly world and heaven as well as connects the church with Nature. In the above listed projects Wright provided additional devices (e.g., cantilevers, projected eaves) to shade the glass and control the glare. He also calculated the depth of these features to help reflect the light into the interior (see more in Chapter 14).

In other religious projects Wright introduced special patterns to the glass, enhancing the geometric motif of the whole house of worship (e.g., Unity Temple, Illinois; Kaufmann Family Chapel, Pennsylvania; Community Christian Church, Missouri). These patterns make the glass, the openings, and the light an integral part of the building.

In other houses of worship Wright used opaque glass (Pettit Memorial Chapel, Illinois), crystal diamond glass (Kaufman Chapel, Pennsylvania), or a combination of glass and other translucent materials (Beth Sholom Synagogue, Pennsylvania). Although these techniques provided a soft diffused light, they also obscured the nature of the glass and the link to the building's exterior.

Wright used painted or stained glass in some of his religious buildings to enhance the spirituality of the edifice (Unity Temple, Illinois; Annie Pfeiffer Chapel, Florida; Minor Chapel, Florida; Trinity Church, Oklahoma; First Christian Church, Arizona). Joseph Siry (2004: 524) claims that Wright's use of this type of glass evokes the cultural memory of stained glass in medieval architecture. Although stained glass may be perceived as a continuation of the spirit of Gothic cathedrals, Wright departed from traditional glass illustrations of Bible stories and used patterns of Nature (e.g., botanical forms, autumn colors) and geometry (derivations from the building's grid). As described before, only in his windows of the Annunciation Greek Orthodox Church in Wisconsin did he include faith symbols. Still, Wright departed from traditional Gothic-style stained glass and created these windows with clear glass that included abstracted patterns of saints (Fig. 4.10.2). In addition, when using colored glass, he always combined the color of the glass with generous amounts of clear opaque glass rather than following the Gothic all-colored glass design. An example of this is the stained glass wall and side upper stained glass windows of the Minor Chapel in Florida (Figs 2.1.1 and 4.12.9).

Floating Roof

To enhance his lighting design's sense of spirituality, Wright's sacred work often included an illusion of a floating roof above the building's walls.[27] This illusion was achieved through the manipulation of light and shadows (Scully 1996: 16; Joncas 1998a: 102). The effect lightens the tint and material of the roof, creating a greater sense of vertical movement in the house of worship. In other words, it enhances the *axis mundi* of the sacred space.

The light from the skylight and the upper windows on all four sides of Unity Temple in Illinois creates the illusion that the temple's concrete roof and its large overhangs are floating over the walls (Figs 1.4 and 3.4.4). This effect draws the worshipers' eyes upward, intensifying their spiritual experience. It also lights and celebrates the architectural features of the temple.

Each of the five small domes of Wright's 1945 design proposal for the Daphne Funeral Chapels in San Francisco, California, rests on a ring of arched openings (Fig. 3.4.13). This creates the visual illusion that the domes are lighter, floating above the main sacred space. When inside the chapel, this effect would evoke an impression of heavenly light, appropriate for a sacred funeral chapel.

Similarly, the shallow dome of the 1956 Annunciation Greek Orthodox Church in Wisconsin rests on arched ribs that provide a ring of light (Fig. 2.3.15). This effect projects an illusion of a floating dome, and resembles the ring of light created by the forty windows pierced in Hagia Sophia's shallow dome, built in the sixth century in Constantinople.[28] In addition, the natural light pouring into the Greek Orthodox Church illuminates the gold luster ceiling and the icon screen. The light bounces off the ceiling and creates a vision of heaven's dome. This effect resembles the original gilded mosaic ceiling of Hagia Sophia's dome, generating the holy atmosphere of the sacred building.

Similarly, the first alternative of Frank Lloyd Wright's 1957 proposal for the Wedding Chapel in California included a shallow dome resting on arched ribs that create a ring of light (Fig. 3.6.4). The pagoda-like roof of the second alternative of Wright's 1957 proposal for the Wedding Chapel in California also seems to float above the building (Fig. 1.7). The bent strip of upper windows allows light from all directions to enter the chapel, creating the floating illusion. The shape of the roof and its eaves, if built, would have added to this illusion while shading the upper windows and controlling for glare.

The stipple-like roof of Wright's 1958 proposal for the Trinity Church in Oklahoma also appears to float above the four triangular bases (Fig. 2.1.4). Huge diamond-shaped windows pierce the pyramidal roof, which leans on the four tips of the massive triangles below it. If built, the church would have been lit from all four sides – creating a special holy light in its sanctuary, and strengthening the worshipers' spiritual experience. In conjunction with its stained glass windows, the design produces the image of a lit roof soaring to heaven.

These examples of Wright's "floating" roofs are also augmented by external lights, which artificially add to the buildings' verticality.

Artificial (Electric) Light

Wright introduced innovative artificial (electric) lighting and light fixture designs as an integral part of his houses of worship. As mentioned before, he was one of the first architects in Chicago to utilize electricity in 1906 as part of his design of Unity Temple.

Wright aimed to complement natural light in darker areas during the day, and to provide the same interior atmosphere during the night as during the day. Still, he emphasized that artificial lighting should be designed "after the building has been properly oriented" for natural light, and to complement daylight (Wright 1954:155).[29] In addition, he worked with external light to illuminate both the sacred path and the worship building itself during the evening/night. This illumination fulfills some of the task lighting for both safety and seeing the way, and also caters to the spiritual tasks of light adding to the mysterious game of light and darkness. Furthermore, in some of his religious buildings Wright designed the light to radiate out of the building at night. With this idea he established his sacred building as a beacon of light to serve as the center of a community.

(a) Interior Artificial Lighting

Wright acknowledged that his holistic design of light fixtures was influenced by the auditorium designs of Adler and Sullivan, "where the electrical lights became features of the plaster ornamentation. The lights were not incorporated, but they were provided for in the decoration as accents of that decoration" (Wright 1928a/1992: 196). This idea is expressed in all of Wright's houses of worship, as the light fixtures are part of the building's ambience or absorbed in it (Wright 1908/1992: 87). "Then, too, there is the lighting fixture, made a part of the building. No longer an appliance nor even an appurtenance, but really architecture" (Wright 1928c/1992: 296). Indeed these fixtures were an integral part of the building's grid and geometric units, and express the sacred form of his projects.

In Unity Temple in Illinois, Wright provided a variety of fixtures, such as larger hanging lamps of both circular and square shapes near the four major columns (Fig. 3.5.5). In addition, he included small, square-shaped background lights in the galleries (Figs 1.4 and 4.12.21). The latter serve as complementary light since the areas beneath the galleries are darker than the central prayer hall. Both light fixtures refer to universal faith symbols – square as earth and reality, and circle as the symbol of heaven (see Part 2 on Faith).

Wright preached that artificial lighting should "come from the same source as natural light" (Wright 1954: 155). He purported that "artificial lighting shone from the same place there at night as well" (Wright quoted by Larkin and Pfeiffer 1993: 70). This concept may be interpreted in two ways. First, light fixtures should be placed in the same area as the daylight source; second, where openings bring light in during the day, so they can let light out during the night, and thus help the sacred building become a beacon of light. These concepts link light fixtures with the *axis mundi* of the sacred space. Examples include the vertical fixtures in Unity Temple, Illinois (Fig. 3.5.5) and in the Annunciation Greek Orthodox Church, Wisconsin (3.8.6).

An additional example is Beth Sholom Synagogue's major triangular chandelier, designed by Wright. It hangs from the translucent ceiling of the sanctuary that provides natural light during the day (Fig. 2.3.9). In addition to representing Jewish Kabalistic characteristics of God (see Part 2 on Faith), this chandelier enhances the vertical aspect of the space. For background lights, Wright installed small triangular spotlights in niches in the ceiling (Fig. 1.13). As part of the triangle grid of the structure and its association with sacred meanings, Wright designed triangle-shaped light fixtures in other parts of the synagogue, such as in the lobby entrance and in the Sisterhood Chapel (Fig 2.2.2). It is interesting to note that a square-based vertical lamp was designed by Wright and placed in the lobby of the synagogue to light a square planter that is located under one of the triangular wall light fixtures (4.12.13). This lamp bounces incandescent light off wood slates and off the wall behind it. The original design of this light fixture was a suspended fixture for a theater. It was later adapted into several variations and placed in both secular and sacred buildings. This square fixture and the planter seem foreign in the building (although a square may be viewed as two triangles). At night light shines out of the synagogue as illustrated by Wright in a sketch (Fig. 1.14).

4.12.13
A Square-based Vertical Lamp was Designed by Wright and Placed in the Lobby of the Sisterhood Chapel of Beth Sholom Synagogue, Pennsylvania.

The Sisterhood Chapel of Beth Sholom Synagogue was designed as a praying hall underneath the major edifice, in the lower part of the synagogue. As such, there are no openings in the chapel, and no natural light source. Wright used artificial light in the chapel and designed the lighting much like daylight design. He used multiple sources of light such as wall and ceiling fixtures. He mimicked a skylight by creating a niche in the ceiling above the *bima*. This niche serves as a light shelf for the artificial light that is incorporated into it (Figs 2.3.11 and 4.12.14). The light is reflected to the ceiling and then bounces down to the holy area of the Ark. Wright's light fixture for the eternal light (*Ner-Tamid*) hangs in the middle of this artificial skylight and serves as its focal point (Fig. 2.3.10).[30]

4.12.14
An Artificial Skylight in the Sisterhood Chapel of Beth Sholom Synagogue, Pennsylvania (note the triangular-shaped light fixtures).

The ceiling light fixtures of Annie Pfeiffer Chapel in Florida were installed close to the exterior walls and in the same position of the walls' small painted glass squares (Fig. 4.12.10). It should be noted that they create better functional light at night than the dimmed natural light during the day. They also serve as complementary lights when it is cloudy outside and the areas under the balcony become darker.

The clearstory windows were roofed over (1979). Light fixtures of the Pilgrim Congregational Church in California were installed in the ridge area of the ceiling and are not sufficient for functional lighting at night. For that reason, the congregation installed simple spotlights that were not part of the original design (Fig. 4.12.15).

As part of his environmentally conscious design and whenever possible, Wright designed the fixtures close to a vent, chimney, or the roof. In addition to creating surfaces to reflect or absorb some of the light, this design helps in venting the heat that is produced by these lights (Banham 1966/1981: 161).

(b) External Lights

Frank Lloyd Wright worked with external lighting to light the exterior parts of his sacred buildings and to radiate light from the interior out to the sky. In his 1940 design of the Community Christian Church (the Church of the Future) in Kansas City, Missouri, he created beams of light that would guide the community toward their worship building at night. More so, this light would literally and metaphorically serve as the center of their life. Wright proposed a perforated roof with eight 1000-watt floodlights, creating a steeple of light with 8000-candle power (Figs 3.4.3 and 4.12.12). In this project, Wright attempted to use the latest electrical lighting techniques to enhance the building's spiritual impact. Budget constraints, blackouts during World War II, trust issues with the client, and insufficient technology were the main reasons that Wright's proposal for the exterior lighting as a Christian metaphor was not realized. However, in December 1994, Dale Eldred and Roberta Ward installed a 1.2 billion candlelight beam, creating a "Steeple of Light" to illuminate the building and its surroundings, and realizing Wright's original idea (Fig. 4.12.16).[31]

As described before, one of Wright's first sketches of Beth Sholom Synagogue in Pennsylvania illustrates his ideas of a sacred building as a beacon of light at night. Electric light beams radiate out of the synagogue's interior through its translucent pyramidal roof. The beams light the synagogue and its surroundings. At night, they showcase the synagogue as the center of the community. It is interesting to note that the translucent pyramidal roof, the source of light during the day, turns out to be the source of light during the night.

In the First Christian Church in Arizona, the exterior lighting on each of the fluted columns illuminates the exterior of the building and the path around it (Fig. 2.3.5). This light deepens the symbolism of the worship center. In the first month of the building's occupation, this lighting system, executed in the 1970s following Wright's lighting design and ideas on the spiritual symbolism of light, won a National Lighting Prize. The lighting creates the same interplay of light and darkness during night-time and daytime (Fig. 4.12.17). In addition, at night, the light that radiates out from the skylight, and the light that shines from the glass in the spire on top of the roof create an illusion of a burning torch (Figs 3.6.16 and 3.6.17). This feature brings us back to the idea that humans need a glimpse of fire (light) to relate to God – another spiritual meaning of light.

A more modest exterior light fixture design is found on the walls of the entrance path to Unity Temple in Illinois. Wright designed this light fixture out of metal and repeated the square pattern of the whole temple (Fig. 3.7.3). This light fixture projects from the exterior wall of the temple, and casts shadows on that wall during the day. At night, the light bounces off the wall to light the path.

4.12.15
The Ceiling Light Fixtures and Additional Spotlights in the Pilgrim Congregational Church, California.

4.12.16
The "Steeple of Light" on top of The Community Christian Church, Missouri (1994).

As stated at the beginning of this chapter, Wright's approach to lighting design was a sophisticated use of multiple sources of natural and electric light. This design made "light blend the building into place with the creation around it" and enhances the sacred space (Wright quoted in Aitken 1998).

As a summary of this approach, I examine in detail Wright's lighting design in Unity Temple, Illinois. This investigation includes digital light simulation and an analysis of the results along the accepted IES lighting design standards for houses of worship.

The selection of Unity Temple for this summary is based on three facts: (a) this is one of Wright's religious buildings that include both the pragmatic and spiritual aspects of his lighting design. Therefore, it can serve as a showcase of his use of multiple light sources and lighting techniques; (b) Unity Temple (1906) was one of Wright's first buildings to include the innovative technology of electrical light and designed light fixtures; and (c) the Unitarian faith is a set of beliefs that stand for unity with no hierarchy, no doctrine, no dogma, and no ultimate religious authority. Therefore, no restrictions are set for church design, and Wright was supported in his experimentation with new forms and innovative technologies such as light.

Wright's Treatment of the Holy Light in Unity Temple

Wright carefully manipulated sunlight through multiple sources to create a natural glow in Unity Temple. As shown before, Wright's techniques to admit daylight into the temple included upper clear glass windows on all four sides of the building, which act like clerestories; slit windows positioned in four corners of the building; and an amber-tinted skylight that distributes even, diffused, soft light into the auditorium. The double glass roof and the tinted glass control the glare in the building. Four large cantilevers shade the upper windows and also control the glare. These cantilevers also act as light shelves reflecting light through the windows to the skylight and down to the ground level of the edifice.

The balanced light from all of these sources filters through the windows and skylight providing the warm tones of sunlight (Kaufman and Raeburn 1960: 78; Larkin and Pfeiffer 1993: 70). In addition, as glare is controlled, the light penetrates deeper and reaches the core of the edifice. Wright also introduced artificial lighting as part of his holistic design and created a daylight ambience at night. The artificial lighting also complemented the natural light during the day in darker areas of the temple, though, due to the limited technology at the time of construction (1906), there was not enough task light (e.g., reading) in these areas (e.g., lower galleries).

To supplement the observations of Wright's design of both task and spiritual lighting in Unity Temple, I evaluated his application of the described lighting techniques in the temple employing computerized lighting simulation software (*Lightscape*). The simulation focused on his original treatment of natural and artificial light design (50 lumen for the lamps).

Lightscape[32] is an advanced lighting and visualization application founded on a physically established simulation of the propagation of light through space (Autodesk 1999). Based on a description of light arriving at a surface, local illumination algorithms portray how individual surfaces reflect or transmit light. Then, the application can predict the intensity, spectral character (color), and distribution of the light leaving that surface. To achieve more accurate images, the program's global illumination algorithms use a combination of ray-traced and radiosity images to render the transfer of light between surfaces in the model. While the ray-tracing algorithm is used for accurate rendering of direct illumination, shadow, specular reflections (e.g., mirrors), and transparency effects, the radiosity calculates the intensity for discrete points in the environment (Autodesk 1999). Integrating both techniques of ray-tracing and radiosity, the simulation results portray highly realistic renderings with accurate measurements of the distribution of light within the scene (Geva and Mukherji 2007, 2009).

To run the program, a three-dimensional Computer Aided Design (CAD) solid walls model of the temple's interior was created and imported into *Lightscape*. Then the model was assigned materials, texture, and physical parameters (such as color transparency, shininess, refractive index), openings, and lighting systems. The lighting systems were defined according to a geographical location, date, time, and sky conditions. The simulations were run on the interior horizontal and vertical surfaces on three time frames (9 a.m., 11 a.m., and 6 p.m.) during the summer and winter solstices (June 21 and December 21 respectively). The surfaces included the floors of the main area and the lower gallery, and the benches on the main floor and the lower and upper galleries. The light on these benches was analyzed in three positions: front, middle, and back of the benches on the east and west sides of the temple to capture the morning and evening light. The vertical surfaces included the pulpit and three walls of the upper and lower galleries.

The output of the solution files consists of a lighting analysis and single images (Fig. 4.12.18), and data for animations such as walk-through images (Fig. 4.12.19). In addition, these analyses display the different ratios of the average, minimum, and maximum values of light. These three ratios are used in conjunction with the average values to roughly measure the uniformity of the distribution of light over a selected surface. Factors such as illuminance, luminance ratios, visual comfort, reflected glare, disability glare, veiling reflections, color, and shadows were used for the illumination considerations.

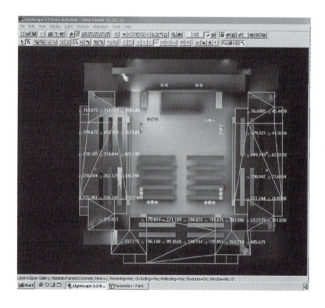 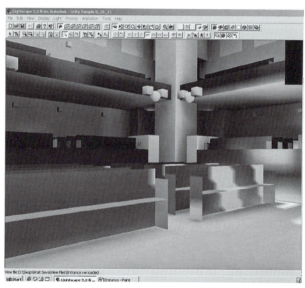

The results of the *Lightscape* simulations illustrate the average lux[33] of the three time frames during summer and winter solstices in different parts of the temple. The findings of the pulpit area simulation show that on both dates the maximum amount of light on the pulpit is at 11 a.m. (6448 lux on June 21, and 3874.85 lux on December 21), with an average of 2977 lux on June 21, and 1442 lux on December 21. The pulpit area appears to be the most lit in relation to other parts of the temple. The main floor results are 809 lux in June and 186 lux in December; the lower gallery floor has 499 lux in June and 226 lux in December. In the summer, the average light on the three walls of the upper gallery read 839 lux, 887 lux, and 1326 lux respectively. In the winter, these walls are lit with 845 lux, 630 lux, and 419 lux respectively. These findings demonstrate Wright's intention to

4.12.18 (left)

Lightscape Simulation: Single Image of Lighting Analysis of Unity Temple, Illinois.

4.12.19 (right)

Lightscape Simulation: Lighting Analysis on 3-D Model of Unity Temple, Illinois for Animations.

focus on the pulpit surface by washing it with light values (Figs 4.12.20 and 3.6.14) that are larger than any other areas in the temple, and to leave the rest of the areas gradually darker (Fig. 4.12.19). While the latter figure illustrates the digital results of the light simulation, Figure 1.4 shows today's actual light in the temple, and Figure 3.6.14 zooms in on the lit pulpit area. Although Wright's design of Unity Temple departed from conventional church design, this finding of his treatment of light follows the tradition of highlighting the altar/pulpit area as the focal point of a church.

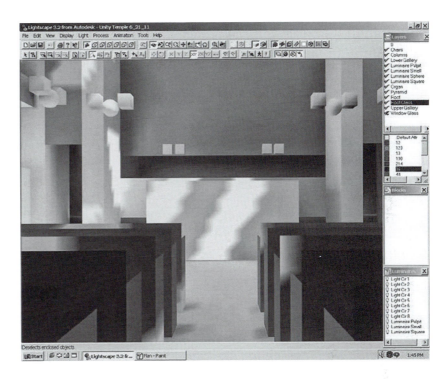

4.12.20

Lightscape Simulation: The Pulpit Surface of Unity Temple, Illinois Washed with Light.

To strengthen the findings that the pulpit area in Unity Temple is more lit than other parts of the temple, and to evaluate the task lighting (e.g., reading the Scriptures, seeing the members of the congregation all around, and fulfilling safety issues), the simulations were run on the benches in different parts of the temple. The results show that the climax of light penetrating the temple is at 11 a.m. on both the summer and winter dates. Since this time still includes the morning light from the east, the light simulations were run on benches in the front of the main floor on the east side of the temple. The results of these simulations show that this area is indeed much more lit (27,017 lux on June 21) than the west side bench area (2764 lux on the same date). The same trend appears in the winter, but with much less light (1748 lux in the front of the main floor on the east side vs. 740 lux in the front of the main floor on the west side). In addition, the front benches on the main floor are more lit than other benches in the temple at the same time. As we move away from the main floor to the galleries, the bench areas become darker, except for the front row benches on the east side of the upper gallery, which are exposed directly to light from above. The benches on the lower gallery are almost without any light on June 21 at 11 a.m., though there is some low light at 9 a.m. and at 6 p.m. On December 21, light on these benches is minimal at 9 a.m., more light appears at 11 a.m., and the benches are in almost complete darkness at 6 p.m. The latter is fitting with the temple's location and its sun angles and early sunset in winter. Moreover, we should take into consideration that at the beginning of the twentieth century, the lamps Wright installed on the back wall of the galleries were small with very low capacity for illumination.

To validate the simulations results, Wright's lighting design of Unity Temple was analyzed along the four recommended light design strategies of the *Illuminating Engineering Society* (IES) standards for houses of worship. Then the values obtained from the lighting simulations of Unity Temple were compared to the quantitative IES standards.[34]

The first IES recommendation of task lighting was partially achieved in Unity Temple. Parts of the temple were too dark for reading even with the slit vertical windows and the background light fixtures. Wright fulfilled the second IES strategy of accent lighting by highlighting the pulpit as the temple's focal point. Wright's interplay of light/shadow, the highlight of the pulpit, and the shapes of the light fixtures fulfilled the third lighting design criterion of architectural lighting. Finally, Wright's design of the illusion of the floating roof, and the glowing soft light, achieved the fourth IES recommendation of celebration light. These findings augment the previous described observations and demonstrate that Wright's treatment of light in Unity Temple fully achieved three aspects of lighting design, focusing more on the spiritual aspects of light in houses of worship; and partially fulfilling the function/task criterion of these standards, since parts of the temple are too dark for reading, seeing, and safety by today's standards.

In addition to the four major IES guidelines for houses of worship lighting, the IES establishes quantitative standards, which are 100 lux for task purposes, such as reading, and, 300 lux for accent lighting,[35] and 25 lux for architectural lighting, which illuminates the sanctuary and its symbols, and enhances the dramatic spiritual effect of light.[36] The results of the simulation analyses show that on average Wright's lighting design in Unity Temple achieved more than the recommended current IES standards, except for the lighting over the benches in the back of the lower gallery.

To overcome the functional lighting deficiency, over time, larger watt light bulbs replaced the originals. The larger watt bulbs doubled the heat, causing some of the original light fixtures to deform or melt. Accordingly, new replicas of Wright's light fixtures had to be installed. Although this solution solved the functional task lighting problem and demonstrated an attempt to maintain Wright's original design, the space is still much more lit, and has lost some of the original dramatic effect of the interplay of light and shadow (Figs 1.4, 3.5.5 and 4.12.21). Therefore, there is less focus on the pulpit's light.

4.12.21
The Natural and Artificial Light in the Galleries of Unity Temple, Illinois.

The dilemma between current functional lighting needs and the original lighting intentions of the architect is part of recent discussions on the preservation and restoration of historic houses of worship that need an upgrade in their lighting system.

In summary, this chapter demonstrates that Frank Lloyd Wright understood lighting concepts and light's spiritual aspects. Lighting design was part of his belief that design and systems should be driven by beauty and truth. Therefore, his design was based on "true light", which in his view was the inner light. His design of light in his sacred architecture aimed to evoke this light, to enhance the building's *axis mundi*, and to connect the worshiper with the Divine. Although his approach was not one of an engineer, this chapter demonstrates that Wright's lighting design can comply with today's most effective techniques of daylight use. His innovative integration of electrical light, his utilization of the best available technology of his time, and his imagined plan for future lighting design beyond the available technology, demonstrate Wright's creativity in using all spiritual aspects of light in his religious structures.

Chapter 13

Acoustics

[M]usic is the language beyond words – of the human heart. The symphony . . . is an edifice of sound.

(Wright 1932a/1977)

The poetic link that scholars observe between construction materials and nature repeats itself in the relationship between music and nature. Elizabeth Hale (2007: 49–50) states: "Nature is a living music scroll, continuously changing and revealing itself. Its pattern is like notes on a page revealing the music within." Joan Halifax (1993: xv) adds, "Each place has a voice. Sending a voice, a voice responds." Wright is part of this choir, claiming that Nature is a visible song (Wright 1932a/1977: 325).

In various cultures all over the ancient world, music was viewed as part of Nature and early teachings (Andrews 2007: 3). Ancient civilizations such as the Egyptians, Greeks, East Indians, Chinese, Native Americans, and Pre-Columbian people all recognized that chant and music represent the voice of their land and elevate the individual and communal spirit to new heights while separating the individual from the mundane (Andrews 2007: 6–7; Hale 2007: 135).

Wright's key design concepts in his acoustic solutions were integrated into the whole design of his religious buildings. These solutions aimed to elevate the visitors' spirits to join the divine harmony.[37] Moreover, his acoustic designs were adapted to his contemporary design ideas, utilizing new and impressive solutions in his time's field of acoustics. Wright's human scale design, his use of appropriate finish materials in the interior of the sacred spaces, and his development of some acoustical methods may be considered as the major elements of his successful acoustic design.

His holistic approach to design crafted the building itself as an instrument of sound, a "kind of extended organ for the production of a sacred sound" (Kieckhefer 2004: 110). J.N. Comper (1947: 10) claims that "the note of a church should be, not that of novelty, but of eternity . . . producing the atmosphere of the heavenly worship". Richard Kieckhefer (2004: 111) interprets Comper's ideas as suggesting freedom from linear design and a particular timeline, i.e., a sense of timelessness. Wright's sacred architecture expresses and accommodates the free spirit of divine music.

Wright's harmonic design with Nature and its geometry and order fits the idea that music is a "science of proportion", which strives for "harmonic proportions on which the universe was thought to be organized" (Cirillo and Martellota 2006: 6). St. Augustine, the Bishop of Hippo (345–430 AD) linked Nature's harmony to music as the divine harmony. He believed that since music's rules are based on mathematics and geometry, they could be applied to visual arts and lift man's spirit in pursuit of divine harmony (Cirillo and Martellota 2006: 7). L.B. Alberti (1404–1472) stated that the very same rules (numbers) that cause sounds to please the ears "can also fill the eyes and mind with wondrous delight" (quoted by Cirillo and Martellota 2006: 8). Wright's wife, Oligivanna Lloyd Wright (1960: 189), described this same effect in Wright's sacred architecture. She wrote about the dedication ceremony of Wright's Beth Sholom Synagogue building in Pennsylvania, "The music of the organ rose to the pyramidal dome, descended and hovered over us. Such great beauty easily turns into pain. As the waves of sound kept rising and falling, some faces glistened with tears."

Indeed, Wright was fond of music and more than once compared his design to a musical composition. In his mind, his designs, like Beethoven's compositions, used repeating thematic motifs and variations on a theme. His use of pure geometrical modules and grid systems may be compared to a composer's use of time signature. His repeated use of decorative details resembles a musical composition's repeated notes: "the bar lines in music act much in the same way as the unit lines in an architectural plan"[38]. Wright's attention to the acoustic needs of his sacred buildings aimed to delight and move the congregations with music.

For example, in addition to a lecture by Wright on 'architecture and religion', the program of the opening ceremony of the Unitarian Meeting House in Wisconsin included a musical performance by Wright's daughter Iovanna on the harp, his grandson Eric on the flute, and the Taliesin Chorus (Hamilton 1991: 16). This event inspired Wright to add a sound baffle to the rostrum to improve the acoustics in the edifice accommodating both music and voice (Hamilton 1990: 182; 1991: 16). Wright acknowledged the power of resonance[39] as an essential component in acoustic design. According to Ted Andrews (2007: 8), resonance "designates the ability of a vibration to reach out through vibrational waves to set off a similar vibration in another body". Sarah Osmen (1990: 28) says that "with resonance the divine experience begins to enter the worshiper" and moves through "the interior of the body to resonate the interior of the building" (Hale 2007: 164).

The mutual relationship between architecture and music is expressed by an acoustic design that accommodates the sound of music. Alternatively, musicians adapt their work to the particular spatial conditions of the place of performance (Cirillo and Martellota 2006). This reciprocal relationship is also influenced by the size and shape of a space, the materials used, and by special acoustic features.

The challenge in acoustic design for houses of worship is finding the balance between the various sounds and silence requirements. A holy space is supposed to accommodate silence, the spoken voice, music (instrumental and/or choir), and chant. These various sounds, as required by different faiths and rituals, all call for different reverberation times that can express a building's resonance. However, these different functions create a conflict between resonance and clarity (e.g., intelligibility of speech) (Roberts 2004; Baumann and Niederstätter 2008; Addis 2009). In other words, these different sound requirements create a conflict between "live" and "dead" acoustics in a sacred space. "Live room" acoustics require a long reverberation that prolongs the sound in the room and helps create a louder effect for singing and organ music. Long reverberation time can enhance "the fluidity, the spontaneity, and the rhythmic unpredictability of sound" (Kieckhefer 2004: 111). However, it can also "degenerate into confusion as new notes interfere with the reflections of early ones" (Addis 2009: 6). "Dead room" acoustics create a short reverberation that enhances the quieter acoustics good for chamber music and speech. The balanced acoustics for a multi-use space should provide the ideal reverberation of two seconds (Roberts 2004: 191).[40]

During most of the nineteenth century, acoustic design followed the guidelines and written material of George Sounders and Ernst Florens Friedrich (Chladni). Sounders (1790) tested his ideas in real auditoria and summarized his observations in a set of recommendations for acoustic design. Chladni (1802) was the author of the first modern comprehensive book on acoustics (Addis 2009: 4). Their recommendations dealt mainly with the distance of the audience from the sound source. Seventy feet was the maximum suggested distance for an audience to still be able to hear sounds and see their source (the stage/pulpit). Other guidelines suggested the proportions and materials of a room, including some special design features such as rotating panels that can change the angles of the reflected sound (Addis 2009: 4). Considered "the father of architectural acoustics", Wallace Clement Sabine expanded on these observations using scientific experiments that were published in his book *Collected Papers on Acoustics* (1922). He established equations calculating the rate of reverberation decay measured in seconds. These guidelines served as the framework of the acoustic work in the Chicago Auditorium (1886–1890) by Dankmar Adler and Louis Sullivan.

Frank Lloyd Wright acknowledged that he learned the main traditional principles of acoustic design when he worked with Adler and Sullivan on that project:

I learned about acoustics from the old Chief . . . And Dankmar Adler invented, of course, the sounding board over the proscenium; and it was his theory that the trumpet was good for the pattern of the house . . . He [Adler] believed that the quicker you could kill the sound and the more instantaneously it was ended – the better the acoustics of the house.[41]

Dankmar Adler created innovative acoustic design measures to supplement the acoustics design guidance available in the 1830s. As an integral part of the interior fabric of the auditorium, he introduced sound boards in the shape of concentric elliptical arches to carry the sound (Wright 1932a/1977: 130). Adler's design of the ventilation system also carried sound and became a feature of the auditorium's acoustic design. He described them as "ornamented in relief, the incandescent electrical lamps and the air inlet openings of the ventilation system forming an essential and effective part of the decoration" (Adler 1892: 429). Working with Adler, Wright gained not only the technical experience of acoustic design, but was also exposed to a comprehensive approach to design, which he employed throughout his entire career.

Frank Lloyd Wright understood sound and silence as integral parts of a sacred space that enhance the sense of the ineffable and numinous: "the choir and the deep longing voice of the cantor resounded in the building [Beth Sholom Synagogue in Pennsylvania] like an echo from Mount Sinai" (O. Wright 1960: 190). Indeed, most of his religious buildings were designed with good acoustics catering to various faith requirements. Wright solved the acoustic conflict between music and speech in his religious buildings. His greatness was his ability to combine several of the available techniques, as recommended by the accepted rules and guidelines for acoustic design, with his new developments in this field. With this combination, he achieved a "divine harmony" and a "divine sound" in his religious projects.

Frank Lloyd Wright's Acoustic Design

In the following sections I describe some of Wright's original acoustic design methods that he implemented with no audio systems, and show their application in his sacred architecture. Since Wright did not detail much of his acoustic design, except for a hint on the final drawings for the Annie Pfeiffer Chapel in Florida, I do not claim to cover all of his acoustic design techniques in my following analyses.[42]

Size and Distance

Wright designed most of his houses of worship as multi-function spaces (e.g., religious services, lectures, concert recitals, and other performances). As such, he needed to overcome the acoustic conflict between music and speech. Wright attempted to avoid this conflict by designing relatively small houses of worship. He freed the prayer halls from structural obstacles that can obstruct the acoustic quality of a space. He placed the preacher/speaker/performer closer to the audience, and often elevated the stage and the pulpit. The latter design approach was derived from the human scale design of his religious projects and from his belief in the unity between clergy and congregation. It should be noted that this aspect of unity is fundamental to Protestant (especially Unitarian) and Jewish concepts. This demonstrates Wright's interwoven design concepts of faith, form, and building technology (see the book's conceptual model, Fig. 1.1).

Examples of this design approach include Wright's design of Unity Temple's edifice as a relatively small space that excluded structural components (a square of 64 feet in plan, with ceiling height of 47 feet). Consequently, the members are no more than forty feet from the pulpit, better than the recommended maximum distance of seventy feet (Fig. 3.5.1). These dimensions create better acoustic conditions for speech and chamber music. However, like the poor lighting conditions under the galleries in the back of the temple, sound is trapped in these dead zone areas. To overcome this effect, Wright elevated the temple's pulpit (Fig. 3.4.9). He used a balanced combination of materials to both move and absorb the sound-waves: concrete for reflectivity, glass for transmitting sound, and carpet and wood (benches, trim) for absorption.

In his larger religious projects such as the Annie Pfeiffer Chapel in Florida, and the Unitarian Meeting House in Wisconsin (Figs. 4.13.1), Wright designed the stage and pulpit closer to the audience, as part of the buildings' grid. This allows the performance to become part of the whole space. In Florida's Annie Pfeiffer Chapel, the triangular platform of the stage extends into the diagonally arranged audience seating and brings the performance out into the center of the chapel (Fig. 3.5.6). In addition, this arrangement allows the preacher to free himself from the confined space of a pulpit (Kieckhefer 2004: 215) and reach closer to the congregation.[43]

The distance of the audience from the stage/pulpit in the Annie Pfeiffer Chapel is shorter than the maximum recommended distance of seventy feet. Wright organized the seating so that "no one in the audience is more than fifty feet away from the rostrum" (Siry 2004: 509). In the renovations following the devastation by the 1944 hurricane, the chapel's number of seats was reduced and the stage jutted out even more. These measures improved the reverberation time in the chapel, enabling Wright to eliminate "Adler's proscenium" (the arch frame)[44].

4.13.1

The Pulpit/Stage of Unitarian Meeting House, Wisconsin.

The First Christian Church in Arizona is another example illustrating the distances between the audience and the stage/pulpit. The church has 700–800 seats located no further than eighty-three feet from the pulpit. Although this distance is rather longer than the recommended distance of seventy feet, the shape and materials of the hall compensate for it. The seating arrangements' angles allow the sound to bounce around the space but never directly back to its source. Moreover, the combination of hard construction materials (concrete and stone) and soft finish materials (plaster, carpet, upholstery) balance the reflectivity and absorbance of the sounds.

Materials

Different materials have different relations to sound. Hard and heavy materials such as concrete and stone absorb very little sound, meaning they are reflective materials. Softer materials, such as wood and plaster, absorb more sound, and therefore reduce the intensity of sound reverberation. Carpet is also considered a soft material that can improve the acoustics by absorbing some of the heavier sound reflections and "deaden[ing] the effect of footsteps" (Baumann and Niederstätter 2008: 57). Medium to soft materials such as porous materials, fabrics, and finish materials (plaster, wood veneer) balance the acoustic properties of a space and reduce high and medium frequencies.[45]

Frank Lloyd Wright understood the effect of materials on the quality of sound and tried to balance the various natures of reflective and absorbent materials in his sacred architecture. Most of his sacred interiors are plastered. As such, the plaster softens the heavy reflectivity from hard materials such as stone and concrete (see, e.g., the interior of Unity Temple). Wright used porous materials to achieve similar acoustic results in areas where plaster was not applied. For example, he used soft stone in the Unitarian Meeting House in Wisconsin (Fig. 4.13.2) and porous (organic) concrete blocks in Annie Pfeiffer Chapel in Florida (Fig. 4.9.3). The latter includes a two-inch air layer between the blocks (Fig. 4.9.4) to prevent the sound from escaping outside. This layer improves some of the acoustic quality in the dead zones of the areas encompassed by these blocks (see also the section on Sound Wells later).

4.13.2
The Porous Stone Walls of the sanctuary. Unitarian Meeting House, Wisconsin.

Wright utilized thermal insulation materials and air as part of his acoustic strategy. While Adler's acoustics design included thermal features (e.g., heating ducts) to carry the sound, Wright used thermal insulation and air either to absorb some of the sound or to block it from escaping the sanctuary. For example, Wright used thermal insulation in the dome ceiling of the Annunciation Greek Orthodox Church in Wisconsin. This material absorbs part of the sound and the reset is reflected to the space as an echo "from heaven". He used the air that is trapped between the double roof of Unity Temple in Illinois (an outside glass roof and an inside skylight) as an insulation layer for thermal purposes, but also to prevent sound loss through the glass of the skylight. In this context, the concrete beams of this skylight (Fig. 2.1.6) help save some of the sound and reflect part of it back to the audience below.

Wright's solution for some of the sound loss due to the glass envelope in the First Christian Church in Arizona was the placement of large and wide concrete columns in the periphery of the building. The columns' hard materials partially reflect the sound back. In Pilgrim Congregational Church in California, Wright blocked some of the potential sound loss through the church's glass wall by designing a wooden ceiling which absorbs most of the sound that is reflected from the hard materials in the church (concrete/stone walls in the apse and the concrete floor).[46]

In other sacred projects Wright designed polished painted concrete floors, which reflect sound just as they reflect light (see, e.g., the Unitarian Meeting House in Wisconsin; the Minor Chapel in Florida; the Pilgrim Congregational Church in California). He managed to balance this sound reflection with upholstered wood benches and other self-designed furniture. These soft materials, as well as human occupants, absorb some of the heavily reflected sounds. In other houses of worship, he used carpet to absorb the unwanted frequencies (see, e.g., Unity Temple in Illinois; First Christian Church in Arizona).

An additional acoustical feature that averts background noises is water. In his 1926 proposal for the Steel Cathedral in New York, Wright designed a sunken hexagonal pit that would hold a fountain throwing water 1000 feet high in the air. This feature was located at the center of the cathedral, uniting the different chapels under one roof. Guthrie, the client for the "Modern Cathedral", described this sunken center as an orchestra pit, praising its potential acoustics, which would create echoes that metaphorically lift the spirit toward heaven.[47] Wright illuminated the water, creating a reflection of countless colors, and used it as an acoustical material that averts background noises. Wright's use of water as an acoustic material was innovative for his time. Moreover, the hexagonal shape of the cathedral's base would allow the sound to bounce around the space, never directly reaching back to its source. This acoustic design proposal was appropriate for this huge cathedral and the amount of people who would circulate in the center of the all-faith building occupying the various chapels. The sounds from one chapel would not disturb the others, and the sounds from the center would not disturb the chapels around it.

Orientation

As described in Figure 1.1 and Figure 4.1, the location and time of a sacred building's construction directly impact on its acoustic design. Location is the source of background sounds, while time influences advancements in technology as well as the changes in background noise. Wright's acoustic design was attentive to background noise. He used the orientation of the building as a technique to decrease outside background noise. He placed the openings of the edifice in areas that are away from the source of noise. Unity Temple in Illinois, Annie Pfeiffer Chapel in Florida, and the Annunciation Greek Orthodox Church in Wisconsin all exemplify the combination of these techniques.

As described in previous chapters, Wright placed Unity Temple on a side street: "The site was noisy. Therefore it seemed best to keep the building closed on the three front sides and enter it from a court to the rear at the center of the lot" (Wright 1932a/1977: 177–184).[48] Wright designed upper windows (clearstories) in the temple that partially block the outside noises.[49] He located the pulpit of the temple at the entrance side of the edifice to be "entirely cut off from the street" (Wright 1932a/1977: 156). He oriented the entrance into the temple's edifice on each side of the pulpit on a lower level "so those entering would be imperceptible to the audience . . . This would preserve the quiet and dignity of the room itself" (Wright 1932a/1977: 156). In addition, he used carpet on the floor to control interior background noises.

In Annie Pfeiffer Chapel in Florida, Wright designed the building with no openings on the ground level (except for the entrance doors). This design decision limited the outside world's interference in the sacred chapel, and blocked the background sounds. Similarly, the domical structure of the Annunciation Greek Orthodox Church in Wisconsin has minimal openings on the ground level. There is the entrance and a strip of arched windows at the top of the edifice. The high placement of these windows, and their close proximity to the insulated absorbent dome, blocks the outside background noise from reaching the audience below.

Latticed Screen Wall

Wright was introduced to the acoustics of the Japanese theater, where a latticed screen wall separates the musicians from the audience. The musicians are placed above and on the sides of the stage. Wright recognized the acoustic effects of this feature and reinterpreted it in his own innovative ways in some of his religious buildings.

He placed the organ pipes behind screen walls. The screen controls some of the echoes by absorbing some of the sound. Therefore, Wright designed these screens from the same medium-to-soft reflective materials that he used in other details of his sacred building. He designed such a screen out of wood for Unity Temple (Fig. 1.4). The wood is the same material used for the trim that decorates all parts of the temple. In addition to the wood's acoustic property, this design illustrates Wright's continuity of materials in his sacred design.

An additional example of having the organ pipes behind a screen wall is the vertical glass and stone screen at the Unitarian Meeting House in Wisconsin (Fig. 4.13.1). Wright built the sides of the screen with the same porous stone used for the whole structure and incorporated operable glass panels as a focal point in the prayer hall. The materials and form of the screen, and the pulpit in front of it, composes the screen as an integral part of the whole church. It should be noted that the porous stone partially absorbs sound. Thus, the organ music is heard in the hall as a balance between the sounds absorbed by these stone surfaces of the screen and the direct sounds coming from the openings in the screen. These openings can be controlled to partially block some of the echoes created behind the screen.

A second use of the lattice screen wall technique in Wright's sacred architecture was his design of a choir screen in Florida's Annie Pfeiffer Chapel choir loft. Since singing is part of the Methodist faith, the choir screen enhances the sound of the choir and organ while dispersing it throughout the edifice. Wright designed a ninety-foot latticed screen above the stage/pulpit, which runs across the mezzanine level (Fig. 4.13.3).

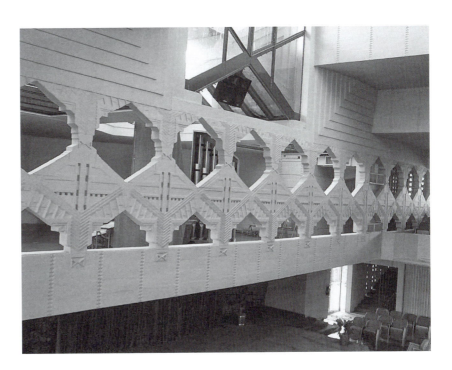

4.13.3
The Choir Screen in Annie Pfeiffer Chapel, Florida.

The design of the screen and its details are an integral part of the grid system of the entire building and corresponds to the same 30 to 60 degree angle of the chapel's plan (see Chapter 9). The screen acts in accordance with Wright's concept of continuity. Plaster was applied on the chapel's upper level's walls and the screen. The hard reflective material of the screen (concrete) is softened by the finish material of the plaster, which also balances the direct sounds from the openings in the latticed screen.

However, the quality of the acoustics of this choir screen was disturbed when air conditioning (AC) was installed in this Florida Chapel. Some of its units were placed behind the acoustic latticed screen (Fig. 4.13.4).

4.13.4
The AC Units Behind the Choir Screen
in Annie Pfeiffer Chapel, Florida.

Although the screen conceals the visual impact of the air conditioning units, their location contributes to the deterioration of the original acoustic quality of the space. To overcome this problem, the congregation installed an audio system. However, the goal of preserving the original architectural integrity was compromised with the location of the two speakers hanging above the screen (Figs 4.13.3, and top of Fig. 4.13.5).

The bell tower of Annie Pfeiffer Chapel in Florida represents another of Wright's uses of the lattice screen wall technique. In the tower, he used a vertical screen and utilized the structural bow-tie elements to screen the sound of the bells (Fig. 3.8.7). This interpretation of the lattice screen wall design shows Wright's ingenuity in combining the building's various systems into an integral part of the design. The sound of the bells was reflected from the concrete plastered walls of the tower and from the solid parts of the screen, while some of the sound poured directly out into the surroundings. Indeed, the bells were heard throughout the whole campus and neighboring areas. Although bell sounds symbolize the sacred aspects of the chapel, and its importance to the Methodist campus, their resonance was so loud that they had to eventually be taken down.

4.13.5
Speakers Hanging at the Top of the
Choir Screen in Annie Pfeiffer Chapel,
Florida.

Sound Wells

In some of Wright's houses of worship, he designed galleries above the rear of the main edifice (e.g., Unity Temple in Illinois; Annie Pfeiffer Chapel in Florida; Minor Chapel in Florida; Annunciation Greek Orthodox in Wisconsin). This design aspect was inspired by his ideas on unity, freedom, and democracy. He designed the galleries so that members of a congregation could see one another and their leader(s), and feel equal in front of each other. However, the areas beneath the galleries became dead zones with poor lighting and less than ideal acoustics. In the Annie Pfeiffer Chapel in Florida, Wright developed and used the technique of "sound wells" to prevent sound-waves from being trapped in these dead zones: "the oblong wells extend through the mezzanine floor and permit sound waves access to all parts of the building with clarity" (MacDonald et al. 2007: 18).[50] Wright designed four sound wells in this chapel, one at each section of the side balconies, and two at the back of the front gallery (Fig. 4.13.6). Fig. 3.6.2 illustrates a cross-section of Annie Pfeiffer Chapel, which includes vertical slots (i.e., "sound wells") that are open to the upper level at the rear of the main floor.

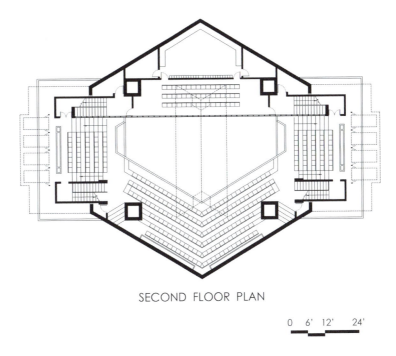

SECOND FLOOR PLAN

0 6' 12'   24'

4.13.6
The Plan of Annie Pfeiffer Chapel's Mezzanine (Galleries) Floor. Please Note the "Sound Wells" on Each of the Side Balconies and Two at the Back of the Front Gallery (redrawn under author's supervision).

The sound wells, in addition to the sound-proofing two-inch air space in between the concrete blocks at the periphery of these areas, provides good acoustic quality in all parts of the chapel. While the concrete blocks and the air layer between them prevent the loss of sound, the sound wells carry it upward and release the sound trapped in the rear areas beneath the galleries (Figs 4.13.7 and 4.14.2). With these techniques, Wright replaced the need for "Adler's proscenium" (the arch frame).

4.13.7
An Example of a "Sound Well" in
Annie Pfeiffer Chapel, Florida.

Once more, Wright's original acoustic design was compromised when air conditioning (AC) units were installed in the chapel. The bottom of the two sound wells near the balcony windows was blocked in order to place the AC units inside these vertical slots (Fig. 4.14.5). Although the use of these wells conceals the view of the AC units, the placement of the units deteriorated the original successful acoustics of the chapel, and adds noise to the space.[51] This conduct exemplifies the conflict of preservation of architectural integrity and innovative building technology, while introducing contemporary building systems. To overcome these acoustic deficiencies, contemporary audio systems were added (Figs 4.13.3 and 4.13.5). As discussed before, the placement of the system's speakers did not consider the original integrity of the chapel.

In summary, one may conclude that Frank Lloyd Wright recognized the ability of sound to lift the human soul and enhance the worshiper's spiritual experience. As such, and because of his love of music, he attempted to provide good acoustics in his sacred architecture. He realized the need to balance speech and music requirements in this type of building. He used techniques and methods that balanced live and dead acoustics creating long and short reverberations without unnecessary echoes. His ingenuity was his combination of the lessons he learned from precedence and the accepted and known guidelines for acoustic design. Furthermore, his ability to combine the conventional techniques of his time with his own innovations improved the acoustics in his houses of worship and helped worshipers hear the preacher and be embraced by the ritual's music. Out of all of the examples described in this chapter, Wright's acoustic design of the Annie Pfeiffer Chapel in Florida stands out and demonstrates his approach of combining several methods and techniques to provide the right acoustics for speech and music.

Although Wright's sacred places were praised for their good acoustics design[52] and show Wright's love for music, over the years sound systems were installed in most of his religious buildings. The plausible reasons for this conduct are related to modern times' advanced audio technology and fashion. One may also assume that these systems assist in helping the congregations' aging members to hear both speeches and music more clearly. At times, the audio systems were installed to overcome deficiencies in the acoustic quality due to the installment of air conditioning units in the buildings (see previous description of Annie Pfeiffer Chapel in Florida).

In some cases the speakers were designed and installed while maintaining the original architectural integrity of the house of worship. For example, in the Sisterhood Chapel of Beth Sholom Synagogue in Pennsylvania, the speakers' design follows Wright's triangular geometry of the building. They were placed in the corners of the ceiling in an attempt to blend with the triangular ceiling and the walls' triangular light lamps (Fig. 4.13.8). In the Pilgrim Congregational Church, California, the speakers were designed with the general motif of the church in mind and placed in a niche above the entrance to the edifice (Fig 4.13.9).

4.13.8
The Triangular-shaped Speakers at the Corner of the Sisterhood Chapel of Beth Sholom Synagogue, Pennsylvania, Blending with the Triangular Light Lamps.

4.13.9
The Speakers' Placement at a Niche Above the Entrance to the Edifice of the Pilgrim Congregational Church, California.

However, the placement of the speakers in Annie Pfeiffer Chapel in Florida compromises the historic integrity of the building and its acoustic quality. The speakers are placed at the skylight's top center, above the choir screen, interfering with the view of the tower above (Figs 4.13.5 and 4.13.3).

This chapter also describes acoustic design as a part of building technology that accommodates sacred ambience and enriches faith requirements. Like lighting design, sound (voice, music, silence) can elevate the spirit of a worshiper. Creating the "holy light" and the "divine music" brings the worshiper closer to God. Wright believed that the worshipers should have a comfortable environment in order to experience this spiritual sensation, which he believed would free their minds from physical constraints. In the next chapter I introduce Wright's environmentally conscious design and his application of it to his sacred architecture.

Chapter 14

Thermal Comfort

It [is] far better to go with the natural climate than try to fix a special artificial climate of your own, Climate means something to man.

(Wright 1954: 178)

The impact of climate on shaping built form has been recognized since ancient times. Vitruvius, a Roman architect from the first century BC, wrote (trans. 1960): "The style of buildings ought manifestly to be different in Egypt and Spain, in Pontus and Rome, and in countries and regions of various characters. For in one part the earth is oppressed by the sun in its course; in another part the earth is far removed from it; in another it is affected by it at a moderate distance." In modern times, scholars such as Fitch (1948, 1961), Olgyay (1963), Banham (1969), Rapoport (1969), Givoni (1976), and Lechner (2001) echo this ancient wisdom, and Rapoport concludes that "the impact of the climatic factor [on built form] will depend on its severity and forcefulness, hence the degree of freedom it allows" (Rapoport 1969: 83). In other words, in temperate areas, which offer a naturally favorable climate, there is a diversity and freedom in the form and style of structures, while in extreme climate conditions the climate becomes the primary factor in influencing architectural form. In addition, the influence of climate on design is also a function of building type (Geva 1995, 2002b). In Western culture, buildings serving functions that closely reflect culture, history, and heritage (such as houses of worship) are less influenced by the local climate than are residential houses, where the primary purpose is providing comfort (Geva 1995, 2002b).

Wright's environmentally conscious design of houses of worship calls for special attention, as Western religions do not necessarily consider thermal comfort as a design factor (see Part 1, this volume; Geva 1995, 2002a, 2009b and Geva and Morris 2010). As discussed in Part 1 of this volume, Wright's expression of harmony with the environment and his human scale were part of his departure from traditional European church design. He followed Eastern cultures' building traditions where houses of worship are comfortable, enabling the worshipers to be fully absorbed by their spiritual experiences. Wright's religious projects were based on human scale. As such, climate consideration was part of his design, providing an all-inclusive comfort level. Wright used passive climatic measures and active heating systems. He believed that climate "means something in relation to one's life in it" and was quoted: "I doubt that you can ignore climate completely, by reversal make a climate of your own and get away with it without harm to yourself" (Wright 1954: 178).

In his early preface to *Ausgefuhrte Bauten und Entwurfe* (1910) Wright wrote:

> In our vast country alternate violent extremes of heat and cold, of sun and storm have to be considered . . . Umbrageous architecture is therefore desirable – almost a necessity both to shade the building from the sun and protect the walls from alternate freezing and thawing.

He then elaborated on the architectural elements that protect a building from harsh weather conditions. In *Modern Architecture* (1931a: 70) Wright repeated his idea of "design with climate". He considered architecture as "an interior space under fine shelter". As part of this concept and of his organic architecture theory that focuses mainly on the synthesis of features of habitation and the harmony with environment, Wright described architecture as a sheltering tree. The tree grows from the earth and provides a refuge from the sun and rain. Grant Hildebrand (1991) further developed Frank Lloyd Wright's notion of architecture as a shelter. He applied Jay Appleton's theory of refuge (an effective shelter) and prospect (a hiding place) to Wright's architecture. Hildebrand's research demonstrates that Wright's architectural patterns for a shelter not only corresponded successfully to Appleton's theory, but provided comfort in a single environmental structure that controls heat, light, view, ventilation, shade, and privacy.

Numerous scholars evaluated some of Wright's early projects using conventional climatic design guidelines (Banham 1966, 1969; Estoque 1981; Lechner 2001). These studies demonstrate that Wright's systems of environmental management (such as natural cross-ventilation, shading devices, and natural light) influenced the design of his exterior and interior architectural forms. In addition to passive cooling/heating methods, Wright also developed and designed heating systems. This development allowed him to free his architecture from conventions such as the traditional Western "box". He could open the traditional confined spaces to allow airflow:

> Another modern opportunity is afforded by our effective system of hot water heating . . . It is also possible to spread the buildings, which once in our climate of extremes were a compact box cut into compartments, into a more organic expression, making a house in a

garden or in the country the delightful thing in relation to either or both that imagination would have it.

(Wright 1910/1986: 15)

The conclusion of these scholars is that the strength of Wright's design is the combination of the building's architectural elements (passive cooling/heating measures) with mechanical devices: "It was the use he [Frank Lloyd Wright] made of mechanics and structural form in combination that marks out the Prairie Houses as triumphs of environmental art" (Banham 1969: 92).

Wright was exposed to the development of the "conditioned air" techniques for heating and cooling while working with Dankmar Adler and Louis Sullivan. They introduced this technique into their auditorium design in the early 1880s (Frampton 1994: 59). They cooled or heated a space with refrigerated or warm air that was sucked into the building through a ten-foot diameter fan, passed over heating coils or blocks of ice and pushed into registers found in the floor or under the space's seating. Wright followed this technique and combined it with the active cooling systems available in 1903 to cool and reduce humidity in his Larkin Building project. According to the "Larkin Company Administration Building Frank Lloyd Wright Architect 1903 Specifications",[53] Wright used an Acme air purifying, cooling apparatus, and an electrically driven Carbonic Anhydride refrigerating machine made by Kroeschell Ice Machine Company in Chicago. This project was recognized as one of "the first examples in the country of fan forced air conditioning in a sealed building" (Aitken 1998: 14).

Still, Wright did not repeat this solution in his design of religious buildings. Rather, he focused on passive measures such as orientation, natural ventilation, shading devices, height of ceilings, skylights, and an open flowing space floor plan. One reason that Wright may not have utilized conditioned air techniques in his sacred architecture is the church interiors' smaller scale compared to the Larkin Building. Another plausible reason may be his belief that Nature is God. Thus, too much artificial climate could suggest a conflict with this idea. Moreover, Wright saw air conditioning as a "dangerous circumstance". He believed that AC produced extreme change in temperature which "tear[s] down a building" and "tear[s] down the human body". Thus, "[t]he less the degree of temperature difference you live in, the better for your constitutional welfare" (Wright 1954: 175–176). Still, since he was fascinated by the development of running hot water and since his first houses of worship were designed for a cold climate he developed heating systems that used hot water and steam. The introduction of these systems, mainly the radiant floor heating system, was innovative in his time (see details below).

In the following sections I look at Wright's solutions for cooling and heating his religious buildings.

Cooling Systems

Wright focused mainly on a combination of passive measures to cool his sacred architecture. He oriented the buildings and their operable windows so as to capture the prevailing winds and provide cross-ventilation. In some of his houses of worship (e.g., Unity Temple and Pettit Memorial Chapel in Illinois; Annie Pfeiffer Chapel and Minor Chapel in Florida), he placed the windows on the upper level close to the ceiling. Since heat rises, this placement helps remove excess heat and humidity. This attention to the need to vent the accumulating heat and humidity was also demonstrated through his design of the translucent exterior pyramidal roof of Beth Sholom Synagogue in Pennsylvania. There, the air layer between the glass and plastic sheets removes the heat build-up in the building. In Pilgrim Congregational Church in California and in the First Christian Church in Arizona, the glass wall envelope includes operable openings that let fresh air in while ventilating the space.

In all his religious projects, Wright designed an open-spaced interior with hardly any partitions to encourage airflow, cooling the entire space. Wright also used hollow structural columns as ducts and vents to cool the space. He designed overhangs and cantilevers to shade the windows and walls. Some scholars argue that these features were designed in an angle that would provide shade in the summer while enabling the sun to penetrate in the winter (Banham 1966/1981: 162; Estoque 1981: 38–51). As described above, Wright was unique in introducing vegetation as part of his sacred architecture design. Some of the plants were part of the exterior design of the building (e.g., Annie Pfeiffer Chapel in Florida) and contributed to the shading effect. These measures were "compatible with Wright's preference for natural cooling over refrigerated air conditioning" (Estoque 1981: 44, 51). Indeed, thermal comfort analyses of some of these buildings illustrate that Wright's focus on passive cooling measures was more successful than his passive heating features. For example, the design of Unity Temple in Illinois provided better climate comfort in the summer than its heating in the winter. In the original design it was too hot (more than 79°F) in only 1 percent of the annual occupancy hours and too cold (less than 68°F) during 53 percent of the annual occupancy hours (Geva 1999).

In my study on the passive cooling systems applied by Wright in Unity Temple, Illinois and in Annie Pfeiffer Chapel, Florida, I analyzed these buildings along accepted "design with climate" guidelines (Geva 1999, 2000, 2002a). Several design guidelines and architectural strategies were developed to accomplish thermal comfort in buildings constructed in different climate zones (Olgyay 1963; Givoni 1976; Robinette 1983; Lechner 2001). These guidelines usually refer to site layout, building form, construction and finish materials, and architectural details. Greater climatic comfort can be achieved in a building that fulfills the design guidelines for a specific climate.

The design of Unity Temple in Illinois fully meets the three major climatic design guidelines for the Chicago area's summer (Lechner 2001: 86). The guidelines that suggest keeping the hot temperatures out and protecting the building from the sun are fulfilled by several passive cooling measures. The thick concrete walls of Unity Temple answer not only the monumental/religious and integrity aspects of the design, but provide a passive cooling effect of thermal mass, where relatively cooler night temperatures enter the building during the day due to the time lag of the heavy walls. Wright's design of the glass-topped atrium serves as a thermal buffer zone that helps control interior temperatures (Aitken 1998: 13). Wright's efficient design of shading devices protects the building from the sun and also helps keep the hot temperatures out (Fig. 3.5.2). The long cantilevered overhangs shade the windows, and the high solid parapet provides some shade on the glazed pitched roof. Wright's design also fully answered the recommended use of natural ventilation to cool the building. He positioned the temple on the site facing the east–west axis and capturing the area's prevailing winds. The main entrance to the complex is open to the courtyard entrance on the other side and provides natural ventilation (Fig. 3.7.8). The upper windows on all sides of the temple are operable, opening to all four sides of the building. As such, they capture the breeze in the area and help exhaust the warm air and moisture that rise toward the ceiling. To increase the rise of hot air, the four massive hollow square columns in the interior of the temple serve as vents and ducts for airflow. Finally, Wright remarked that electric lights should be turned off during the day so that their heat would not counter the cooling effects (Aitken 1998: 14).[54]

Like Unity Temple in Illinois, Florida's Annie Pfeiffer Chapel's openings (windows and huge doors) were designed to be operable. The doorways located on each side of the ground level (Fig. 1.12) and the openings facing the two balconies of the second level (Fig. 4.13.6) let in air and light while removing heat and humidity. This natural ventilation measure prevented dampness and thereby minimized mildew problems that are associated with the effects of humidity on the organic mixture of the building's concrete blocks.

All openings are shaded with overhangs (Fig. 3.8.7). The exterior walls of the upper level are finished with a light tan color that reflects the sun. Thus, Wright's climate-conscious design of this chapel fulfills two of the major design guidelines for the Florida climate zone. These guidelines recommend cooling and removing excess moisture in the summer, and protecting the building from the summer sun (Lechner 2001: 108). In addition, as in Unity Temple, Wright included four hollow structural columns, which serve as vents. Figure 1.5 shows the hollow column with its openings in the upper part, and Figure 4.14.1 illustrates the bottom openings of the hollow columns. These openings control the entrance/exit of air through the vent/duct.

4.14.1
Annie Pfeiffer Chapel, Florida: the
Hollow Column With its Openings in
the Bottom Part.

Furthermore, Wright designed four major "sound wells" at the rear of each section of the balcony seats (see Chapter 13 on Acoustics). Two of them are located near the upper level windows (Figs 4.13.6 and 4.13.7). These "wells" acted as major vents that extract the rising heat from below and remove it through the open windows (Fig. 4.14.2).

However, when the windows and doors of the building were closed, the huge skylights in Annie Pfeiffer Chapel trapped the heat created by the sunlight. There is no indication whether the operable openings (windows/doors) on the upper level were left open to cross-ventilate the chapel during services and other activities.[55] It is documented that in 1945 and 1946, Dr. Spivey, from the Southern Florida Methodist College, wrote to Wright to complain about the excessive sunlight penetrating the chapel, making it uncomfortable to sit in. He asked Wright to solve the problem (Siry 2004: 518–519 and n. 82; MacDonald et al. 2007: 28). There is no indication of what Wright's answers were to Dr. Spivey. Still, we do know that soon after construction, the chapel's four small skylights, located on the sides of the central skylight, were masked from inside the space (beneath) with framed covers (see Chapter 12 on Light; and Fig. 1.5). This helped to reduce some of the glare and heat. It is also known that Wright's design of plants hanging from the bell tower's trellises was intended to filter some of the glare and sunlight coming from above (Figs 3.4.7 and 3.8.7). However, it is not known if the original plan, which called for these plants, was fulfilled. Historic photographs of the chapel from the 1940s (when Dr. Spivey wrote the letters to Wright) show the tower as almost bare, with no lavish plants cascading from above as proposed by Wright (MacDonald et al. 2007: 19). Interestingly, while a 1962 photo by Ezra Stroller shows hanging vegetation from the tower (Christ-Janer and Foley 1962: 196), there are no documents revealing whether the plants were maintained properly to help shade part of the skylight and reduce some of the uncomfortable conditions due to the penetrating sun. As mentioned before, when I visited the chapel in 2002, there was no indication of growing plants.

4.14.2
Annie Pfeiffer Chapel, Florida: an
Example of a "Sound Well" That Acts
Like a Major Air Vent.

The third criterion of "climate-conscious design" in Florida to avoid additional sources of humidity was only partially fulfilled in the Annie Pfeiffer Chapel. The Florida Southern College campus was planned around Lake Hollingsworth in Lakeland, Florida. This lake obviously provides an additional source of humidity to the area. However, the Annie Pfeiffer Chapel is located 800 feet inland and was mostly blocked from the lake by the density of the citrus trees. These trees also provided some shade in the area (Fig. 4.14.3).

4.14.3

The Remaining Citrus Trees near Annie Pfeiffer Chapel, Florida.

To overcome some of the thermal discomfort in the chapel, and to cater to modern convenient thermal comfort, environmental modifications were introduced over the years. In the late 1960s and early 1970s, a heating, ventilation, and air conditioning (HVAC) system of a direct expansion air conditioning and electric strip heat was installed in the chapel behind the choir screen (Fig. 4.13.4), at the entrance corridors (Fig. 4.14.4), and in the "sound wells" (4.14.5).

With this installation the full-length doors to the balconies were replaced by casement windows. All openings were sealed to tighten the infiltration rates. The shelves to hold the AC units on the bottom blocked the side sound wells, and the original seating of 800 seats was reduced to 450. In addition to these internal changes, the citrus grove around the building was minimized and most of it was replaced with grass.

4.14.4 (left)
An Installment of a Heating,
Ventilation, and Air Conditioning
(HVAC) System at the Entrance
Corridor of Annie Pfeiffer Chapel,
Florida.

4.14.5 (right)
An Installment of an HVAC System
Inside the "Sound Wells" of Annie
Pfeiffer Chapel, Florida.

The fixed windows and tight infiltration block the cross-ventilation in the building and create a mildew problem in the porous blocks. Due to condensation caused by operating the HVAC system, the small colored pieces of glass, which pierce the concrete blocks, started to fall out. To overcome this situation, the building currently relies on a constant temperature controlled by the HVAC system to keep the interior cool and dry. In fact, the AC runs 24/7 even during the summer when the college is closed and the building is not in use. The installment of the AC units inside the "sound wells" near the windows damaged the functionality of the "wells" to act as vents that remove some of the heat and humidity that accumulates on the ground level under the gallery. Although the "wells" screen the AC units, thereby maintaining the architectural integrity of the chapel, this renovation compromises some of the original passive cooling effects. This highlights current preservation conflicts between the introduction of new technologies and its compromise of original building technology.

The reduced number of seats in the chapel decreases the number of people occupying the building. This in turn helps to cool the chapel. However, when the building is in full use during the fall, winter and spring, the reduced number of people decreases their total radiant heat, which originally helped warm the building in the winter. Thus, the building must rely on its heating system. Finally, the loss of most of the citrus grove reduced the building's shading while also increasing the effects of the humidity from the lake and from the lawn around the building's spray irrigation. The installment of the HVAC system in the chapel and the accompanied changes did not necessarily consider the original integrity of the building's thermal properties (see also Chapter 13 on Acoustics). In addition, empirical thermal comfort analyses show that it did not greatly improve the thermal conditions in the chapel (see section below on Computerized Energy Simulations).

4.14.6
The Outdoor AC Unit of the Annunciation Greek Orthodox Church, Wisconsin. Note the Unit on the Right Side of the Picture.

The same trend may be observed with the installment of an HVAC system in the Annunciation Greek Orthodox Church in Wisconsin. Although there was an attempt to hide the outdoor AC unit behind some trees and to screen it from the entrance to the Church, its positioning could have been more sensitive to the architectural integrity of the building (Fig. 4.14.6).

An example of a sensitive approach may be seen in the Pilgrim Congregational Church in California. The HVAC system was installed using Wright's original heating system under the floor. The floor vents are located near the operable windows of the glass wall. Despite the AC installment, the congregation prefers to open the windows and use fans to cool the space in the relatively moderate summers of California (Fig. 4.11.3).

Heating Systems

To achieve climatic comfort level in the winter, Wright used traditional heating systems (e.g., fireplace, radiators) and developed new systems (e.g., radiant heat floor) as an integral part of his design. It seems that his "investment" in the heating system was more extensive than in his design solutions for passive heating systems.

Passive Heating Measures

Norbert Lechner (2001) summarized three general recommendations for "climate-conscious design" in the winter: keep heat in, let the winter sun in, and protect from cold winter winds. He then details strategies for each of these guidelines as related to specific climate zones.

Wright's design of windows, skylights, and translucent pyramidal roofs in his sacred architecture fulfilled the criterion of letting in the winter sun. As mentioned earlier, some argue that Wright calculated the relationship between the length of the cantilevers and the angle of the winter/summer sun. This way, the design enables the sun to shine into the building during winter (Estoque 1981; Banham 1966/1981).

The use of air as insulation helped Wright to partially achieve the criterion of keeping in the heat. He utilized air between the double roof (glazed pitched roof outside and skylight inside) of Unity Temple in Illinois, as well as between the glass and plastic sheets of Beth Sholom Synagogue in Pennsylvania. The skylights in these atriums also serve as a buffer that keeps the heat inside. Wright used two inches of "an interior insulating air space between" the layers of the concrete blocks of Annie Pfeiffer Chapel and Minor Chapel in Florida (Wright 1954: 200–201; Fig. 4.9.4). However, since Wright focused on natural cross-ventilation in the summer, his designs did not protect his projects from cold winter winds. Furthermore, since he did not use insulation materials in most of his religious buildings, the guidelines for keeping in the heat and protecting the interior from the cold winds could not be fully fulfilled. More so, when he developed the radiant heat floor system (see below), he claimed, "When you have the floor warm – heat by gravity – insulation of the walls becomes comparatively insignificant" (Wright 1954: 159).

Still, it is interesting to note that Wright became aware of the utility of insulation with thermal materials later in his career (Wright 1945: 158–160). For example, in the Minor Chapel in Florida (1954), his drawing of the chimney area detail specified two inches of asbestos insulation between the concrete slab and the copper roof. He also pointed out that the best place for insulation in a warm climate is overhead; it keeps the heat out while providing shade. In cold weather the insulation in the overhang maintains the flow of vertical circulation of rising heat from the floor (Wright 1954: 158–159). He also acknowledged that in northern regions snow could contribute additional insulation.

In his writings on "insulation and heating" (1954: 158–160), Wright mentioned the importance of insulated roofs: "the overhead is where insulation should occur in any building . . . whereas the insulation of the walls and the air space within the walls becomes less and less important". When the building consists of a heating system, he observed that:

overhead insulation is extremely important: heat rises and if it finds a place overhead where it can be cooled off and dropped, you have to continuously supply a lot of heat. If however, the overhead is reasonably defensive against cold, you can heat your house very economically.

Indeed, in 1959 he used thermal insulation in the Greek Orthodox Church in Wisconsin. The church's ceiling includes metal flake on Air-O Therm asbestos (Storrer 1993: 428–429). This material began to sag and fall apart, and was replaced with an insulation layer of foamed-in-place urethane.

Fireplaces

In Wright's eyes the fireplace served as a symbol of comfort, safety, light, and as the heart of a space: "It comforts me to see the fire burning deep in the solid masonry . . . A feeling that came to stay" (Wright 1932a/1943: 141). This poetic take on the fireplace has been mentioned in literature throughout the years. Recently, Per Petterson portrayed his core feelings on the fireplace in his 2003 novel *Out Stealing Horses*:

> [I] leave the room in twilight so the yellow flames in the stove flicker brightly over the floor and walls. The sight of them slows my breathing down and makes me calm as it must have done for men through thousand of years: let the wolves howl, here by the fire it's safe.
>
> (Petterson 2003: 183)

Wright's use of the fireplace in his sacred architecture was a tool for heating the place, but also for connecting humans with the eternal meaning of fire. It was unique to include a fireplace in the design of houses of worship. This demonstrated another point of Wright's departure from traditional European church design. The fireplace appears in the following religious buildings: Unity Chapel in Wisconsin; Unity Temple complex (in the House) in Illinois; Pettit Chapel in Illinois (Fig. 4.14.7); Unitarian Meeting House in Wisconsin (Fig. 4.14.8); Minor Chapel in Florida; and Pilgrim Congregational Church in California (Fig. 4.14.9). In small spaces like Wisconsin's Unity Chapel and Illinois's Pettit Memorial Chapel, Wright used the fireplace as the only means of heating. In other projects the fireplace was combined with other heating techniques.

Radiant Floor Heating

One of the reasons that Wright may have focused more on passive cooling systems rather than passive heating systems in his design of sacred buildings is his fascination with the hot water heating system. Wright explained that this early 1900s development was another modern opportunity to free his sacred architecture from traditional constraints: "By this means, the forms of buildings may be more completely articulated, with light and air on several sides" (Wright 1910/1992: 113). This fascination led Wright to introduce hot water and steam as a means to heat an interior space. He used it in radiators or in radiant floor heating systems, which he called "gravity heat". The latter system uses steam or hot water pipes under the building's floor. The pipes lay on a gravel bed covered with four-inch-thick poured concrete. These pipes heat the floor, and since heated air naturally rises, this system would heat the building's space.

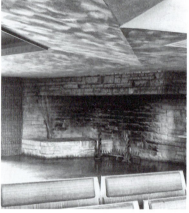

4.14.7 (left)
The Fireplace of the Pettit Chapel, Illinois.

4.14.8 (above)
The Fireplace of the Unitarian Meeting House, Wisconsin.

4.14.9
The Fireplace of the Pilgrim Congregational Church, California.

We call it gravity heat because the pipes filled with steam or hot water are all in a rock ballast bed beneath the concrete floor – we call the ballast with concrete top, the floor mat. If the floor is above the ground it is made of two-inch-square wood strips spaced three feet and eight inches apart. The heating pipes are in that case set between the floor joists.

(Wright 1954: 99–100)

It should be noted that Wright was one of the first architects in America to introduce the radiant floor heating system, which originated in China and spread to Japan and Korea and from there to America. He attempted to install this system in Unity Temple in 1906 without success.[56] In 1938 he installed the system with greater success in the Annie Pfeiffer Chapel in Florida (Fig. 4.14.10). The heating was "supplied by copper coils embedded in gravel beneath the floor mat, through which hot water was pumped" (MacDonald et al. 2007: 18).

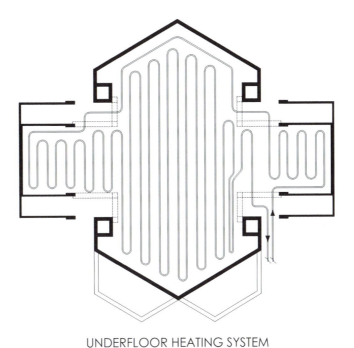

UNDERFLOOR HEATING SYSTEM

0   6' 12'   24'

4.14.10
The Radiant Floor Heating System Plan of Annie Pfeiffer Chapel, Florida (redrawn under author's supervision).

In 1947 he incorporated this system in his design of the Unitarian Meeting House in Wisconsin. Wright wrote the specifications for the radiant floor heating system at the Unitarian Meeting House on the drawing of the church's basement layout (sheet 1). This heating system includes water circulated by automatic electric pumps through pipe coils located beneath the floor slab. Oil-fired hot water boilers with an automatic thermostat sensitive to occupancy load, solar gain, etc. would correspond to outdoor temperatures. In 1958 this system was part of the design of the Pilgrim Congregational Chapel in California.

In addition to the radiant heating floor system, and as mentioned before, in some of his churches Wright designed hollow main structural columns to serve as vents and ducts for heating airflow (Larkin and Pfeiffer 1993: 70). In the 1902 auditorium (church) in Lincoln Center in Chicago, Illinois, four hollow piers were designed to host the mechanical services (Siry 1991b: 266).[57] Similarly, Wright introduced four hollow columns in Unity Temple in Illinois (1906) and later in Annie Pfeiffer Chapel in Florida (1938).

In summary, the strength of Wright's environmentally conscious design was in his use of multiple techniques for cooling and heating. Specifically, Wright attempted to create a microclimate in his sacred architecture using a combination of the building's architectural elements (passive cooling/ heating measures) and other active measures such as the fireplace and radiant floor heating system. He saw the heating system as an integral part of the building: "Here was the complete opportunity to digest all that paraphernalia in the building – creating not a heated interior but creating climate – healthful, dustless, serene. And also, the presence of heat thus integral and beneath makes lower temperatures desirable" (Wright 1954: 100).

To corroborate these observations and validate the qualitative analyses, I have utilized computerized energy simulations to analyze the climate conditions and thermal comfort of Unity Temple, Illinois and Annie Pfeiffer Chapel, Florida.

Computerized Energy Simulations

In my studies of the environmentally conscious design of Wright's early architecture in Oak Park, Illinois (Geva 1999),[58] I compare the thermal comfort of Wright's Unity Temple (1906) and two family residences in Oak Park (Mrs. Gale's House – 1909, and Wright's Original House – 1889). I examined how Wright shaped the design of the different building types (i.e., religious versus residential architecture), which were built in the same location and in the same period, to accommodate specific climatic constraints. The main findings of this study showcase Wright's sensitivity to climate conditions in his design. My study demonstrates that Unity Temple is compatible with the climate of the Chicago area even by today's standards and is more comfortable than Wright's residential buildings built in the same location and in the same period. In addition, the results of the digital analyses corroborate the qualitative analyses and show that Wright focused on cooling the houses of worship more than on heating them.

I ran digital simulations on these buildings and empirically assessed the comfort level and energy required to achieve the designated thermal conditions in the Chicago area. In this study, and in an additional project where I compared the thermal comfort of Unity Temple, Illinois and the Annie Pfeiffer Chapel, Florida (see details below), I utilized ENER-WIN – an hour-by-hour computerized energy simulation software (Degelman and Soebarto 1995; Degelman 1997, 2002, 2006).[59] The program's input file is based on given climatic data (the program includes more than 2000 cities in the world); building description (the program consists of a catalog of envelope materials and their thermal values, and numerous daily user profiles based on ASHRAE standards[60]); and economic data (which is not relevant to this study). The input files of the projects' buildings (Unity Temple, Mrs. Thomas H. Gale House, and the original Home of Frank Lloyd Wright in Illinois and later, Annie Pfeiffer Chapel in Florida) were run in two ENER-WIN modes. The first mode is defined as a passive simulation, which is mainly applied to structures without heating, ventilation and air conditioning (HVAC) systems. In this mode, the simulations evaluate the building's acceptable comfort level in percentage of time out of the annual occupancy, and in discomfort degree hours (DDH) (Al-Homoud 1994). The second mode is the active simulations mode, which assesses the energy performance of buildings using HVAC systems in energy units. The latter simulations can also be run on buildings without HVAC (such as historic buildings) by simulating them *as if* they include mechanical/electrical systems. The output of these simulations includes a building's source energy in thousand BTUs per square foot (kBtu/sq.ft.)[61] and energy loads in million Btus (MBtus).[62]

The findings of the passive mode simulations run on Unity Temple show that the temple is more comfortable than the two single-family houses. Unity Temple's discomfort level is 62,882 annual DDH, while the discomfort level of Mrs. Gale's House is 110,309 annual DDH, and Wright's original home exhibits 121,230 annual DDH. In all three buildings, most of the thermal discomfort may be attributed to the cold weather in Chicago.

The results of the active mode simulations run on Unity Temple show an annual source energy of 129.6 kBtu/sq.ft., which is better than the Building Energy Performance Standard (BEPS) for this type of building in Chicago (141 kBtu/sq.ft.). The annual source energy of the residences (142 kBtu/sq.ft. for the Gale House, and 153.6 kBtu/sq.ft. for Wright's original house) are greater than the BEPS for residence types of building in Chicago (103–110 kBtu/sq.ft.).

The findings that Unity Temple is more comfortable than the two residences may be interpreted in two ways. One possibility is that the Unitarian congregation supported Wright's new ideas of relating faith, form, and building technology. As such, they allowed him to explore non-traditional design and new technologies, and in turn achieve better thermal comfort. Another explanation may be attributed to Wright's concern with climatic comfort when a building was to be used by a larger number of people. However, since there is no evidence for these explanations in the literature or in archival documents, it is difficult to draw a decisive conclusion.

The simulations' results also demonstrate the major impact of Chicago's cold winters on the buildings' thermal conditions. Wright tried to overcome this cold discomfort by lowering the ceiling height in his residential projects and including heating systems such as fireplaces, radiators, and a radiant floor heating system in his designs. In Unity Temple, he installed heating ducts hidden in uninsulated terracotta under the floor and in the four hollow major columns. Unfortunately, this system never functioned, and radiators were added prior to the building's opening.[63]

Further investigation of the energy loads in Unity Temple shows that the major contributors to higher heating loads in the chapel are the roof (724.5 MBtu), exterior walls (524.6 MBtu), and infiltration/ventilation (292.77 MBtu). The major contributor to the cooling loads is the solar heat that radiates through the windows (124.2 MBtu). However, the thermal mass effect of the concrete walls decreases the cooling load by 146.22 MBtu, neutralizing the solar effect. These findings strengthen the conclusion that Wright better addressed the cooling measures than the heating systems.

To substantiate the idea that insulation could improve thermal comfort in the temple, especially during the winter, I simulated Unity Temple *as if* it includes an insulated roof (U-Factor of 0.069)[64] and a reduced infiltration rate (1.0 Air Changes per Hour (ACH)). The simulations resulted in an improvement of 12 percent in climatic comfort (55,393 annual DDH) and 21 percent in energy performance (102.2 kBtu/sq.ft. source energy).

The second study utilizing computerized energy simulation to evaluate Frank Lloyd Wright's environmentally conscious design is a comparison of the thermal comfort of Unity Temple in Illinois and Annie Pfeiffer Chapel in Florida. The selection of these two religious buildings was based on the fact that their design showcases Wright's experiments with innovative building technology that responded to local environments and accommodated his unique design (Geva 1999, 2000, 2002a). In addition, their different locations make these buildings an interesting case for this comparison. Unity Temple was built in 1906 in Oak Park, Illinois, a distinctive climate zone with windy, cold winters and hot, humid summers. Annie Pfeiffer Chapel was constructed in 1938 in Lakeland, Florida, as the first building on the Florida Southern College campus. The site of the chapel has bright sunlight, a hot humid climate, and lush vegetation.

Running ENER-WIN on Wright's original design of Annie Pfeiffer Chapel, which included Wright's proposal for partial shading and cross-ventilation, showed that the building would have been thermally comfortable (between 68°F and 79°F) during 60 percent of the annual occupancy hours. If the original design had an HVAC system, its annual source energy would have been 133.2 kBtu/sq.ft. This latter finding is better than the BEPS for this type of building in Central Florida (164 kBtu/sq.ft.) (Geva 2000, 2002a). These results, which are better than the BEPS, are similar to the findings in Unity Temple.

Most of the thermal discomfort in the Annie Pfeiffer Chapel (a total of 13,872 DDH) may be attributed to cold weather. Although the winters in Florida are mild, it is too cold in the chapel (less than 68°F) during 28 percent of the annual occupancy hours (11,526 DDH-Cold). On the other hand, it is too hot (more than 79°F) only 12 percent of the annual occupancy hours (2,346 DDH-Hot). These findings strengthen the conclusion that Wright paid more attention to the hot conditions of Florida and was less concerned with passive heating measures. Instead, he focused on installing a radiant floor heating system under the chapel's floor, and duct systems in the major columns (Fig. 1.14.10).

Running an ENER-WIN active mode on Annie Pfeiffer Chapel *as if* the original design had included an HVAC system shows that the major contributor to the cooling loads of Wright's original design of the chapel is the number of people occupying the building (in the original design Wright included 800 seats). However, the load created by radiant heat from people (81 MBtu) is neutralized by the effect of the concrete block walls that decreases the total cooling load by 85 MBtu. The major contributors to the heating loads in the chapel are the roof (153.7 MBtu), and the rates of infiltration/ventilation (87 MBtu). The radiant heat from people decreases the heating load by 73 MBtu. Like Unity Temple's, these results enhance the findings of the previous qualitative analyses, which suggest that the lack of insulation and weathering materials causes the building to be less thermally comfortable in the winter than in the summer.

As previously described, an HVAC system was installed in the Annie Pfeiffer Chapel at the end of the 1960s. This change was accompanied by some interior alterations. To assess the effective change in the chapel's thermal comfort I ran the simulation on the current conditions of the building. The results show an increase in the total discomfort level from 13,872 total DDH in Wright's original design to 15,257 total DDH in the current condition. Currently, the building is colder in the winters than the original design (too cold 29 percent of the annual occupancy hours). It has the same comfort level relative to the original conditions in the summer (too hot 12 percent of the annual occupancy hours). The major contributor to the cold conditions in the chapel is the reduction in the number of people occupying the chapel (less radiant heat from people). These findings show the strength of Wright's environmental design where he considered the space's size and the number of people in it.

Developing energy conservation strategies, which suggest better solutions for climate conditions in the chapel, was the third phase of my project. It is recommended to incorporate some of Wright's original energy components with an effective use of the HVAC systems. Running ENER-WIN on the chapel with the combination of efficient air conditioning, operable windows that allow natural cross-ventilation when the weather permits, and plants hanging from the bell tower for shading effect, resulted in a major thermal improvement. The source energy was reduced to 62.5 kBtu/sq.ft., and the discomfort level in the chapel was reduced to 6,528 DDH. These findings represent a major improvement of approximately half of the previous results. The building's comfort level increases to 71 percent of the annual occupancy hours. It is too cold during 22 percent of the annual occupancy hours versus the original design of 28 percent, and the current conditions of 29 percent. It is too hot 7 percent of the annual occupancy hours versus 12 percent in the original design and current stage of the chapel.

However, it should be acknowledged that the analysis of the chapel's thermal comfort does not refer to glare issues in some parts of the chapel. Sunlight moves during the day and highlights different sections of the chapel through the clear skylight, while other parts are shaded. As mentioned in Chapter 12 on Light, the area of the stage and its pulpit is lit most of the time (Fig. 3.5.6). In my visit in the chapel, I got the impression that the place is well lit, but still gives a sense of dimmed lighting. The latter may be attributed to the small, colorful glass pieces that are installed within the concrete block walls in the background of the auditorium and which create a "jewel-box" appearance.

Wright understood the relationship between light and thermal comfort and tried to approach it with multiple techniques (Aitken 1998: 14). The use of a skylight and the shape of an atrium (e.g., Unity Temple, Anne Pfeiffer Chapel) not only symbolizes a gathering in a communal space (Laseau and Tice 1992: 117), but also provides natural light and contributes to the thermal comfort or discomfort in the building. The defused balanced natural light, which is filtered by colored glass or by vegetation, decreases the need for electric light during the day and thus reduces its generated heat. In his attempt to bring light deeper into the interior of the Larkin Building, Wright remarked that electric lights should be turned off during the day. This helps to cool the building. Wright's approach to environmental design in his sacred buildings shows that he "simultaneously incorporates multiple techniques for controlling light and temperature" (Aitken 1998: 14).

In summary, it may be concluded that Wright's design of houses of worship exhibits environmental consciousness. He created climatic conditions that may be considered comfortable even by today's standards (BEPS), though his designs were attentive to hot weather more than to cold conditions. He solved the cooling needs of these buildings with passive measures of architectural features, while experimenting with new technologies such as hot water and steam for heating systems. He focused on the development of radiant floor heating more than on designing passive heating measures. This approach was obvious when he dismissed the use of insulation when installing the radiant floor heating system. Still, in some of his houses of worship he included air layers as thermal and acoustical insulation. It is interesting to note that he proposed a roof garden to be included in his design of the Community Christian Church in Missouri (1940). This solution would serve to insulate the roof and reduce the cooling/heating loads. This idea was a very innovative and sustainable design at the time, and Wright may be commended for his futuristic environmental approach. However, due to the conservative position of his clients in Missouri and because of budget constraints, this roof garden was never built.

As with light and acoustics, Wright solved climate issues by using a combination of techniques and methods. His ingenuity was in utilizing the combination of passive cooling/heating measures with heating systems such as radiant floor heating, radiators, and fireplaces. He designed this combination as an integral part of his holistic design and added to the sacred ambience of his religious projects.

Summary of Part 4 (Building Technology)

The book's conceptual model (Fig. 1.1) illustrates the mutual relationship between building technology, form, and sacred ambience. It shows that sacred form and ambience influence the selection of materials and systems; while building technology determines often the form and its ambience. Figure 1.4 under this part of the book depicts a more specific diagram of these relationships, showing the mutual relationship between materials, structures, and systems (e.g., light, acoustics, thermal comfort) and how they influence the sacred form and ambience. In addition, the diagram illustrates the impact of the building's context (e.g., environment and time) on the sacred ambience and on the development of building technology.

Following this diagram the first three chapters of Part 4 examine Wright's use of materials and structural systems and their relation to form along his main design concepts of nature, democracy and freedom, and his holistic approach to design. Wright's innovative use of traditional and new materials reinforced his departure from traditional European church design while still catering to different faith requirements.

The next three chapters include the building systems that accommodate Wright's design of the sacred ambience: light, acoustics, and thermal comfort. These chapters emphasize the ingenuity of Wright's utilization of multiple techniques and methods to create the ambience of a sacred building. This approach to building technology enriched the systems' effectiveness and enhanced the spiritual atmosphere of the sacred ambience. Moreover, it proved again Wright's holistic design where the whole is the equilibrium of its parts. Indeed, Wright's design of the ambience factors was interwoven with his use of materials and structural systems in creating the sacred building.

In all aspects of building technology, Wright demonstrated a poetic approach to his selection of materials and systems. In his eyes, building technology expressed truth and beauty as much as form, and therefore he often expressed it in or as the architecture of the house of worship. These ideas were embedded in Wright's attempts, while producing a space that could lift the soul of the worshipers and accommodate the faith required spiritual experiences.

In this part of the book I also demonstrate Wright's environmentally conscious approach to sacred design. The use of local materials for construction and finishes and his treatment of light and climate systems were ahead of its time. By today's terminology, his projects would have been labeled "sustainable architecture".

Wright's sustainability development was drawn from his design aspects of nature, democracy and freedom, and from his holistic approach. For example, Wright used local materials such as stone, wood, sand, and aggregates that were part of the natural surroundings of the buildings. He designed natural light as the major "holy" light, believing that he brings Nature/God into the sacred space. He also advocated the use of natural light during the day and turning off electric lights that increase cooling loads in a building.

By its nature, climate, like light, directly relates to local environment and is influenced by temporal changes. Wright attempted to create a micro-climate in his sacred spaces, focusing on passive measures to cool/heat the building and combining it with active heating systems. Thus, he developed his energy strategies by combining passive and active measures for effective energy use. The strength of this combination is recognized today as the most efficient energy strategy, and therefore it is fundamental to current sustainable design trends. Moreover, Wright believed that this design frees the worshipers from any physical discomfort and enables them to be absorbed into the space's spiritual ambience, the essence of the house of God.

The relation of the ambience factors to democracy and freedom may be observed in Wright's human scale design of unity and simplicity. In addition, Wright departed from traditional European church design and provided equality in the worship services. Every member could see the others as well as the religious leader(s); everyone could hear the music and the voice of the leaders and the community; everyone would feel as comfortable as possible so as to fully enjoy the spiritual space. In other words, every worshiper becomes part of the community and its sacred building.

Notes

1 Wright in a letter to *The Magazine of Art* (1953) published in an Appendix in Tselos (1969: 72).

2 As mentioned in Chapter 6, the four-foot module became a standard filled by three sixteen-inch blocks (Storrer 1993: 98).

3 For a description of the repertoire of modern technology developed during the end of the nineteenth century and the beginning of the twentieth century, see works by scholars such as Cecil D. Elliott (1992), Kenneth Frampton (1994); and Rowland Mainstone (2001).

4 In the early 1960s the entire structure of Unity Temple, including its decoration, was coated with Portland cement paint, hiding the original texture and color (Bell 1974: 162). In the 1970s shot-Crete application mix was applied to the structure to resemble the original texture (Bell 1974: 162).

5 Wright wrote this intention on his drawing sheet of masonry details for the construction of the Unitarian Meeting House.

6 The choice of the specific green color of the roof at the First Christian Church does not meet Wright's original intention to use copper and its specific color as a roofing material.

7 These articles appear as part of Wright's series entitled 'In the Cause of Architecture III–VIII: The Meaning of Materials' (Wright 1928c) and were reprinted in Pfeiffer, Bruce (ed.) (1992) *Frank Lloyd Wright Collected Writings* Vol. 1: 269–309.

8 The articles in the *Southern* are as follows: 'Florida Rock Used in Chapel Construction' (January 28, 1939: 1); 'Blocks are in the Making' (September 8, 1939: 3); and 'Chapel is Going up in Hurry' (December 9, 1939: 1, 4).

9 Wright's perception of the relation between wood and religion reflects Japanese religious principles.

10 The coquina was from Florida's east coast, near St. Augustine. This material was used architecturally since the Spanish colonial times (Siry, 2004: 515).

11 Arla Lind (1995: 42) claims that Wright never used the Luxfer prism glass in his buildings.

12 'Chip Off the Old Block', an article published under Refurbishment/Case Study One Column in *RIBA Journal* (August 1993: 40–41).

13 The structural system of Annie Pfeiffer Chapel's roof did not rely solely on the cantilevers for the central lantern's support. The system consists of an arrangement of reinforced concrete beams including three concrete bow-ties on the east–west end of the tower. Still, in the first years of the building's existence, structural cracks appeared in the beams under the balcony. Following the October 1944 hurricane that damaged the church's tower and skylight, the repairs made

used substantially more reinforcing steel than was specified in the original design (MacDonald et al. 2007: 31).

14   This information is found in a December 2, 1940 article in *Time Magazine* (38–40) and in Wright's autobiography (1932a/1977).

15   Charles E. Roberts was a mechanical engineer and inventor as well as president of the American Steel Screw Company.

16   Harold Grove chaired the building committee, and Helen served as coordinator of the project.

17   This information is taken from documents held in Pilgrim Congregational Church's archives.

18   Contributors to the church's construction who are mentioned in the church's brochure include Del Hansen, who worked on the excavation, and Gwynn Bland and Gray Smith, who worked on the forms for the concrete bents of the church's roof.

19   Hamilton (1990: 185) reported that "the battens worked, but the roofs leaked anyway, and portions have required repair". One of the reasons for the problems with this roof may be attributed to the fact that due to budget constraints the roof was constructed with a thinner copper than Wright's specified thickness.

20   The God Brahman, one of the chief Hindu Gods, is known as the creator of all living beings.

21   Louis Kahn followed Wright's idea that the light is the beautifier of the building, and said, "To me natural light is the only light, because it has mood – it provides a ground of common agreement for man – it puts us in touch with the eternal. Natural light is the only light that makes architecture."

22   Vincent Scully (1962) demonstrates the strength of the interplay of light and shadow in sacred architecture in Greek temples.

23   It should be noted that upper overhangs/cantilevers shade the openings in both buildings.

24   The placement of the windows at the tops of the walls contributes to the separation of the sacred interior space from the mundane.

25   Dr. Spivey, Wright's client and President of Southern College in Florida, "pleaded [with] Frank Lloyd Wright to correct this problem in the rebuilt chapel" following the damages of the 1944 hurricane (MacDonald et al. 2007: 28).

26   During my visit to Annie Pfeiffer Chapel in Florida there was no evidence of plants hanging from the tower.

27   Le Corbusier designed a strip of light between the walls and the roof of his Notre Dame du Haut, Ronchamp, France (1955), creating an illusion of a floating roof.

28   Emperor Justinian built Hagia Sophia between 532 and 537 AD in Constantinople (today Istanbul, Turkey).

29   This approach is fundamental to *IES* contemporary lighting design strategies where the emphasis is on natural light as the main source of illumination while artificial light is secondary.

30   The design of the light fixture for the eternal light is based on the triangular module of the building.

31   As reported in the journal *Historic Preservation* (May/June 1995: 15); and in *ARTnews* (March 1995: 38).

32   The selection of *Lightscape* program was based on the available digital lighting simulation software in 1999 when this project was conducted.

33 Lux (lx) is the measured unit of illuminance and luminous emittance.

34 These light design standards and guidelines may be found in the *IES Lighting Design Handbook*. They and others are also summarized by Lechner (2001).

35 According to the *IES* standards, accent lighting is approximately three times the "reading" target illuminance (*IES Lighting Handbook*).

36 According to the *IES* standards, architectural lighting is approximately 25 percent or less of the "reading" target illuminance (*IES Lighting Handbook*).

37 'Eye Music' *Frank Lloyd Wright Quarterly* (1998) 9 (2): 4–9, p. 4.

38 Ibid, p. 6–8.

39 Resonance requires three major elements: the original vibrating source (the sound itself), a transmitting medium (the space); and a receiver of the vibration (Andrews 2007; Hale 2007: ix).

40 A comparison chart of standard acoustic ranges for various building types indicates that worship spaces should include a range of 500–1k Herz reverberation time, which places this building type between classrooms and symphony halls (Roberts 2004: 191).

41 Wright quoted in 'Musical Sites' *Frank Lloyd Wright Quarterly* (1998) 9 (2): 4–9, p. 19.

42 Since there is not much information on his acoustic design in his unbuilt proposals, one may assume that he intended to use the same methods in these projects as he used in his built houses of worship.

43 The original pulpit of the Annie Pfeiffer Chapel in Florida was a fixed place, a "ship's prow pulpit". Following the hurricane of 1944, which partially destroyed the chapel, a new and movable pulpit was built (MacDonald et al. 2007: 27).

44 From 'Musical Sites' *Frank Lloyd Wright Quarterly* (1998) 9 (2): 4–9, p. 19.

45 People occupying a space serve as "materials" that reduce the reflection of hard materials on one hand, and balance some of the absorption of sound on the other hand.

46 The plastered wall of this area, which gently reflects the sound back to the audience, prevents the loss of sound through the open circulation isle on the side of the church.

47   The article by Guthrie, the rector of St. Mark's-in-the-Bouwerie in New York City, appeared in the *San Francisco Examiner* (April 13, 1925: 1).

48 As mentioned earlier, numerous scholars attributed the temple's orientation on the site (the main elevation facing the side street) to the temple's complex plan. This orientation was the only way the plan could fit the building site (Nute 1996: 95).

49 When the windows on all four sides of Unity Temple are open for ventilation, outside noise does get into the building.

50 I could not detect any sound wells in Wright's other religious projects.

51 Since these sound wells were also designed as vents (see Chapter 14), the placement of the AC units also violates Adler's concept of using thermal features for advancement in a space's acoustics.

52 Joseph Siry (2004: 512) describes the praises of good acoustics in Annie Pfeiffer Chapel in Florida.

53 Frank Lloyd Wright Memorial Foundation's Archives.

54 While Wright's comment referred to the Larkin Building, it also applies to his other buildings, such as Unity Temple.

55 In the 1943 *Intrlachen* yearbook it is stated that the chapel served as a multi-function hall holding weekly activities such as lectures and concerts in addition to services.

56 Concrete debris was found in parts of the ducts during the renovation of Unity Temple in the 1970s. Some speculate that this was the main reason why Wright's original heating system did not function.

57 Wright collaborated with Architect Dwight H. Perkins on the design of Lincoln Center in Chicago, Illinois from 1898 until 1903 (Siry 1991a).

58 In 1997, my study entitled "Frank Lloyd Wright's Architecture: A Computerized Energy Simulation Study" was awarded *The James Marston Fitch Award* for innovative research in historic preservation in America. Based on this research I presented and published a paper in 1999. An additional project where I compared Unity Temple in Illinois to Annie Pfeiffer Chapel in Florida was presented and published in 2002.

59 ENER-WIN was selected due to its friendly interface and the familiarity of the author.

60 ASHRAE: American Society of Heating, Refrigerating, and Air Conditioning.

61 Source Energy: energy consumed by the power plant to produce the total energy used by the building.

62 The building's cooling/heating loads measure how much energy is required to cool or heat the building.

63 See note 56.

64 The insulation of the roof was calculated as if it was included on the beams of the concrete slab, leaving the skylight in place. There is no practical way to include insulation in the temple's concrete walls without damaging the historic integrity of the temple. Therefore, I did not include insulated walls in these simulations.

Part 5
CONCLUSION

5
CONCLUSION

Buildings like people must first be sincere, must be true, and then withal as gracious and loveable as may be.

(Wright 1908 quoted in Pfeiffer 1992: 88)

In this book I introduce a conceptual model that illustrates the relationships between faith, form, and building technology in sacred architecture (Fig. 1.1). This model shows that faith directly influences form and sacred ambience. It also explores the mutual relationship between form and building technology and sacred ambience; and how environmental conditions and time both influence form and progress in building technology. Part 1 of the book elaborates on the various aspects that comprise these relationships.

In Parts 2, 3, and 4, I apply the conceptual model to Frank Lloyd Wright's sacred architecture, and examine the major elements of the model: faith, form, and building technology as found in his sacred projects. This investigation is conducted along Wright's main design concepts of nature, freedom and democracy, and his holistic approach to design, that integrates programmatic tasks, building production, and spiritual experiences.

His design of the sacred path enhances the procession of the worshipers toward the sacred plan and separates their experience from the mundane. This separation is strengthened by Wright's design of the abstracted *axis mundi* – the world's vertical axis, a link between earth and sky and bringing man closer to the Divine. Furthermore, the worshipers are absorbed by the "holy" light and "divine" sounds in Wright's sacred buildings. In other words, Wright created spaces that elevate the soul while portraying true emotions. This aspect of his design illustrates the ability of architecture to help man's soul consider spiritual beauty and art: "only by receiving true emotion from architecture will man be able to consider art" (Goetitz quoted in Pelletier 2008: 11). His design of these elements not only enhances the spiritual experience of his religious projects, but highlights the poetic aspects of his sacred architecture.

Wright catered to each faith's functional and spiritual needs through abstraction. This abstraction was one of the most important new and powerful qualities in Wright's sacred architecture. Wright's abstraction of geometry was driven from Nature. Since Wright strongly believed that God could be revealed through Nature, these abstractions enrich the spirituality of his religious projects. Wright believed that ancient religious monuments were strongly connected to Nature and its forces. Thus, he also based his abstractions on his interpretation of the shapes and symbolism of these monuments. This inspiration helped Wright depart from conventional European church design and to express his search for an American style that would reflect freedom, democracy, and the American landscape. "Ultimately Wright came to see all his buildings as part of one fabric – a new vision of democratic architecture for free man in a free society" (Owings Jr. 2003: 5). The concept of architecture as an expression of freedom and environment (Nature) is relevant to today's globalization. It can manifest itself in sustainable designs that relate to global and local conditions, and cater to the ultimate desire of human beings to be free.

Furthermore, his understanding of the essence of a building's materials and the power of using light and sound as beautifiers of religious buildings contribute to the multiple meanings of these abstractions. Wright's relationship between form and building technology can serve as an example of modern architecture, as his interpretations stand the test of time based on current trends in architecture.

Wright believed that truth and beauty are the dominant factors in determining architectural forms and in the selection of a building's materials and systems. This belief is similar to a traditional Navajos chant, "Beauty before me, Beauty behind me, Beauty above me, Beauty below me, I walk in beauty." This chant expresses the quality of nature as it surrounds humans. For Wright, Nature was interpreted as God. Thus, we can see its beauty as sacred, "aligned with the gods, the body, mind, and voice [which] made sacred again. Every morning. Every day" (Hale 2007: 136). Some, like Terry Patterson (1994) criticized this notion of beauty as being the main focus of Wright's design and construction. Still, in the context of his sacred architecture, Wright showed how beauty and truth evoke and enhance the spiritual experience. He believed that "Truth is a divinity in architecture" (Wright 1953b/1995: 62). He used beauty to reveal order, harmony, balance, and rhythm as part of Nature's laws. His sacred projects take architecture to another dimension, focusing on the human spirit itself and humanity's freedom, and creating the vital force that characterizes the sacredness within a space. Describing Beth Sholom Synagogue in Pennsylvania, Olgivanna Lloyd Wright wrote (1960: 192): "The temple fulfills the indestructible wish of the human soul to share in divine beauty and to feel the presence of God."

She adds that the uniqueness of Frank Lloyd Wright's design is in its being "a new architectural expression whose roots are dipped into the long measures of Time". This relationship between Wright's sacred architecture and time may be interpreted in two ways. First, time serves as a reference to ancient religious monuments, which became an inspiration to Frank Lloyd Wright's sacred architecture. The second interpretation of the above quote can describe Wright's sacred architecture as eternal. This notion brings us to the concluding points that highlight what makes Wright's sacred architecture so special, unique, and significant to preserve.

In addition to my description of Wright's poetic design of sacred architecture, the following three concluding points should be acknowledged. First, the continuous use of Wright's built sacred architecture; second, the importance of these buildings to American culture; and the third point is the mutual relationship between Wright's sacred architecture and his secular projects. All of these concluding points demonstrate the significance of his sacred architecture and may serve as the basis for preserving Wright's built religious buildings and cherishing his unbuilt sacred architecture.

The Continuous Use of Wright's Houses of Worship

Wright's built projects have been used continuously for worship services, surviving almost unaltered since their construction and dedication. They still function as houses of worship for the same faith, serving as each congregation's icon through generations.

Members of these congregations are proud of these buildings, which still accommodate their physical and spiritual needs: "They [Annie Pfeiffer and Danforth (Minor) Chapels] have been with my family from birth to death" (Shari Szabo quoted in MacDonald et al. 2007: 23). The Annie Pfeiffer Chapel is mentioned and illustrated in every yearbook of the Southern Florida College. As described before, some of the buildings include personal contributions by members of the congregation, who were heavily involved in the construction of their church (e.g., The Unitarian Meeting House and the Pilgrim Congregational Church). Although it is a fact that this involvement stemmed mainly from the congregations' economic constraints, we should acknowledge the contribution of working the soil and nature as a reflection of the ideals of American democracy (Owings Jr. 2003: 6–8). These ideals also foster the attachment and pride of the congregations to their houses of worship.

Most of Wright's religious buildings were preserved over the years and continue to be maintained by their congregations. These houses of worship exhibit the combination of the "ordinary" (familiar and measurable elements that relate mainly to each faith's rituals) and the complex secular activities (e.g., schools, community events). Furthermore, these buildings display their faith's and congregation's symbols and spiritual meanings (the "extra" of the religious building). Thus, one can see that Wright's sacred work employs a holistic approach to the design and utilization of the programmatic and the extraordinary in architecture.[1]

Wright's design of houses of God provides the worshiper with a special kind of energy that "gives us something we cannot find elsewhere" (Osmen 1990: 11). Wright designed buildings of worship where people can come and daydream about God rather than being constrained by religious doctrine. The human scale of these buildings and the combination of sacred and secular functions make them vibrant and alive in a time when many houses of worship are closing and parishes are selling their property.

Wright's Sacred Architecture and its Contribution to American Culture

America recognized the value of Frank Lloyd Wright's sacred architecture and its contribution to American culture. Most of his built houses of worship are listed on the National Register of Historic Places and on the American Institute of Architects (AIA) Best Buildings list. For example, Unity Temple has been designated a National Historic Landmark[2] since 1971. In 1991, *Architectural Record* chose Unity Temple as the sixth most significant building in the United States in the twentieth century. In addition, the AIA selected it as one of seventeen buildings by Frank Lloyd Wright that should be maintained as his architectural contribution to American culture.

The AIA and the National Trust for Historic Preservation singled out Wright's Beth Sholom Synagogue in Pennsylvania in 1959 and the Unitarian Meeting House in Wisconsin in 1960 for their invaluable contribution to American culture. In 1973 the Unitarian Meeting House was placed on the National Register of Historic Places, while the synagogue was designated a National Historic Landmark in 2007. Both buildings were added to this important list for their national significance as the most important works of the great American architect Frank Lloyd Wright.

Other examples include the Annunciation Greek Orthodox Church in Wisconsin, which was added to the National Register of Historic Places in 1974 for its architectural and engineering significance; and the Pettit Chapel in Illinois, which was posted on the National Register in 1978.

Wright's Florida Southern College in Lakeland was placed on the National Register of Historic Places in 1975. The importance of Wright's buildings on this campus, which include the Annie Pfeiffer Chapel and the Minor

Chapel, raises concerns in the international community about their condition, and therefore the buildings were posted on the World Monument Fund's 2008 World Watch list in "urgent need of immediate attention and assistance, and worthy of preservation" (MacDonald et al. 2007: 8).

Wright's religious buildings were posted on these lists among his other secular buildings, which were recognized for their unique architecture, engineering, and cultural values. Indeed, Wright claimed that all of his architecture is sacred, and therefore we can trace a continuous mutual flow among all his designs.

The Mutual Influences Between Frank Lloyd Wright's Sacred and Secular Projects

Referring to Wright's design process, Bruce Pfeiffer (1990: 80) wrote that "there were instances when an idea was put on paper and developed but not realized, yet, it served as the seed for another project". The relation between Wright's sacred built and unbuilt projects as well as their influence on or by secular projects reveal the strength of Wright's design concepts of architecture as related to nature, democracy and freedom, while demonstrating an equilibrium of the separate parts of the design into the whole. Although the mutual relationship between Wright's sacred and secular designs can be developed into a separate manuscript, I want to introduce a few examples of the "recycled" designs of his sacred architecture.

My archival study of Wright's sacred projects reveals that some of his sacred forms were influenced either by an unbuilt proposal for another religious building (not of the same faith), or by a secular type of building. Moreover, some of his religious building projects became the platform for the development of some of his secular projects.

The following examples show Wright's "reuse" of some of his designs of a specific house of worship in the designs of other faiths' religious building. Wright's 1906 Unity Temple design in Oak Park, Illinois inspired his two proposed alternatives for the Christian Catholic Church in Zion, Illinois (1911 and 1915). These proposals include an interior view (Fig. 5.1), a transverse section (Fig. 5.2), and elevations (Fig. 3.6.11) similar to Unity Temple. In this fashion, a Unitarian house of worship became the basis for the design of a Catholic church.

Wright's 1920s proposal for the Johnson Desert compound and shrine inspired his 1958 design of the tower and steeple for the Pilgrim Congregational Church in Redding, California (Fig. 3.6.21). The unbuilt project for the All Faith Steel Cathedral in New York (1926) inspired the 1959 design of the Jewish Synagogue in Pennsylvania. Wright's 1950s design proposal for the Southern Christian Seminary became the basic design for a different denomination twenty-two years later – the First Christian Church of Phoenix. The built Danforth Chapel, known as the Minor Chapel, in Lakeland, Florida was designed as a Methodist church in 1954 (Figs. 5.3 and 3.5.8) and became one of the 1956 design proposals for a Christian Science Church in Bolinas, California (an unbuilt project) (Figs 5.3, 5.4 and 5.5). The 1956-built Annunciation Greek Orthodox Church in Wisconsin inspired Wright's 1957 first proposal for the Wedding Chapel in California (Fig. 3.6.4).

5.1
Frank Lloyd Wright's 1911 (ca) Design Proposal for the Interior of the Christian Catholic Church in Zion, Illinois (© 2009 Frank Lloyd Wright Foundation, Scottsdale AZ/Artists Rights Society (ARS), New York).

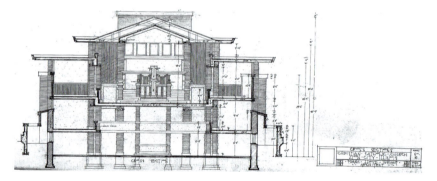

5.2
A Transverse Section of Wright's 1911 (ca) Design Proposal for the Christian Catholic Church in Zion, Illinois (© 2009 Frank Lloyd Wright Foundation, Scottsdale AZ/Artists Rights Society (ARS), New York).

In a way, these examples are inconsistent with Wright's statement that the design of houses of worship should accommodate the harmonious needs of each faith and his idea that "Every great religion had produced its own special type of architecture" (Clark 1871). Still, these examples of Wright's "recycled" sacred architecture can be reasoned away in light of Wright's claim that his religious architecture is inspired by fundamental and universal elements such as Nature as God's creation, democracy and freedom, and his holistic approach to design. As such, he argued that he could build any church or house of worship: "I attend the greatest of all churches. And

I put a capital N on Nature and call it my church . . . But because my church is elemental, fundamental, I can build for anybody a church" (Frank Lloyd Wright in a television interview 1957, cited in Pfeiffer 1990: 87; Legler 1997: 5).

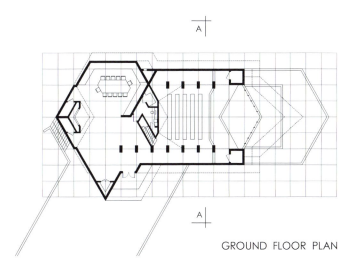

5.3
The 1954 Floor Plan of the Minor Chapel (Danforth Chapel), Florida (redrawn under author's supervision).

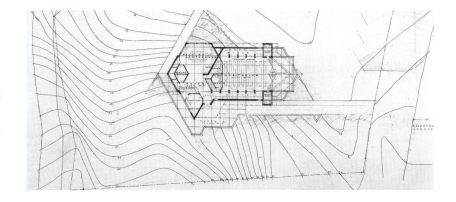

5.4
Frank Lloyd Wright's 1956 Floor Plan Proposals for a Christian Science Church in Bolinas, California (© 2009 Frank Lloyd Wright Foundation, Scottsdale AZ/Artists Rights Society (ARS), New York).

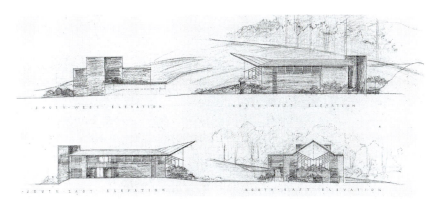

5.5
Frank Lloyd Wright's 1956 Elevations Proposal for a Christian Science Church in Bolinas, California (© 2009 Frank Lloyd Wright Foundation, Scottsdale AZ/Artists Rights Society (ARS), New York).

A close examination of the plan of Minor Chapel in Florida (Fig. 5.3), which was later transformed into a design proposal for the Christian Science Church in California (Fig. 5.4), shows not only the "recycling" of the design for a different religious denomination, but a design in different environments: a building in hot-humid Florida on an almost flat terrain inspired a proposal of a building to be built in temperate California on a hilly site. Again, one may argue that this is in some way inconsistent with Wright's environmentally conscious design. Yet, a careful study of the drawings shows that although the north arrow points in the same direction, Wright was sensitive enough to position the buildings according to the local climate and terrain conditions. Moreover, in temperate climates like that of California, one can design buildings that are more attentive to cultural/religious demands while catering less to the local climate.

Examples of the fluid connection between Wright's secular and sacred architecture can be seen in several of his projects. The entrance of his 1897 studies for the unbuilt All Souls' Church in Chicago, Illinois (Fig. 5.6), and his 1911 proposal no.1 for the Christian Catholic Church in Zion, Illinois (Fig. 3.3) inspired his 1948 design for the entrance to the Morris Gift Shop in San Francisco, California (Fig. 5.7).

The 1938 Annie Pfeiffer Chapel plan influenced the plan of a proposal for a small school in Wright's project of The Living City. In that project, Wright also proposed a pyramidal Roadside Market. Alofsin (1989: 35) claims that in addition to the influence of Wright's 1926 design of the Steel Cathedral in New York, the 1938 market proposed design inspired the pyramidal form of Beth Sholom Synagogue, built in 1954. An additional example of the influence of a sacred design on the secular is Wright's design proposal for a sports club and play resort for Huntington Hartford in Hollywood, California (Fig. 5.8). The design of a cluster of shallow domical structures around a central vertical element can be seen in the aerial perspective that appeared a year after Wright's design proposal for the Daphne Funeral Chapels, San Francisco, California (Fig. 3.4.13).

5.6 (left)
Frank Lloyd Wright's 1897 Studies for the All Souls' Church in Chicago, Illinois (an unbuilt project). (© 2009 Frank Lloyd Wright Foundation, Scottsdale AZ/Artists Rights Society (ARS), New York).

5.7 (right)
Frank Lloyd Wright's 1948 Morris Gift Shop in San Francisco, California.

5.8
Frank Lloyd Wright's Proposal for
a Sports Club and Play Resort for
Huntington Hartford in Hollywood,
California. (© 2009 Frank Lloyd Wright
Foundation, Scottsdale AZ/Artists
Rights Society (ARS), New York).

These examples of the reuse of elements from sacred buildings in secular
projects resemble the ancient and classical traditions where the sacred,
the pinnacle of form and building technology, influenced the secular style
and construction.

It is also interesting to note the similarities between the plans and grid
system of the Unitarian Meeting House in Wisconsin (1947) and the Palmer
House in Michigan (1950). This example reinforces Wright's belief that
the house is a sacred building (see Part 3, Form). This belief can also be
observed in Wright's use of cruciform plans both in his Prairie-style houses
(Storrer 1993: 91) and in the plans of some of his churches (e.g., Unity
Temple complex, Unitarian Meeting House, Pettit Chapel). In addition,
Susan Wydick (1987: 26) claims that both Wright's residential designs and
his designs of houses of worship accommodate programmatic requirements and cater to environmental conditions. His houses of worship
respond to faith requirements, as well as to the building's site and local
environmental conditions.

Some scholars point out the influence of Wright's secular projects on his
sacred architecture. One such example is the influence of the Larkin
Building (1902) in Buffalo, New York, on the design of Unity Temple (1906)
in Oak Park, Illinois. Like the Larkin Building, Wright's Unity Temple was
built as an enclosed building and its partite arrangement was developed
directly from the secular office building (Levine 1996: 37–46).

Another example of details reuse is Wright's Luxfer Prism Office building
in Chicago, Illinois (1896–1897), which shows a façade of units of glass,
resembling the treatment of the skylight of Unity Temple (1906) built in
Oak Park, Illinois. Although the skylight is horizontal and made of amber

glass rather than prism glass, it is based on the same idea that units of glass can cover a whole surface.

Some argue that the design of the Annunciation Greek Orthodox Church in Wauwatosa, Wisconsin is a reduced version of Wright's Monona Terrace in Madison, Wisconsin (Levine 1996: 500, n. 1470).[3]

Although all of these examples of the mutual relation of Wright's sacred and secular projects may provoke questions about the consistency in his writings and design work, they can be explained in two ways. As mentioned before, Wright claimed that all of his projects are sacred. His sacred architecture is sophisticated yet direct, beautiful, and honest (Wydick 1987: 26). Wright created "buildings with a sense of repose and calm and to achieve this it was essential that every aspect of the design . . . be in perfect harmony" (Brooks 1979: 13). We may also view these relationships as either the recycling of ideas or as "variation on a theme" (Laseau and Tice 1992: 11) by an artist/architect who strongly believed in his design concepts of Nature, Democracy and Freedom and that the design of the whole is the equilibrium of its parts.

Writing this book became a special journey and a long process. Each part of this journey shed a different light on Wright's work and enriched my experience. My field trips to all of his built religious buildings deepened my appreciation for his sensitive design of architectural and technical details as part of a holistic approach to design. I saw how his sacred architecture evokes a celebration of spirit and a unification of community.

My archival study at the Frank Lloyd Wright Foundation exposed me to his unbuilt projects. These designs are unique and express his belief in truth and beauty. The research of his written material and the materials written by other scholars informed me of his wealth of ideas and design solutions. In all, this journey was so rich and intriguing that it felt like an endless hoisting of water from a deep well. Every time I turned a page, I found an additional dimension to write about and include in the book. As Olgivianna Lloyd Wright wrote about her husband's work (1960): "just as you think you have reached it, there will be another branching out into another direction and dimension."

Notes

1 For more details on the extraordinary in art and architecture, see Martine Heidegger's work *History of the Concept of Time: Prolegomena* (1985 trans.), and "The Origin of the Work of Art" in *Poetry, Language, Thought* (1971 trans.).
2 A building designated a National Historic Landmark is automatically listed in the National Register of Historic Places.

3   A short description of the church appeared in *Architectural Forum* (October, 1956: 17) under *News*, 'Wright Sketches 510 Story Office Tower, Round, Blue-Roof Greek Orthodox'. Visiting both buildings, I believe that rather than a recycling of the Monona Terrace design, Wright's design of the Greek Orthodox Church reflects the congregation's faith, and its dome serves as a tribute to the Byzantine's domical churches.

Appendix

Frank Lloyd Wright's Sacred Architecture: List of Projects

Building	Location	Year*	built (B) unbuilt (UB)
Unity Chapel	Spring Green, Wisconsin	1886**	B
Unitarian Chapel	Sioux City, Iowa	1887	UB
All Soul's Church	Chicago, Illinois	1897	UB
Abraham Lincoln Center	Chicago, Illinois	1900/1903***	UB
Unity Temple	Oak Park, Illinois	1906	B
Petit Mortnary Chapel	Belvidere, Illinois	1906	B
Christian Catholic Church	Zion, Illinois	1911	UB
Christian Catholic Church	Zion, Illinois	1915	UB
Johnson Desert Compound and Shrine	Death Valley	1921/1923/1924-1925****	UB
Steel Cathedral	New York, New York	1926	UB
Memorial Chapel ^^	unknown	1930	UB
Cathedral and Cemetery	Broadcare City, Illinois	1934	UB
Memorial to the Soil Chapel (Chapel for Newman Family)	Cooksville, Wisconsin	1936	UB
Annie Pfeiffer Chapel	Florida Southern College, Lakeland, Florida	1938	B
Community Christian Church	Kansas City, Missouri	1940	B
Methodist Church ^^	Spring Green, Wisconsin	1940	UB
Daphne Funeral Chapels	San Francisco, California	1945	UB
Unitarian Meeting House	Shorewood Hills, Wisconsin	1947	B
Dwelling for Harvey G. John Jr.	Oconomowoc, Wisconsin	1949	UB
Southwest Christian Seminary	Phoenix, Arizona	1950	UB

Building	Location	Year*	built (B) unbuilt (UB)
First Christian Church	Phoenix, Arizona	1973	B
Kaufman Rhododendron Chapel	Mill Rum, Pennsylvania	1952	UB
Danforth Chapel (Minor Chapel)	Florida Southern College, Lakeland, Florida	1954	B
Beth Sholom Synagogue	Elkins Park, Pennsylvania	1954	B
Christian Science Reading Room 1	Riverside, Illinois	1954	UB
Christian Science Reading Room 2	Riverside, Illinois	1954	UB
Christian Science Church 1	Bolinas, California	1956	UB
Christian Science Church 2	Bolinas, California	1956	UB
Annunciation Greek Orthodox Church	Wanwatosa, Wisconsin	1956	B
Wedding Chapel 1&2	Berkeley, California	1957	UB
Taliesin Unity Chapel	Spring Green, Wisconsin	1958	UB
Trinity Chapel	University of Oklahoma, Norman, Oklahoma	1958	UB
Pilgrim Congregational Church	Redding, California	1958	B
Christian Science Church ^^	Chicago, Illinois	1959	UB
Holy Trinity Greek Orthodox Church	San Francisco, California	1959	UB

* the year is based on the Frank Lloyd Wright Archives.
** Joseph Silsbee-Wright on team (See Form)
*** built by Dwight H. Perkins (See Building Technology)
**** the question of the dates of the design appears in Part 1 note 7
^^ Projects mentioned by Patrick J. Meehan (1984). I could not find any information on these projects to cross validade this data.

Bibliography

Addis, Bill (2009) 'A Brief History of Design Methods for Building Acoustics' *The Third International Congress on Construction History Proceedings*, Vol. 1: 1–10, Cottbus, Germany: Brandenburg University of Technology, Chair of Construction History and Structural Preservation.

Adler, Dankmar (1892) 'The Chicago Auditorium' *Architectural Record*, 1, (4) (April–June).

Ahn, You-Kyong (2007) 'Adaptive Reuse of Abandoned Historic Churches: Building Type and Public Perception', Ph.D. Dissertation, College Station, TX: Texas A&M University.

Aitken, Donald (1998) 'Frank Lloyd Wright: Daylighting Master', *Frank Lloyd Wright Quarterly*, 9 (3): 3–17.

Al-Homoud, M.S. (1994) *Design Optimization of Energy Conserving Building Envelopes.* Ph.D. dissertation, College Station, TX: Texas A&M University.

Alofsin, Anthony (1989) 'Broadacre City: The Reception of A Modernist Vision, 1932–1988', *Center: A Journal for Architecture in America*, 5: 8–43.

Alofsin, Anthony (1993) *Frank Lloyd Wright: The Lost Years, 1910-1922*, Chicago, IL: The University of Chicago Press.

Alofsin, Anthony (1994) 'Frank Lloyd Wright and Modernism' in Terence Riley and Peter Reed (eds) *Frank Lloyd Wright. Architect*, New York: Museum of Modern Art: Distributed by Harry N. Abrams, pp. 32–57.

Alofsin, Anthony (1996) 'Wright and The Glimmer of Japan' in Melanie Birk (ed.) *Frank Lloyd Wright's Fifty Views of Japan: The 1905 Photo Album,* Rohnert Park, CA: Pomegranate Artbooks, pp. 9–13.

Altman Irvin, Chemers M. (1980) *Culture and Environment*, Monterey, CA: Brooks/Cole Publishing Company.

Ameri, Amir H. (1997) 'Housing Ideologies in the New England and Chesapeake Bay Colonies, c 1650–1700', *The Journal of the Society of Architectural Historians*, 56 (1): 6–15.

Andrews, Ted (2007) *Sacred Sounds: Music & Healing Through Words & Music* (5th edn), Woodbury, MN: Llewellyn Publications.

Anfam, David (2007) 'To See, or Not To See' in K.C. Eynaten, Kate Hutchins, and Don Quaintance (eds) *Not-Seen: Search for Understanding: The Rothko Chapel Art Series*, Houston, TX: A Rothko Chapel Book, pp. 65–87.

Arnold, Eberehard (1975) *Light and Fire and The Holy Spirit*, New York: The Woodcrest Service Committee, Inc.

Ash, Mitchell G. (1995) *Gestalt Psychology in German Culture, 1890–1967: Holism and the Quest for Objectivity*, Cambridge, UK: Cambridge University Press.

Autodesk (1999) *Lightscape Release 3.2: Learning Lightscape,* San Rafael, CA: Autodesk Inc.

Banham, Reyner (1966) 'Frank Lloyd Wright as Environmentalist', *Arts and Architecture,* 83: 26–30; reprinted in Brooks, Allen (1981) *Writing on Wright: Selected Comments on Frank Lloyd Wright,* Cambridge, MA: MIT Press.

Banham, Reyner (1969) *Architecture of the Well-Tempered Environment,* Chicago, IL: University of Chicago Press.

Barrie, Thomas (1996) *Spiritual Path, Sacred Place: Myth, Ritual, and Meaning in Architecture,* Boston, MA: Shsambhala.

Barrie, Thomas (2010) *The Sacred In-Between: The Mediating Roles of Architecture,* London and New York: Routledge.

Barrows, John Henry (ed.) (1893) *The World's Parliament of Religions,* 2 vols, Chicago, IL. Parliament Pub. Co.

Barthel, Diane L. (1996) *Historic Preservation: Collective Memory and Historical Identity,* New York, and Brunswick, NJ: Rutgers University Press,

Bastea, Eleni (ed.) (2004) *Memory and Architecture,* Albuquerque, NM: University of New Mexico Press.

Baumann, D. and C. Niederstätter (2008) 'Acoustics in Sacred Buildings' in Rudolf Stegers *Sacred Buildings: A Design Manual* (translated from German), Basel, and Boston, MA: Birkhäuser, pp. 54–59.

Behrens, Roy R. (1986) *Illustration as an Art,* Englewood Cliffs, NJ: Prentice Hall.

Behrens, Roy R. (2000) 'Revisiting Gottschaldt: Embedded Figures in Art, Architecture and Design', *Gestalt Theory,* pp. 97–106.

Bell, Robert A. (1974) 'Shotcrete Restoration of a Historic Landmark', *Concrete Construction* (April): 161–163.

Benedikt, Michael (2008) *God, Creativity, and Evolution – The Argument from Design(ers),* Austin, TX: The Center for American Architecture and Design, University of Texas at Austin.

Berlage, Hendrik (1912) *Een Drietal Lezingen in Amerika Gebouden,* Rotterdam, Nederland: W.L. and J. Brusse.

Bernier, Ronald R. (2007) *Monument, Moment, and Memory: Monet's Cathedral in Fin de Siecle France,* Lewisburg, PA: Bucknell University Press.

Birk, Melanie (ed.) (1996) *Frank Lloyd Wright's Fifty Views of Japan: The 1905 Photo Album,* Rohnert Park, CA: Pomegranate Artbooks.

Blake, Peter (1969) *Frank Lloyd Wright: Architecture and Space,* Baltimore, MD: Penguin Books Inc. (4th edn paperback).

Boyd, Thomas J. (1959) 'Seamless-Roll Terne Roofing', *Progressive Architecture* (June): 172–175.

Brauer, David (2007) 'Space as Spirit' in K.C. Eynaten, Kate Hutchins, and Don Quaintance (eds) *Not-Seen: Search for Understanding: The Rothko Chapel Art Series,* Houston, TX: A Rothko Chapel Book, pp. 43–53.

Brooks, Allen H. (1979) 'Wright and the Destruction of the Box', *Journal of the Society of Architectural Historians,* 38 (March): 7–14.

Campbell, Joseph (1988) *The Power of Myth,* New York: Doubleday Publishers.

Cartledge, Mark J. (2007) *Encountering the Spirit: The Charismatic Tradition,* Maryknoll, NY: Orbis Books.

Casey, E.T. (1988) 'Structure in Organic Architecture' in Bruce B. Pfeiffer and Gerald

Nordland (eds) *Frank Lloyd Wright in the Realm of Ideas*, Carbondale, IL: Southern Illinois University Press.

Chambers, Wm. S., Jr. (1942) '"Innovations in College Chapel Architecture." Anne Pfeiffer Chapel, Florida Southern College', *Architectural Concrete*, 1: 16–17.

Ching, Francis (1996) *Architecture: Form, Space, and Order*, New York: Van Nostrand Reinhold.

Chladni, Ernst (1802) *Die Akustik*, Leipzig, Germany. Breitkopf und Hartel.

Christ-Janer, Albert and Mary Mix Foley (1962) *Modern Church Architecture*, New York: McGraw-Hill.

Cirillo, Ettore and Francesco Martellota (2006) *Worship, Acoustics, and Architecture*, Essex UK: Multi-Science Publishing Company.

Cirlot, Juan Eduardo (1971) *A Dictionary of Symbols* (2nd edn), New York: Philosophical Library.

Clarahan, M.M. (2004) 'Inspired Illumination: Sanctuary Lighting Must Do More than Simply Chase the Shadows Away', *Your Church* 50: 42–44.

Clark, James (1871) *Ten Great Religions: An Essay in Comparative Theology*, 2 Vols. Boston MA: Houghton Mifflin.

Cohn, Robert L. (1981) *The Shape of Sacred Space: Four Biblical Studies*, Chico, CA: Scholars' Press.

Collier, L.G. (1979) 'The Cultural Geography of Folk Building Forms in Texas' in F.E. Abernethy (ed.) *Built in Texas*, Waco, TX: E-Heart Press, pp. 20–43.

Comper, John Ninian, Sir (1947) *Of the Atmosphere of a Church*, London: Sheldon Press.

Connerton, Paul (1989) *How Societies Remember*, New York: Cambridge University Press.

Conover, Moore, E. (1948) *The Church Builder*, New York: Interdenominational Bureau of Architecture.

Cram, Ralph Adams (1924) *Church Building: A Study of the Principles of Architecture in Their Relation to the Church* (3rd edn), Boston, MA: Marshall Jones Company.

Cram, Ralph Adams (1925) *The Substance of Gothic: Six Lectures on the Development of Architecture from Charlemagne to Henry VIII*, given at the Lowell Institute, Boston (November and December, 1916) (2nd edn), Boston, MA: Marshall Jones Company.

Craven, Thomas (1934) *Modern Art – The Men, The Movements, The Meaning*, New York: Simon & Schuster; Reprinted paperback edition (2007) by Milward Press.

Critchlow, Keith (1980) 'What is Sacred in Architecture', *Geometry in Architecture – Lindisfarne Letter 10*, West Stockbridge, MA: The Lindisfarne Association Press.

Crosbie, Michael J. (2000) *Architecture For The Gods*, New York: Watson-Guptill Publications.

Cubitt, Geoffrey (2007) *History and Memory*, Manchester: Manchester University Press.

Davis, Patricia T. (1974) *Together They Built a Mountain*, Lititz, PA: Sutter House.

De Long, David G. (ed.) (1998) *Frank Lloyd Wright and The Living City*, Weilam Rhein, Germany: Vitra Design Museum.

Degelman, Larry O. (1997) *Enerwin Manual*, http://www.enerwin.com

Degelman, Larry O. (2002) *Enerwin Manual*, http://www.enerwin.com

Degelman, Larry O. (2006) *Enerwin Manual*, http://www.enerwin.com

Degelman, Larry and Veronica Soebarto (1995) 'Software Description for ENER-WIN: A Visual Interface Model for Hourly Energy Simulation in Buildings'. *Fourth*

International IBPSA Conference: Building Simulation Proceeding, Madison, WI, pp. 692–696.

Deva, Krishna (1995) *Temples of India,* Vol.1, New Delhi: Aryan Books International.

Doremus, Thomas (1985) *Frank Lloyd Wright and Le Corbusier: The Great Dialogue*, New York: Van Nostrand Rheinhold.

Dow, Arthur W. (1899) *Composition: A Series of Exercises Selected from a New System of Art Education*, Boston, MA: J.M. Bowles; reprinted (1913) (7th edn), Garden City, NY: Doubleday, Page & Company.

Dubbelde, Dave (2006) 'Influence of Culture, Faith, Environment, and Building Technology on the Built Form: The Case of Nineteenth Century Catholic Churches in Galveston, Texas', Ph.D. Dissertation, College Station, TX: Texas A&M University.

Durkheim, Emile (1912) *The Elementary Forms of the Religious Life*, London: George Allen & Unwin (English translation 1915), Oxford: Oxford University Press (English translation 2008).

Elgin, Kathleen (1971) *The Unitarians, The Freedom to Worship Series*, New York: David McKay Company, Inc.

Eliade, Mircea (1954) *The Myth of the Eternal Return: Cosmos and History*, London: Arkana.

Eliade, Mircea (1958/1996) *Patterns in Comparative Religion*, New York: Sheed and Ward Inc., 1996 edition published by University of Nebraska Press, Lincoln, Nebraska.

Eliade, Mircea (1959/1987) *The Sacred and The Profane – The Nature of Religion*, New York: Harcourt, Brace and World.

Eliade, Mircea (1992) *Symbolism, The Sacred and The Arts*, ed. Diane Apostolos-Cappadona, New York: Continuum Publishing Company.

Elliott, Cecil D. (1992) *Technics and Architecture: The Development of Materials and Systems for Buildings*, Cambridge, MA: MIT Press.

Emerson, Ralph W. (1841) 'The Over-Soul (Essay IX)', *Essays: First Series* published in http://www.emersoncentral.com/oversoul.htm (accessed, January 29, 2009).

Enderlein, Volkmar (2004) 'Architecture' in M. Hattstein and P. Delius (eds) *Islam: Art and Architecture* [translation from German], Cologne, Germany: Kolnemann, pp. 64–79.

Eng, Tan Twan (2008) *The Gift of Rain*, New York: Weinstein Books.

Estoque, Justin (1981) 'Heating and Cooling Robie House', *APT Bulletin*, 19 (2): 38–51.

Everett, Charles Carroll (1909) in Edward Hale (ed.) *Theism and the Christian Faith: Lectures Delivered in the Harvard Divinity School*, New York and London: Macmillan.

Fenollosa, Ernest (1896a) 'The Nature of Fine Art: I', *The Lotos*, 9 (9) (March): 672.

Fenollosa, Ernest (1896b) 'The Nature of Fine Art: II', *The Lotos*, 9 (10) (April): 760–761.

Fenollosa, Ernest (1896c) *The Masters of the Ukiyo-e*, New York: Knickerbocker Press.

Fitch, James Marston (1948) *American Building; The Forces that Shaped It*, Boston, MA: Houghton Mifflin.

Fitch, James Marston (1961) *Architecture and the Esthetics of Plenty*, New York: Columbia University Press.

Fitch, James Marston (1982) *Historic Preservation: Curatorial Management of the Built World,* New York: McGraw-Hill.

Fitchen, John (1994) *Building Construction Before Mechanization*, Cambridge, MA: MIT Press.

Frampton, Kenneth (1994) 'Modernization and Mediation: Frank Lloyd Wright and the Impact of Technology' in T. Riley and P. Reed (eds.) *Frank Lloyd Wright. Architect*, New York: Museum of Modern Art: Distributed by Harry N. Abrams. pp. 58–79.

Frampton, Kenneth (2005) 'The Text-tile Tectonic: The Origin and Evolution of Wright's Woven Architecture' in Robert McCarter (ed.) *On and By Frank Lloyd Wright: A Primer of Architectural Principles*, London and New York: Phaidon Press, pp. 170–189.

Frampton, Kenneth and Kunio Kudo (1997) *Japanese Building Practice: From Ancient Times to the Meiji Period*, New York: Van Nostrand Reinhold.

Frampton, Kenneth (Author) and John Cava (Editor) (2001) *Studies in Tectonic Culture: The Poetics of Construction in Nineteenth and Twentieth Century Architecture*, Cambridge, MA: MIT Press.

Frazer, Sir James George (1935) *The Golden Bough: A Study in Magic and Religion* (3rd edn), New York: Macmillan.

Futagawa ,Yukio (ed.) (1984) *Frank Lloyd Wright*, Tokyo: A.D.A. Edita.

Gadamer, Hans-Georg (1986) *The Relevance of the Beautiful and Other Essays*, Cambridge,UK: Cambridge University Press.

Gaebler, Max D. et al. (1952) 'A Church in the Attitude of Prayer', *Architectural Forum*, 97 (December): 85–92.

Gelfenbien, Gary Paul (1987) *Spheres of Light: Light as the Common Element of The Byzantine East and The Gothic West*, Ann Arbor, MI: University Microfilms International Company.

Geva, Anat (1994) 'Computerized Energy Simulation: A method for Testing Environmental Design Theory,' *Environmental Design Research Association (EDRA) Annual Proceedings: Banking on Design?* 25 (March): 107–112

Geva, Anat (1995) 'The Interaction of Climate, Culture, and Building Type on Built Form: A Computer Simulation Study of Energy Performance of Historic Buildings', Ph.D. dissertation, College Station: Texas A&M University.

Geva, Anat (1998) 'The Use of Computerized Energy Simulations in Architectural Research in Historical Context', A*ssociation of Collegiate Schools of Architecture (ACSA) Southwest Regional Meeting Proceedings: Searches in Architectural Reproduction* (October): 184–197.

Geva, Anat (1999) 'Frank Lloyd Wright's Oak Park Architecture: A Computerized Energy Simulation Study', *ACSA (Association of Collegiate Schools of Architecture) Technology Conference Proceedings: Technology In Transition: Mastering The Impacts*, Montreal, Canada (June): 151–157.

Geva, Anat (2000) 'Climatic Considerations and Energy Performance of Frank Lloyd Wright's Ann Pfeiffer Chapel, Florida Southern College', *APTI (Association for Preservation Technology International)* and the *National Park Service Conference Proceedings: Preserving the Recent Past II* (October): 3/39–3/45.

Geva, Anat (2002a) 'Passive Energy Systems in Frank Lloyd Wright's Sacred Architecture', *PLEA International (Passive and Low Energy Architecture) Conference Proceedings: Design with the Environment* (July): 861–866.

Geva, Anat (2002b) 'Lessons from the Past: The Interactive Effect of Climate and Culture on 19th Century Vernacular Architecture in South Central Texas', *Association of*

Collegiate Schools of Architecture (ACSA) Technology Conference Proceedings: Technology and Housing, Portland, Oregon: 288–297.

Geva, Anat (2005) 'The Use of Computerized Energy Simulations in Assessing Thermal Comfort and Energy Performance of Historic Buildings' in C.A. Berbbia and A. Torpiano (eds) *Structural Studies, Repairs and Maintenance of Heritage Architecture IX*, Southampton and Boston, MA: WIT Press: 587–596.

Geva, Anat (2009a) 'The Quest of Origin: 19th Century Sacred Architecture of Immigrants in South Central Texas', in Iris Aravot and Eran Neuman (eds) *Back to the Things Themselves: Architectural Experience, Memory and Thought* (in press).

Geva, Anat (2009b) 'The Utility of Computerized Energy Simulations in the Study of Religious Identity', Proceedings of *The Third Construction History Society International Congress*, Cottbus, Germany, Vol. 2: 679–688.

Geva, Anat and Andrew Garst (2005) 'The Holy Light: A Comparison of Natural and Artificial Light in A Sacred Setting', *SiGradi IX IberoAmerican Congress of Digital Graphics Proceeding: Vision and Visualization*, Lima, Peru: 695–699.

Geva, Anat and Anuradah Mukherji (2007) 'A Study of Light/Darkness in Sacred Settings: Digital Simulations', *International Journal of Architectural Computing*, 5 (3): 507–521.

Geva, Anat and Anuradha Mukherji (2009) 'Frank Lloyd Wright's Treatment of Light in Unity Temple: Digital Model and Simulations', *SiGradi – X IberoAmerican Congress of Digital Graphics Proceeding: From Modern to Digital*, Sao Paulo, Brazil: Universidade Presbiteriana Mackenzie.

Geva, Anat and Jacob Morris (2010) 'Empirical Analyses of Immigrants' Churches Across Locations: Historic Wendish Churches in Germany, Texas, and South Australia', *ARRIS: The Journal of the Southeast Chapter of the Society of Architectural Historians*, 21: 38–61.

Givoni, Baruch (1976) *Man, Climate and Architecture*, 2nd edn, New York: Van Nostrand Reinhold.

Glassie, Henry (1966) 'The Pennsylvania Barn in the South: Part II', *Pennsylvania Folklife* 15(4):12–25.

Glassie, Henry (1968) *Pattern in the Material Folk Culture of the Eastern United States*, Philadelphia, PA: University of Pennsylvania Press.

Glassie, Henry (1972) 'Folk Art' in Richard M. Dorson (ed.) *Folklore and Folklife: An Introduction*, Chicago, IL: University of Chicago Press, pp. 253–280.

Glassie, Henry (1974) 'The Variation of Concepts within Tradition: Barn Building in Otsego County, New York', *Geoscience and Man* 5:177–235.

Glassie, Henry (1975) *Folk Housing in Middle Virginia: A Structural Analysis of Historic Artifacts*, Knoxville, TN: University of Tennessee Press.

Gothold, Zeev (1977) 'Traditions and Customs in Synagogues Building and Design in Israel' (in Hebrew) in D. Kasuto *and Shachnti Betochchem*, Jerusalem, Israel: Ministry of Education and Culture, pp. 14–51.

Grabsky, Phil (1999) *The Lost Temples of Java,* London: Orion Books.

Graf, Otto Antonia (2005) 'Enspacement: The Main Sequence From 4 to 6' in Robert McCarter (ed.) *On and By Frank Lloyd Wright: A Primer of Architectural Principles*, London and New York: Phaidon Press, pp. 144–169.

Green, Aaron G. (1988) 'Organic Architecture: The Principles of Frank Lloyd Wright' in

Bruce Pfeiffer and Gerald Nordland (eds) *Frank Lloyd Wright in the Realm of Ideas*, Carbondale, IL: Southern Illinois University Press.

Green, Michael (2005) *One Song a New Illuminated Rumi*, Philadelphia, PA: Running Press.

Gura, Philip F. (2007) *American Transcendentalism: A History*, New York: Hill and Wang.

Guthrie, William N. (1927) *Offices of Mystical Religion*, New York and London: The Century Co.

Gutmann, Joseph (1983) *The Jewish Sanctuary*, Leiden: Brill.

Halbwachs, Maurice (1980) *The Collective Memory* (English translation), New York : Harper & Row.

Hale, Elizabeth (2007) *Sacred Space, Sacred Sound*, Wheaton, IL: Theosophical Publishing House.

Halifax, Joan (1993) *The Fruitful Darkness: Reconnecting with the Body of the Earth*, San Francisco, CA: Harper, San Francisco.

Hamilton Mary J. (1990) 'The Unitarian Meeting House', in Paul E. Sprague (ed.) *Frank Lloyd Wright and Madison: Eight Decades of Artistic and Social Interaction*, University of Wisconsin-Madison, WI: Elvehjem Museum of Art, pp. 179–188.

Hamilton Mary J. (1991) *The Meeting House: Heritage and Vision*, a booklet, Madison, WI: The Friends of the Meeting House.

Hayes, Bartlett H. (1983) *Tradition Becomes Innovation: Modern Religious Architecture in America*, New York: Pilgrim Press.

Heatwole, Charles A. (1989) 'Sectarian Ideology and Church Architecture,' *Geographical Review*, 79 (1): 63–78.

Heidegger, Martin (1971) *Poetry, Language, Thought*, New York. HarperCollins Inc.

Heidegger, Martin (1985) *History of the Concept of Time: Prolegomena* (trans.), Bloomington, IN: Indiana University Press.

Hertz, David M. (1995) *Frank Lloyd Wright in Word and Form*, New York: G.K. Hall & Co.

Hildebrand, Grant (1991) *The Wright Space: Pattern & Meaning in Frank Lloyd Wright's Houses*, Seattle, WA: University of Washington Press.

Hitchcock, Henry R. (1942) *In the Nature of Materials,* New York: Da Capo Press.

Hitchcock, Henry-Russell and Philip Johnson (1932) *The International Style: Architecture since 1922*, New York: W.W. Norton.

Hoffman, Donald (1986) *Frank Lloyd Wright Architecture and Nature*, New York: Dover Publications.

Hoffman, Donald (1995) *Understanding Frank Lloyd Wright's Architecture*, New York: Dover Publications.

Humphrey, Caroline and Piers Vitebsky (2005) *Sacred Architecture*, New York: Barnes & Noble Books, reprinted from Little, Brown (1997).

Johonnot, Rodney J., Pastor (1906) *The New Edifice of Unity Church, Oak Park, Illinois*, Oak Park, IL: The New Unity Church Club. Reprinted edn Oak Park, IL: Oak Park Unitarian Universalist Church (1984).

Joncas, Richard (1998a) 'Buildings for Worship' in David G. De Long (ed.) *Frank Lloyd Wright and The Living City*, Weilam Rhein, Germany: Vitra Design Museum, pp. 100–113.

Joncas, Richard (1998b) 'Buildings for the Arts' in David G. De Long (ed.) *Frank Lloyd Wright and The Living City*, Weilam Rhein, Germany: Vitra Design Museum, pp.130–147.

Jung, C.G. (1966) *Collected Works: The Archytypes and the Collective Unconscious*, Vol. 9, Part 1 (translation), Princeton, NJ: Bollingen Paperbacks.

Kaufmann, Edgar (1978) 'Frank Lloyd Wright: Plasticity, Continuity, and Ornament', *Journal of Architectural Historians*, 37 (1) (March): 34–39.

Kaufmann, Edgar and Ben Raeburn (1960) *Frank Lloyd Wright: Writings and Buildings*, New York: New American Library.

Kieckhefer, Richard (2004) *Theology in Stone: Church Architecture from Byzantium to Berkeley*, New York: Oxford University Press.

Knecht, Barbara (2001) 'An Innovative Approach Leads to a Solution for the Unity Temple's Crumbling Exterior', under 'Tech Briefs' in *Architectural Record* (April): 173–174.

Kniffen, F. (1936) 'Louisiana House Types', *Annals of the Association of American Geographers* 27: 179–193.

Kniffen, F. (1976) 'American Cultural Geography and Folklife' in D. Yoder (ed.) *American Folklife*, Austin: University of Texas Press, pp. 51–70.

Kruty, Paul and Paul Sprague (2005) *Prelude to the Prairie Style: Eight Models of Unbuilt Houses by Frank Lloyd Wright, 1893–1901*, Urbana-Champaign, Il: School of Architecture, University of Illinois at Urbana-Champaign.

Kultermann, U. (1979) 'The Oculus of the Pantheon in Rome', *Architecture and Urbanism* (November): 110: 79–88.

Lamm, Julia A. (1996) *The Living God: Schleiermacher's Theological Appropriation of Spinoza*, University Park, PA: Pennsylvania State University Press.

Lane, Belden (1988) *Landscapes of the Sacred: Geography and Narrative in America Spirituality*, Baltimore, MD: Johns Hopkins University Press.

Larkin, David and Bruce B. Pfeiffer (eds) (1993) *Frank Lloyd Wright: The Master Works*, New York: Rizzoli International Publications.

Laseau, Paul and James Tice (1992) *Frank Lloyd Wright: Between Principle and Form*, New York: Van Nostrand Reinhold.

Lawlor, Robert (1982) *Sacred Geometry – Philosophy and Practice*, London: Thames and Hudson.

Lechner, Norbert (2001) *Heating, Cooling, Lighting* (2nd edn), New York: John Wiley & Sons.

Legler, Dixie (1997) 'Divine Architecture', *Frank Lloyd Wright Quarterly*, 8 (1): 5.

Lévi-Strauss, Claude (1963) *Structural Anthropology*, New York: Basic Books.

Levine, Neil (1996) *The Architecture of Frank Lloyd Wright*, Princeton, NJ: Princeton University Press.

Licht, K.D.F. (1966) *The Rotunda in Rome: A Study of Hadrian's Pantheon*, Copenhagen, Denmark: Gyldendal.

Lind, Arla (1995) *Frank Lloyd Wright's Glass Designs*, San Francisco, CA: Archetype Press Books.

Lipman, Jonathan (2005) 'Consecrated Space: Wright's Public Buildings' in Robert McCarter (ed.) *On and By Frank Lloyd Wright: A Primer of Architectural Principles*, London and New York: Phaidon Press, pp. 264–285.

Lloyd, G.E.R. (1968) *Aristotle: The Growth and Structure of his Thought*, Cambridge, UK: Cambridge University Press.

MacCormac, Richard (2005) 'Form and Philosophy: Froebel's Kindergarten Training and Wright's Early Work' in Robert McCarter (ed.) *On and By Frank Lloyd Wright: A*

Primer of Architectural Principles, London and New York: Phaidon Press, pp. 124–143.

MacDonald, Randall M., Nora E. Galbraith, and James G. Rogers (2007) *The Buildings of Frank Lloyd Wright at Florida Southern College*, Charleston, SC: Arcadia Publishing.

MacDonald, W.L. (1976) *The Pantheon: Design, Meaning, and Progeny*, Cambridge, MA: Harvard University Press.

Mainstone, Rowland J. (2001) *Development in Structural Form*, 2nd edn, Oxford and Boston, MA: Architectural Press.

Mann, A.T. (1993) *Sacred Architecture*, Shaftesbury, Dorset and Rockport, MA: Element.

Mannion, Msgr. M.F. (1997) 'Ten Theses on a Church Door', *Catholic Culture*, available at http://www.catholicculture.org/culture/library/view.cfm?id=121&repos=1& subrepos=&searchid=285528 (accessed January 30, 2009).

Mark, Robert (1990) *Light, Wind, and Structure: The Mystery of the Master Builders*, Cambridge, MA: MIT Press.

Martienssen, Heather (1976) *The Shapes of Structure*, London, Oxford, and New York: Oxford University Press.

McCarter, Robert (1997) *Unity Temple: Frank Lloyd Wright*, London and New York: Phaidon Press.

McCarter, Robert (ed.) (2005a) *On and By Frank Lloyd Wright: A Primer of Architectural Principles*, London and New York: Phaidon Press.

McCarter, Robert (2005b) 'Abstract Essence: Drawing Wright from the Obvious' in Robert McCarter (ed.) *On and By Frank Lloyd Wright: A Primer of Architectural Principles*, London and New York: Phaidon Press, pp. 6–21.

McCarter, Robert (2005c) 'The Integrated Ideal: Ordering Principles in Wright's Architecture' in Robert McCarter (ed.) *On and By Frank Lloyd Wright: A Primer of Architectural Principles*, London and New York: Phaidon Press, pp. 286–337.

McNally, S.J.D (1985) *Sacred Space: An Aesthetic for the Liturgical Environment*, Bristol, IN: Wyndham Hall Press.

Meehan, Patrick J. (ed.) (1984) *The Master Architect: Conversations with Frank Lloyd Wright*, New York: John Wiley & Sons.

Michell, George (1987) 'Introduction' in *Temples and Tenements: The Indian Drawings of Deanna Petherbridge*, Calcutta, India: Seagull Books.

Millet, Marietta S. (1996) *Light Revealing Architecture*, New York: Van Nostrand Reinhold.

Mirsky, Jeanette (1976) *Houses of God* (Phoenix edn), Chicago, IL: University of Chicago Press.

Moore, Fuller (1985) *Concepts and Practice of Architectural Daylighting*, New York: Van Nostrand Reinhold.

Moore, Niamh and Yvonne Whelan (2007) *Heritage, Memory and the Politics of Identity: New Perspectives on the Cultural Landscape*, Aldershot: Ashgate Publishing.

Mukherji, Anuradah (2001) 'The Holy Light: A Study of Natural Light in Historic Hindu Temples in The Southern Region of Tamilnadu, India', Master of Science Thesis, College Station, TX: Texas A&M University.

Nora, Pierre (1996) 'From Lieux de memoire to Realms of Memory' in Pierre Nora *Realms of Memory: Rethinking the French Past*, New York: Columbia University Press, Vol. 1: xxvii–xxiv (trans.).

Nute, Kevin (1996) 'Wright the Architect' in Melanie Birk (ed.) *Frank Lloyd Wright's Fifty Views of Japan: The 1905 Photo Album,* Rohnert Park, CA: Pomegranate Artbooks, pp. 89–101.

Nute, Kevin (2000) *Frank Lloyd Wright and Japan*, (2nd edn – paperback), London and New York: Routledge.

Okakura, Kakuzo (1906) *The Book of Tea*, Boston, MA: Fox, Duffield & Company.

Olgyay, Victor (1963) *Design with Climate: Bioclimatic Approach to Architectural Regionalism*, Princeton, NJ: Princeton University Press.

Osmen, Sarah A. (1990) *Sacred Places*, New York: St. Martin's Press.

Otto, Rudolf (1917) *The Idea of the Holy* (Das Heilige), Breslau (English translation) New York: Oxford University Press 1936, 1970.

Owings, Rank N. Jr. (2003) 'Frank Lloyd Wright and The Regionalists: Visions for America', *Frank Lloyd Wright Quarterly*, 14 (1): 4–15.

Patterson, Terry (1994) *Frank Lloyd Wright and The Meaning of Materials*, New York: Van Nostrand Reinhold.

Patton, Kenneth (1947) 'The Church of Tomorrow', *Christian Register*, 126, (June): 241, 268.

Pelletier, Louise (2008) 'Modeling the Void: Mathias Goeritz and the Architecture of Emotions', *Journal of Architectural Education*, 62 (2): 6–13.

Petterson, Per (2003) *Out Stealing Horses* (trans.), New York: Picado.

Pevsner, Nikolaus (1968) *The Sources of Modern Architecture and Design*, New York: F.A. Praeger.

Pfammatter, Ulrich (2008) *Building the Future: Building Technology and Cultural History from the Industrial Revolution until Today*, Munich: Prestel.

Pfeiffer, Bruce B. (1988) *Frank Lloyd Wright Monographs*, Tokyo, Japan: A.D.A. Edita Publishers.

Pfeiffer, Bruce B. (1990) *Frank Lloyd Wright Drawings: Masterworks From The Frank Lloyd Wright Archives*, New York: Harry N. Abrams.

Pfeiffer, Bruce B. (ed.) (1992) *Frank Lloyd Wright Collected Writings*, Vol.1 (1894-1930) New York: Rizzoli International Publications.

Pfeiffer, Bruce B. (ed.) (1995) *Frank Lloyd Wright Collected Writings*, Vol. 5 (1949-1959) (paperback). New York: Rizzoli International Publications.

Pfeiffer, Bruce B. (1999) *Treasures of Taliesin: Seventy-Seven Unbuilt Designs* (2nd, rev. edn), San Francisco, CA: Pomegranate Artbooks.

Pfeiffer, Bruce B. and Nordland, Gerald (eds) (1988) *Frank Lloyd Wright in the Realm of Ideas*, Carbondale, IL: Southern Illinois University Press.

Plato (2000) *Timaeus* (trans. Donald Zeyl), Indianapolis, IN: Hackett Publishing.

Plummer, Henry (1987) 'Poetics of Light', *Architecture and Urbanism* (December): 8–11.

Pringle, Allen (1893) 'The Great Parliament of Religions', *The Open Court* (Chicago), 7 (322) (November): 3855.

Pugin, Augustus (1836/1969) *Contrasts*, New York: Humanities Press.

Pugin, Augustus (1844) *Glossary*, London: H.G. Bohn.

Rapoport, Amos (1969) *House Form and Culture*, Englewood Cliffs, NJ: Prentice-Hall.

Rickert, John (1967) 'House Façades of the Northeastern United States: A Tool of Geographic Analysis', *Annals of the Association of American Geographers*, 57 (2): 211–221.

Riley, Terence and Peter Reed (eds) (1994) *Frank Lloyd Wright, Architect*, New York: Museum of Modern Art.

Robinette, Gary O. (ed.) (1983) *Energy Efficient Site Design*, New York: Van Nostrand Reinhold.

Roberts, Nicholas W. (2004) *Building Type Basic for Places of Worship*, New York: John Wiley & Sons.

Robinson, Julia W. (1989) 'Architecture as a Medium for Culture: Public Institution and Private House' in Setha M. Low and Erve Chambers (eds) *Housing, Culture, and Design*, Philadelphia, PA: University of Pennsylvania Press, pp. 253–275.

Rogers, Steven B. (2001) 'The Frank Lloyd Wright Campus at Florida Southern College: A Child of Sun', *Frank Lloyd Wright Quarterly,* 12 (3): 4–23.

Ross, Denman (1907) *A Theory of Pure Design*, Boston, MA: Houghton Mifflin.

Sabine, Wallace C. (1922) *Collected Papers on Acoustics,* Cambridge, MA: Harvard University Press, reprinted (2010) by Nabu Press.

Saifullah, M.S.M., Ghoniem Muhammad, Squires, Abd al-Rahman and Ahmed Mansur (2001) 'The Qiblah of Early Mosques: Jerusalem or Makkah?', available at http://www.islamic-awareness.org/History/Islam/Dome_Of_The_Rock/qibla.html (accessed January 12, 2010).

Schwarz, Rudolf (1958) *The Church Incarnate: The Sacred Function of Christian Architecture* (trans), Chicago, IL: H. Regnery.

Scully, Vincent (1962) *The Earth, the Temple, and the Gods: Greek Sacred Architecture*, New Haven, CT: Yale University Press.

Scully, Vincent, Jr. (1988) 'Introduction' in Carol R. Bolon, Nelson Robert and Linda Seidel (eds) *The Nature of Frank Lloyd Wright,* Chicago, IL: University of Chicago Press.

Scully, Vincent (1991) *Architecture: the Natural and the Man-Made*, New York: St. Martin's Press

Scully Vincent, Jr. (1996) *Frank Lloyd Wright* (14th printing: paperback), New York: George Braziller.

Serageldin, Ismail and Steele, James (1996) *Architecture of the Contemporary Mosque*, London: Academy Editions.

Shainberger, Joseph (1977) 'Design of Synagogues Through History' (in Hebrew), in D. Casuto and Shachnti Betochchem, Jerusalem, Israel: Ministry of Education and Culture, pp. 78–89.

Siry, Joseph M. (1991a) 'The Abraham Lincoln Center in Chicago', *The Journal of Architectural Historians*, 50 (3): 235–265.

Siry, Joseph M. (1991b) 'Frank Lloyd Wright's Unity Temple and Architecture for Liberal Religion in Chicago 1885–1909', *The Art Bulletin*, 73 (2): 257–282.

Siry, Joseph M. (1996) *Unity Temple: Frank Lloyd Wright and Architecture for Liberal Religion*, Cambridge, UK: Cambridge University Press.

Siry, Joseph M. (2004) 'Frank Lloyd Wright's Annie Pfeiffer Chapel for Florida Southern College: Modernist Theology and Regional Architecture', *The Journal of Architectural Historians*, 63 (4): 498–539.

Siry, Joseph M. (2008) 'The Architecture of Earthquake Resistance: Julius Kahn's Truscon Company and Frank Lloyd Wright's Imperial Hotel.' *The Journal of the Society of Architectural Historians*, 67 (1): 78–105.

Smith, William R. (1894) *Lectures on the Religion of the Semites*. First series, *The Fundamental Institutions*, London: A. & C. Black.

Sounders, George (1790) *A Treatise on Theaters*, London. Reprinted (1968) Salem, NH: Ayer Co. Pub.

Sperling, G. (1998) 'The "Quadrivium" in the Pantheon of Rome' in K Williams (ed.) *NexusII: Architecture and Mathematics*, Firenze, Italy: Edizioni Dell'erba, p. 129.

Stanton, Phoebe (1985) 'Religious Architecture' in *Built in the U.S.A.: American Buildings from Airports to Zoos*, Washington, DC: Preservation Press, pp. 139–144.

Storrer, William A. (1993) *The Frank Lloyd Wright Companion*, Chicago, IL: University of Chicago Press.

Suzuki, Daisetz T. (1999) *Sengai: The Zen of Ink and Paper*, Boston, MA: Shambhala.

Tabb, Phillip (1996) *Sacred Place: The Presence of Archetypal Patterns in Place Creation*, a booklet, Boulder, CO: The Academy for Sacred Architectural Studies.

Tabb, Phillip (2007) 'Semantic Cosmologies of Ronchamp and Rothko Chapel' in K.C. Eynaten, Kate Hutchins, and Don Quaintance (eds) *Not-Seen: Search for Understanding: The Rothko Chapel Art Series*, Houston, TX: A Rothko Chapel Book, pp. 89–99.

Tanizaki, Junichiro (1977) *In Praise of Shadows*, New Haven, CT: Leete's Island Books.

Tauscher, Cathy and Peter Hughes (2008) 'Jenkin Lloyd Jones', available at http://www 25.uua.org/uuhs/duub/articles/jenkinlloydjones.html (accessed June 2, 2008).

The Catholic Encyclopedia (2010) http://www.newadvent.org/cathen (accessed January 12, 2010).

Trachtenberg, Marvin and Isabella Hyman (1986) *Architecture: From Prehistory to Post-Modernism*, Englewood Cliffs, NJ: Prentice-Hall, and New York: H.N. Abrams.

Tselos, Dimitri (1953) 'Exotic Influences in the Architecture of Frank Lloyd Wright', *Magazine of Art*, 46: 160–169.

Tselos, Dimitri (1969) 'Frank Lloyd Wright and World Architecture', *The Journal of the Society of Architectural Historians*, 28 (1) (March): 58–72.

Turner, Harold W. (1979) *From Temple to Meeting House: The Phenomenology and Theology of Places of Worship*, The Hague and New York: Mouton.

Turner, Paul Venable (1984) *Campus: An American Planning Tradition*, Cambridge, MA: MIT Press.

Upton, Dell (ed.) (1986) *America's Architectural Roots, Ethnic Groups That Built America*, Washington, DC: The Preservation Press.

Vitruvius (1st century AD) (1960) *The Ten Books on Architecture*, New York: Dover Publications.

Vlach, John M. (1991) *By the Work of Their Hands: Studies in Afro-American Folklife*, Charlottesville, VA: University Press of Virginia.

Vlach, John M. (1993) *Back of the Big House: The Architecture of Plantation Slavery*, Chapel Hill, NC: University of North Carolina Press.

Volwahsen, Andreas (1969) *Living Architecture: Indian*, London: Macdonald & Co.

Von Franz, Marie Louise (1972) *Creation Myths*, Dallas, TX: Spring Publications.

Wagner, P.L. (1972) *Environments and People*, Englewood Cliffs, NJ: Prentice-Hall.

Wallace, Mike (1957) *The Mike Wallace Interviews with Frank Lloyd Wright*, available at http://www.hrc.utexas.edu/multimedia/video/2008/wallace/wright_frank_lloyd_t.html

White, James F. (1962) *The Cambridge Movement: The Ecclesiologists and the Gothic Revival*, Cambridge: Cambridge University Press.

Wilber, Ken (2006) *Integral Spirituality*, Boston, MA: Shambhala.

Wright, Frank Lloyd (1896) 'Architect, Architecture, and the Client', (unpublished speech); reprinted in Bruce B. Pfeiffer (ed.) *Frank Lloyd Wright Collected Writings*, Vol. 1 (1992), pp. 27–38, New York: Rizzoli International Publications.

Wright, Frank Lloyd (1900) 'A Philosophy of Fine Art', (unpublished speech); reprinted in Bruce B. Pfeiffer (ed.) *Frank Lloyd Wright Collected Writings*, Vol. 1 (1992), pp. 39–44, New York: Rizzoli International Publications.

Wright, Frank Lloyd (1901) 'The Art and Craft of the Machine' *The Catalogue of the Fourteenth Annual Exhibition of the Chicago Architectural Club (March 1901)*; reprinted in Bruce B. Pfeiffer (ed.) *Frank Lloyd Wright Collected Writings*, Vol. 1 (1992), pp. 58–69, New York: Rizzoli International Publications.

Wright, Frank Lloyd (1907) 'A Fireproof House for $5,000', *The Ladies' Home Journal* (April); reprinted in Bruce B. Pfeiffer (ed.) *Frank Lloyd Wright Collected Writings*, Vol. 1 (1992), pp. 81–83, New York: Rizzoli International Publications.

Wright, Frank Lloyd (1908) 'In the Cause of Architecture', *Architectural Record*, 23 (3) (March): 155–221; reprinted in F. Gutheim (ed.) (1975) *In the Cause of Architecture*, New York: McGraw-Hill; and in Bruce B. Pfeiffer (ed.) (1992) *Frank Lloyd Wright Collected Writings*, Vol. 1, pp. 84–100, New York: Rizzoli International Publications.

Wright, Frank Lloyd (1910) 'Introduction (preface)' in Ernst Wasmuth (ed.) *Ausgefuhrte Bauten und Entwurfe von Frank Lloyd Wright*, Berlin: Wasmuth; reprinted in English (1986) *Studies and Executed Buildings,* New York: Rizzoli International Publications; reprinted in Bruce Pfeiffer (1992) *Frank Lloyd Wright Collected Writings*, Vol.1, pp. 101–115, New York: Rizzoli International Publications.

Wright, Frank Lloyd (1912) *The Japanese Print: An Interpretation*, Chicago, IL: Ralph Fletcher Seymour Company; reprinted in Bruce Pfeiffer (ed.) (1992) *Frank Lloyd Wright Collected Writings*, Vol. 1, pp. 116–125, New York: Rizzoli International Publications.

Wright, Frank Lloyd (1914) 'In the Cause of Architecture: Second Paper', *Architectural Record*, 35 (5) (May): 405–413; reprinted in Bruce Pfeiffer (ed.) (1992) *Frank Lloyd Wright Collected Writings*, Vol.1, pp. 126–137, New York: Rizzoli International Publications.

Wright, Frank Lloyd (1925) 'In the Cause of Architecture: The Third Dimension', *Wendigen*; reprinted in Bruce Pfeiffer (ed.) (1992) *Frank Lloyd Wright Collected Writings*, Vol. 1, pp. 209–214, New York: Rizzoli International Publications.

Wright, Frank Lloyd (1927a) 'In the Cause of Architecture IV: Fabrication and Imagination', *Architectural Record*, 62 (4) (October): 318–321; reprinted in Bruce Pfeiffer (ed.) (1992) *Frank Lloyd Wright Collected Writings,* Vol. 1, pp. 241–244, New York: Rizzoli International Publications.

Wright, Frank Lloyd (1927b) 'In the Cause of Architecture. Part III: Steel', *Architectural Record*, 62 (2): 163–166; reprinted in Frederick Gutheim (ed.) (1975) *In the Cause of Architecture*, New York: McGraw-Hill; reprinted in Bruce Pfeiffer (ed.) (1992) *Frank Lloyd Wright Collected Writings*, Vol. 1, pp. 234–240, New York: Rizzoli International Publications.

Wright, Frank Lloyd (1928a) 'In the Cause of Architecture I: The Logic of the Plan', *Architectural Record*, 63 (1) (January): 49–57; reprinted in Bruce Pfeiffer (ed.)

(1992) *Frank Lloyd Wright Collected Writings*, Vol. 1, pp. 249–254, New York: Rizzoli International Publications.

Wright, Frank Lloyd (1928b) 'In the Cause of Architecture II: What "Styles" Means to The Architect', *Architectural Record* (February): 145–151; reprinted in Bruce Pfeiffer (ed.) (1992) *Frank Lloyd Wright Collected Writings*, Vol. 1: 263–268, New York: Rizzoli International Publications.

Wright, Frank Lloyd (1928c) 'In the Cause of Architecture III: The Meaning of Materials – Stone', *Architectural Record*, 63 (4) (April): 350–356; 'In the Cause of Architecture IV: The Meaning of Materials – Wood', *Architectural Record*, 63 (5) (May): 481–488; 'In the Cause of Architecture V: The Meaning of Materials – The Kiln', *Architectural Record*, 63 (6) (June): 555–561; 'In the Cause of Architecture VI: The Meaning of Materials – Glass', *Architectural Record*, 64 (1) (July): 10–16; 'In the Cause of Architecture VII: The Meaning of Materials – Concrete', *Architectural Record*, 64 (2) (August): 98–104; 'In the Cause of Architecture VIII: The Meaning of Materials – Sheet Metal and A Modern Instance', *Architectural Record*, 64 (4) (October); all reprinted in Bruce Pfeiffer (ed.) (1992) *Frank Lloyd Wright Collected Writings*, Vol. 1, pp. 269–309, New York: Rizzoli International Publications.

Wright, Frank Lloyd (1928d) 'Towards A New Architecture', *World Unity* (September); reprinted in Bruce Pfeiffer (ed.) (1992) *Frank Lloyd Wright Collected Writings*, Vol. 1, pp. 317–318, New York: Rizzoli International Publications.

Wright, Frank Lloyd (1929) 'The Line Between the Curious and the Beautiful' (unpublished essay); reprinted in Bruce Pfeiffer (ed.) (1992) *Frank Lloyd Wright Collected Writings*, Vol. 1, pp. 329–332, New York: Rizzoli International Publications.

Wright, Frank Lloyd (1931a) *Modern Architecture*, Princeton, NJ: Princeton University Press; reprinted (1959) Southern Illinois University Press.

Wright, Frank Lloyd (1931b) 'Modern Architecture, Being The Kahn Lectures' (published lectures), Princeton, NJ: Princeton University; reprinted in Bruce Pfeiffer (ed.) (1992) *Frank Lloyd Wright Collected Writings*, Vol. 2, pp. 19–79, New York: Rizzoli International Publications.

Wright, Frank Lloyd (1931c) 'Two Lectures on Architecture' (published lectures), the Art Institute of Chicago; reprinted in Bruce Pfeiffer (ed.) (1992) *Frank Lloyd Wright Collected Writings*, Vol. 2: 82–101, New York: Rizzoli International Publications.

Wright, Frank Lloyd (1932a) *An Autobiography*, New York: Horizon Press; reprinted (1943) New York: Duell, Sloan and Pearce; reprinted (1945) London: Faber and Faber and Hyperion Press; reprinted (1977) New York: Horizon Press; reprinted in Bruce Pfeiffer (ed.) (1992) *Frank Lloyd Wright Collected Writings*, Vol. 2, pp. 102–382, New York: Rizzoli International Publications.

Wright, Frank Lloyd (1932b) 'The Disappearing City'; reprinted in Bruce Pfeiffer (ed.) (1993) *Frank Lloyd Wright Collected Writings*, Vol. 3, pp. 70–112, New York: Rizzoli International Publications, (first published by W. F. Payson. New York, 1932).

Wright, Frank Lloyd (1939) *An Organic Architecture: The Architecture of Democracy*, London: Lund Humphries & Co.; reprinted in Frank Lloyd Wright (1970) *The Future of Architecture* (paperback), New York: Meridian Books-New American Library, pp. 239–316.

Wright, Frank Lloyd (1940) 'The New Frontier: Broadacre City', *Taliesen Magazine* (October); reprinted in Bruce Pfeiffer (ed.) (1994) *Frank Lloyd Wright Collected Writings*, Vol. 4, pp. 45–66, New York: Rizzoli International Publications.

Wright, Frank Lloyd (1943a) 'An Autobiography Book Five: Form', reprinted in Bruce
        Pfeiffer (ed.) (1994) *Frank Lloyd Wright Collected Writings*, Vol. 4, pp. 121–240,
        New York: Rizzoli International Publications.

Wright, Frank Lloyd (1943b) 'An Autobiography Book Six: Broadacre City'; reprinted
        in Bruce Pfeiffer (ed.) (1994) *Frank Lloyd Wright Collected Writings*, Vol. 4,
        pp. 241–254, New York: Rizzoli International Publications.

Wright, Frank Lloyd (1945) *When Democracy Builds* (rev. edn), Chicago, IL: University
        of Chicago Press.

Wright, Frank Lloyd (1946a) 'Review of The Church Beautiful', *Christian Register*
        (August); reprinted in Bruce Pfeiffer (ed.) (1994) *Frank Lloyd Wright Collected
        Writings*, Vol. 4, pp. 298–299, New York: Rizzoli International Publications
        reprinted in *Frank Lloyd Wright Quarterly* (1997), 8 (1) (winter): 6.

Wright, Frank Lloyd (1946b) 'The Architect' a lecture published in 1947 in *The Work of
        Mind*, Chicago, IL: University of Chicago Press; reprinted in Bruce Pfeiffer (ed.)
        (1994) *Frank Lloyd Wright Collected Writings*, Vol. 4, pp. 285–293, New York:
        Rizzoli International Publications.

Wright, Frank Lloyd (1946c) 'Why I Believe in Advancing Unitarianism' published by the
        American Unitarian Association (May 1946); reprinted in Bruce Pfeiffer (ed.)
        (1994) *Frank Lloyd Wright Collected Writings*, Vol. 4, pp. 296–297, New York:
        Rizzoli International Publications.

Wright, Frank Lloyd (1949) *Genius and the Mobocracy*, New York: Duell, Sloan and
        Pearce; reprinted in Bruce Pfeiffer (ed.) (1994) *Frank Lloyd Wright Collected
        Writings*, Vol. 4, pp. 335–382, New York: Rizzoli International Publications.

Wright, Frank Lloyd (1952) 'A Church in the Attitude of Prayer', *Architectural Forum*
        (December): 85–92.

Wright, Frank Lloyd (1953a) *The Future of Architecture*, New York: Horizon Press;
        reprinted in paperback (1970), New York: Meridian Books-New American Library.

Wright, Frank Lloyd (1953b) *The Future of Architecture*, New York: Horizon Press;
        reprinted in Bruce Pfeiffer (ed.) (1995) *Frank Lloyd Wright Collected Writings*, Vol.
        5, pp. 60–61, New York: Rizzoli International Publications.

Wright, Frank Lloyd (1954) *The Natural House*, New York: Horizon Press.

Wright, Frank Lloyd (1955) *An American Architecture*, New York: Horizon Press.

Wright, Frank Lloyd (1957) *A Testament*, New York: Horizon Press.

Wright, Frank Lloyd (1958a) *The Living City*, New York: Horizon Press; reprinted
        (1963) New York: Mentor; reprinted in Bruce Pfeiffer (ed.) (1995) *Frank Lloyd
        Wright Collected Writings*, Vol. 5, pp. 251–344, New York: Rizzoli International
        Publications.

Wright, Frank Lloyd (1958b) 'Is It Good-Bye To Gothic?', *Together Magazine* (May);
        reprinted in *Frank Lloyd Wright Quarterly* (1997), 8 (1) (winter): 8–9; and in Bruce
        Pfeiffer (ed.) (1992) *Frank Lloyd Wright Collected Writings*, Vol. 5, pp. 227–233,
        New York: Rizzoli International Publications.

Wright, Frank Lloyd (1960) *Frank Lloyd Wright: Writings and Buildings*, edited by Edgar
        Kaufmann and Ben Raeburn, New York: A Merdian Book: New American Library.

Wright, Frank Lloyd (1967) *The Japanese Print*, New York: Horizon Press.

Wright, Frank Lloyd (1975) *In the Cause of Architecture: Essays by Frank Lloyd Wright
        for Architectural Record, 1908–1952*, edited by Frederick Gutheim, New York:
        McGraw-Hill.

Wright, Frank Lloyd (1986) *Letters to Clients* (selected and with commentary by Bruce Brooks Pfeiffer), Fresno, CA: Press at California State University, Fresno.

Wright, Frank Lloyd and Brownell Baker (1937) *Architecture and Modern Life,* New York: Harper & Brothers; reprinted in Bruce Pfeiffer (ed.) (1993) *Frank Lloyd Wright Collected Writings*, Vol. 3, pp. 216–249, New York: Rizzoli International Publications.

Wright, Oligivanna Lloyd (1960) *The Shining Brow: Frank Lloyd Wright*, New York: Horizon Press.

Wydick, Susan (1987) *Frank Lloyd Wright and Folk Architecture*, Springfield, IL: Dana-Thomas House Foundation.

Yi-Fu, Tuan (1974) *Topophilia: A Study of Environmental Perception, Attitudes and Values*, Englewood Cliffs, NJ: Prentice-Hall.

Yi-Fu, Tuan (1978) 'Sacred Space: Explorations on an Idea' in Karl Butzer *Dimensions of Human Geography,* University of Chicago Department of Geography Research Paper, pp. 84–99.

General Web References

WordNet: a lexical database for the English language
http://wordnet.princeton.edu/perl/webwn

The Merriam-Webster Dictionary online
http://www.merriam-webster.com/dictionary/temple

Index